Sheila MacLeod was born on the Isle of Lewis in the Outer Hebrides, but she has lived for most of her life in the South of England. She went to Somerville College, Oxford, where she read English and then worked briefly at the Clarendon Press. Apart from working at the Clarendon Press she has never had a full-time job, but has taught Arvon fiction courses and weekends at various places, a part-time year at Richmond College and now has students from the Antioch Centre for British Studies.

For the most part, Sheila MacLeod has concentrated on fiction but she has also written two television plays and done a fair amount of journalism.

She lives in London.

SHEILA MACLEOD

Lawrence's Men
and Women

PALADIN
GRAFTON BOOKS
A Division of the Collins Publishing Group

LONDON GLASGOW
TORONTO SYDNEY AUCKLAND

Paladin
Grafton Books
A Division of the Collins Publishing Group
8 Grafton Street, London W1X 3LA

Published in Paladin Books 1987

First published in Great Britain by
William Heinemann Ltd 1985

ISBN 0-586-08549-1

Printed and bound in Great Britain by
Collins, Glasgow

Set in Ehrhardt

Contents

Introduction

It is a hot, still day in July or August 1953 or 1954 or even 1955. The location is the soporifically wooded village of Hermitage, near Newbury, in Berkshire. The substantial redbrick house, once known as The Corner House, has been renamed Erisort House as a tribute to the Hebridean origins of its present occupants. Lying on the front lawn, a pre-anorexic teenage girl is reading D. H. Lawrence – all the shorter fiction in two fat volumes – with a growing sense of unease which sometimes approaches panic. And yet something compels her to read on. It is the terrible grown-up world of sexual and emotional passion, which is at once an object of horror and an object of her intensest interest.

That confused and unhappy teenager was of course myself. I was reading Lawrence at my father's suggestion, indeed insistence, the sort of insistence a benevolent Victorian paterfamilias might have used to induce his daughters to read the Bible: for their own good and betterment. My parents, who spoke as familiarly of Lawrence and Frieda as if they were almost alter egos, were Leavisite enthusiasts. Volumes of Lawrentiana borrowed from the public library were (along with the collected editions of *Scrutiny*) a regular if shifting feature of their household effects. We had moved from London to Hermitage, rather than to the neighbouring village of Hampstead Norris where my father taught at the local school, because the Lawrences had often stayed there in what was now the milkman's cottage.

It is difficult for me now to reconcile that enthusiasm with the image I have of my parents who were both rather restrained and by no means permissive people. I think it must have been difficult for me then, although it was not a difficulty I recognized consciously. Here in the pages of Lawrence's work the secret world of adults, which was never openly spoken about, was laid bare. This was a world beyond my experience, even as a seasoned reader, and, I gradually came to suspect, beyond my capabilities. And yet something about it somewhere rang mysteriously true. Lawrence made me and my life seem puny, inadequate. And yet I could sense too that there was something bigger inside me, waiting to break out.

Descriptions of 'nature' bored me, so I skimmed through them and concentrated instead on the relationships between human beings. Although I had no way of knowing what adults got up to together in secret, I was uneasily aware that no one I knew behaved like Birkin and Gerald, Ursula and Gudrun, in *Women In Love*. Nor did anyone in my experience talk in their nakedly articulate fashion about their own or other people's feelings. Here was writing of such emotional intensity (and, underneath, the passionate current of sexuality) that I was daunted as well as puzzled.

But even then I think what daunted me most, in a dim and rather dazed way, was Lawrence's composite portrait of adult womanhood. The beginning of *Aaron's Rod*, where Aaron walks out on his wife and children just before Christmas, enraged and frightened me to an extent I would not have been able to admit. I didn't want to know what happened to Aaron. I wanted to know what happened to Lottie Sisson without her husband and to Millicent and Marjory without their father. It was as if Lawrence had wiped them out, relegated them to some sub-world not worth writing about. But this world of women and children was the only world I knew.

At this stage Lawrence's men didn't interest me because I wanted to know about *myself*, to understand what I was and what I might become. Ursula in *The Rainbow*, eldest daughter as she too is, was someone I could admire, someone with whom I could tentatively identify, but her later succumbing to Rupert Birkin filled me with dismay. There seemed to be no way of knowing about myself except through men: it was through men that women became 'fulfilled' and attained true womanliness. And all this not, as I had previously imagined, because they had children together, but through the mysterious agency of sex, which was supposedly something wonderful, but at the same time too shameful to be mentioned in everyday conversation.

Both Ursula's sister Gudrun and Lou Carrington in *St Mawr*

abandoned their men, Gudrun to pursue her career as an artist
and Lou to live alone on a rat-infested ranch in New Mexico. But
Gudrun was clearly neurotic and Lou, though rich enough to do
as she pleased, was doomed to loneliness. There seemed to be no
other way towards 'fulfilment' (which I vaguely took to mean some
sort of self-realization) than to subject oneself to male violation,
whether of the body or of the mind. And I now see a connection
between my saturation in Lawrence and my subsequent anorexia,
during which I determined to keep my body to myself denying that
it was capable of any sort of desire – even that for food.

When I became an undergraduate at Oxford in 1958 I was
surprised to find that the New Left (with which by now I had
allied myself) were also Leavisite Lawrentians, earnestly discussing
'relationships', 'commitment', and 'pro-life values' but not, as I
remember, passion. Their claims on Lawrence's behalf were less
literary than political, Lawrence himself being less a 'priest of love'
than a triumphant example of class mobility. This Lawrence was
very much the miner's son, promoting grass-roots values against
the depersonalizing forces of capitalism. He was a voice in the
wilderness, crying out that all men were capable, whatever their
social status, of living life to the fullest – and he would show them
the way. All men. There was the rub. The full life of the creative
intellect was tacitly assumed to be a masculine preserve. Men who
had made it to Oxford from working-class homes could identify
themselves with Lawrence but women from similar backgrounds,
like myself, were somehow supposed to become so many Friedas.

Around this time I began writing short stories, partly in a spirit
of 'I'll show 'em', and gained a certain notoriety from my first
published story which was about a girl losing her virginity (to use
the contemporary phraseology) to an American GI at Greenham
Common. Young men and women in 1959–60 did not write about
such things, except perhaps through a haze of romanticism. Nor
was it fashionable to expose one's vulnerability, especially in
relation to sex. But my narrator (writing in her diary) was both
frank and vulnerable. These qualities I had learned, at least in
part, from D. H. Lawrence. But there was something defiant about
her too, as there was in the very act of writing the story, and this I

had learned from myself. The notion that I couldn't be a 'real' woman and a writer had always irked me in a subterranean sort of way. Now it was becoming deeply hurtful.

In 1960 the Penguin edition of *Lady Chatterley's Lover* stood trial at the Old Bailey on a charge of obscenity, that is, a tendency to 'deprave and corrupt'. Like most people I had read only the expurgated version and so the full text, now legally cleared, came as something of a revelation – and a release. This Lawrence was, as befits the beginning of the 1960s, a prophet of sexual freedom. And although it was stressed by expert witnesses at the trial that liberty was not the same as licence and that Lawrence's attitude to sex was actually somewhat puritanical, so he remained throughout the decade. Whether you were in favour of letting it all hang out or just some good wholesome fucking, Lawrence was your ally and your advocate. And it was all right to call it fucking because, if the act were not shameful, so neither was the word.

When I read the unexpurgated version some two or three years after the trial, I was mainly impressed by Lawrence's ability to write from Connie's point of view. By this time I was no longer anorexic but married and pregnant. Sex was no longer a mystery belonging to the grown ups but something which seemed to have been invented by my own generation who now turned to Lawrence not for enlightenment but as an historical exercise in which the past served to confirm the present. We knew it all. And so, supposedly, did Lawrence. Even so I found many of the expurgated passages absurd or over the top. I was no longer asking myself: is this the way it's supposed to be? I was telling myself (and Lawrence): this is not necessarily how it is.

My unease was now of a different calibre. Something somewhere was deeply wrong with *Lady Chatterley's Lover* and it wasn't the explicitness or the four-letter words. I suspected that it was the allocation to sexuality of the position of central importance in the scheme of things. Not that I found sexuality unimportant. I just knew that there were other forms of pleasure, other means of transcendence. I also knew by now that there were relationships other than monogamously heterosexual ones, especially mother-hood and friendship, which were of vital importance to me. There seemed to be something desperate in the isolation and self-absorption of Connie and Mellors. By extension there seemed to be something obsessive and therefore questionable in Lawrence's insistence on sexuality as the power which informs the universe, the only power through which we know we are alive. And I defined my unease as a justifiable instance of liberal response.

What strikes me as odd now is that I never really questioned the nature of the sexuality advocated in *Lady Chatterley's Lover*. If I had, I should have seen the differences between Lawrence's views of male and female sexuality and, in the process, become sharply aware of the differences in his attitudes towards men and women. But somehow, until the advent of the Women's Movement, I couldn't think in those terms, just as before the Impressionists people couldn't see the brown fogs over London as subjects worthy of painting. But it was of course Lawrence's treatment of women which was causing my latterday unease.

In my subsequent and sporadic re-reading of Lawrence I was struck by his paradoxical attitude towards women. So often he shows uncannily intuitive insight into his female characters: as often his understanding comes to an abrupt halt, wiped out by a wave of apparent misogyny, usually in the form of a recantation or a sudden reversal of fortune. What starts out as a sympathetic and accurate portrait degenerates into a series of unconvincing stereotypical reactions, and the instinct of the novelist is sacrificed to the forced moral conclusions of the polemicist.

Since the early 1970s feminists have been attacking Lawrence as the epitome of sexism and his theories of sexuality as male-centred and insensitive or dismissive towards women. I have scarcely been able to find a woman in the 1980s who has a good word to say for him. And indeed there is much in Lawrence's fiction that is enough to send any self-respecting woman (feminist or no) into paroxysms of dismissive rage. (I do not exaggerate: Lawrence still arouses strong emotions, a facility which is one of his greatest strengths as well as an indication of his dogmatism.) But as so often with Lawrence, that is not the whole story, and his work, especially the later fiction, is riddled through and through with paradox.

Lawrence is one of the most maddening writers who ever wrote. Sometimes he writes so gloriously well – only to sink immediately into bathos. Sometimes every word rings profoundly true on one page, and on the next we are presented instead with a series of half-baked notions and shrilly dogmatic assertions. As a thinker he is full of contradictions, and never more so than when writing about the relations between men and women. Although he saw his life's work as 'sticking up for the love between men and women', he often seems more interested in the love between men and men, and was capable of suggesting that the sexes stay apart until they have learned to be kind with one another. His work is fraught with the struggle between the male and female principles, any decisive resolution between the two being as decisively overturned. If the male principle triumphs, it will not be for long. The assumption, sometimes tacit, sometimes overt and as overtly resented, is that the woman or feminine (even in Lawrence himself) is stronger and will prevail.

This then is my starting point in attempting to determine Lawrence's attitudes towards both men and women: Lawrence himself and his view of himself. This after all was Lawrence's own starting point: a man who saw himself as self-consciously if precariously male. The close relationship with his mother and, later, the equally close but now openly embattled relationship with his wife, were the strongest and most important in his life. Both were relationships in which it seems he often lost sight of himself, and which he was compelled to fight against in the name of individual identity. Because both were relationships with women a large part of that identity was bound up with ideas about maleness and masculinity. Lawrence believed that men should be manly and women womanly. Although his definitions and explications of these concepts are inconsistent, he remained firm on one point: that the two are separate and opposed. But they are also complementary, and this is why their union is of such central and vital importance: 'life itself'.

Lawrence's friend, the novelist Catherine Carswell, claimed that he was easy to read but hard to understand. Although I see what she means in that Lawrence's fiction is at once more complex and less dogmatic than it at first appears, this assertion is not altogether true. There is little that is easy about Lawrence, least of all living with him as I have been attempting to do for the last eighteen months. To read Lawrence intensively is to inhabit a world in which perception, language and emotion are all relentlessly heightened, and ideas flow in seemingly never-ending if repetitive succession. No wonder I was so stimulated and disturbed by him when I was twelve, thirteen, fourteen. Here indeed is a feast for the emotionally and intellectually hungry adolescent. But it is a vast and complicated grown-up banquet rather than what used to be called a square meal.

My re-reading has been undertaken from the standpoint of a woman in her forties, a woman who is a novelist and a mother – two roles which Lawrence would have been at pains to deny me in the interests of my womanly fulfilment. Because I know him to be wrong on both counts, I no longer feel threatened by him. It seems to me now that Lawrence's outbursts of misogyny spring from a failure in self-confidence which in turn depends upon a reluctant but eventually unshakeable belief in the frailty of the male and the comparative unquenchable strength of the female. All the elaborate theorizing in the essays and the longer non-fiction works such as *The Crown* or *Fantasia of the Unconscious* is designed to deny as much, but in the novels the point is again and again finally conceded. The victory, though, is never a simple matter and may well be Pyrrhic.

Relations between men and women are not after all about victory and defeat, but about working out a *modus vivendi*. Such is the substance of Lawrence's final concessions, and his fiction consti-tutes a series of alternative strategies towards this end. We may reject many or all of them with varying degrees of alacrity, but it seems to me that we cannot afford to dismiss his central concern with male–female relationships. Unless we are homosexual separ-atists of either sex, we all want them to work better than they so often do. And we all recognize that, in the words of the title of one of Lawrence's own essays, we need one another. I don't believe that either men or women have come to terms with such needs today, much less worked out the optimum means for their fulfilment. But Lawrence has laid some of the groundwork for us, not least in taking such matters with the utmost seriousness as well as a fundamental but unfashionable optimism, and it seems to me a worthwhile exercise to explore and evaluate what he has to offer us.

PART ONE
Men

1

The passion to be masculine

The words 'manly' and 'manliness' are rarely used today, and then probably with some sense of irony. The very idea of someone being manly in all seriousness has an old-fashioned air to it, conjuring up a picture of a fine upstanding young fellow, clean-limbed, stiff-upper-lipped and straight out of the pages of John Buchan or the Biggles books. Or perhaps the picture is that of a Charles Atlas, fairly bursting with masculine strength and health. It is, at any rate, a somewhat risible one, perhaps especially to women.

D. H. Lawrence uses both words often, and with the utmost seriousness. They leap off the page at you, insistent and a little desperate. The idea, indeed ideal, of manliness is clearly important to Lawrence, for all his professed scorn of both ideas and ideals. As an idea it is propounded again and again in his essays, and discussed with earnest anxiety, perhaps with anger, by most of the major male characters in his novels. As an ideal it is what those same characters strive towards, forever refining and redefining its terms until, in *Lady Chatterley's Lover*, Lawrence had arrived at something which seemed capable of attainment.

Why was manliness of such vital importance to Lawrence? Norman Mailer, who understands Lawrence very well, provides us with a clue.

He illumines the passion to be masculine as no other writer, he reminds us of the beauty of desiring to be a man, for he was not much of a man himself, a son despised by his father, beloved of his mother, a boy and young man and prematurely ageing writer with the soul of a beautiful woman.

The passion to be masculine. The beauty of desiring to be a man. I must confess that until I read those phrases, the concepts had never occurred to me. Certainly I have never felt any corresponding passion to be feminine, and the desire to be a woman seems to me not beautiful, but strangely irrelevant. I am feminine, I am a woman, and that's that. At the same time I can see how painful, how terrible, it must be to have any doubts on the matter. Gender identity is very much a part of total identity. With a few very rare exceptions we are all born as bodies which are essentially sexed, male or female, and to doubt or deny as much amounts to denying the fact of our bodies, the fact that we are bodies at all.

It seems to me that women in general have fewer doubts about gender identity than men do. Of course there are women, just as there are men, who wish to deny that they are bodies; and of course there are women, just as there are men, who wish to dispute the gender identity bestowed on them at birth; but the nagging, undermining uncertainty to which many men fall prey is foreign to most women. If I change the fan-belt in my car, if I chair a meeting, I may well be aware that I am doing something which was previously considered a man's job, but I never feel that I am not therefore a woman (I am much more likely to say to myself, 'Huh, I can do this as well as any man – if not better!') or that I am in some mysterious way being unwomaned. In fact there is no such word as 'unwomaned' – but there is of course such a word as 'unmanned'. The implication is that womanliness is something which cannot be taken away from you: it is both self-evident and enduring. Manliness appears in comparison as a frail, elusive thing. Given that maleness is no less obvious than female-ness at birth, why should this be so?

There are several reasons, some historical, some biological. Women's work has long been downgraded and devalued when compared to men's work; male muscular strength has been prized above the female capacity for physical endurance; men have been the owners of wealth and property, the wielders of authority, the holders of power, the achievers, the doers, the go-getters, while women have been barred from such apparently desirable positions or behaviour. And so on. In sum, to be a man is something of an effort, something to be fought for bit by bit and, when won, defended with the utmost vigilance. It is also something which can be weighed or measured, something quantifiable and, as such,

open to comparisons. The same applies to the biological reasons
for the seeming frailty of the male: not only do women live longer
than men, but for women the sexual act involves no effort to prove
oneself, whereas a man believes (rightly or wrongly) that he has to
perform, and that his performance can be assessed as well as his
erection measured. What a dreadful, anxiety-inducing business it
all sounds! Is any of it really necessary?

Well, yes and no. It is often difficult for women to take such
matters seriously, but I think we should try – not in order to please
and appease men, but in order to understand the world better.
Lawrence's passion to be masculine is often depicted as something
quite foreign to the world of women. In *John Thomas and Lady
Jane* (a previous version of *Lady Chatterley's Lover*) the gamekeeper
Parkin, who is a more vulnerable and so rather more sympathetic
figure than his successor Mellors, asks Connie Chatterley if she
can allow him to see himself as someone she can look up to,
someone who is bigger than she is. He needs as much, he says, he
can't help it. In context, his request is as much a plea on behalf of
the working-class male when faced with the economic and social
superiority of the aristocratic female as a demand for male domination. Parkin is trying to restore what he sees as an imbalance in
the relationship, an imbalance which robs him of part of his sense
of identity – and therefore his sense of himself as a man. Connie
acquiesces readily: it is of no importance to her who is bigger than
whom because ideas of domination and submission do not matter
to her. But she knows that they matter to Parkin. And she wants
Parkin to be the sort of man he wants to be.

The extent to which Lawrence worked through this material so
as to bring out the underlying meaning is evident from an anecdote
which Frieda Lawrence tells in her memoir, *Not I But the Wind* . . .
During the course of one of their many rows Lawrence pushed
her against the wall, his hands round her throat, shouting that he,
the man, had to be 'master' in their relationship. To which Frieda
replied, 'Is that all? You can be master as much as you like. I don't
care.' Her reply amazed Lawrence, who immediately let go of her:
the quarrel was at an end, and the question of mastership effectively
scotched. The unreasoning rage of the goaded man has become,

in the hands of the novelist, a rather pathetic statement which rings psychologically true. The passion to be masculine, to fill that role called 'man', must be seen in its social and psychological contexts rather than in terms of propaganda.

In *Sexual Politics* Kate Millett says on a note of triumph that here Frieda 'quite outwitted' Lawrence. Not at all. Frieda's response seems to be uncalculated, and an example both of her compassion and her imaginative sympathy – qualities singularly lacking in Millett's own essay on Lawrence. I mention Kate Millett at this point because her book is still widely read, and the chapter on Lawrence seems to have led a great many women to dismiss Lawrence the novelist unread besides rejecting Lawrence the moralist as an enemy. This is a mistake. *Sexual Politics* is a piece of propaganda for lesbianism and masturbation and is full of hatred for heterosexuality. Hardly the basis for an open-minded approach to D. H. Lawrence.

We can, however, be grateful to Millett for one thing: Norman Mailer's illuminating essay on Lawrence in *The Prisoner of Sex*, which was written as a riposte to *Sexual Politics*. It seems to me that Mailer understands Lawrence better than does Millett not only because Mailer is a man, but because he is a novelist. Mailer sees that Lawrence's passion to be masculine is not just a dictatorial ploy but a profound psychological need. It is not simply the single-minded pursuit of a recognizable goal, but a matter of trying out different strategies in order to see the nature and shape of the goal more clearly. To write a novel is in itself an admission of uncertainty, of tentativeness. The essayist may and can pontificate, advocate, argue and cite facts and figures in order to prove his/her points. But the novelist cannot prove anything, no matter how passionately he/she may believe it: novelists must put their most cherished beliefs to the ultimate test, that of exemplifying them in the lives of men and women who may or may not, by virtue of their very humanity, be able to accept or endorse them. To write a novel is to admit that what concerns you most deeply is neither self-evident nor susceptible to proof.

What I am trying to say, as far as manliness is concerned, can be summed up in Lawrence's own dictum, 'Never trust the artist, trust the tale.' There is perhaps no writer to whom this could be applied more profitably than Lawrence himself. Mailer goes on to describe him as a man

locked into the body of a middling male physique, not physically strong, of reasonable good looks, a pleasant to somewhat seedy-looking man, no stud. What a nightmare to balance that soul! to take the man in himself, locked from youth into every need for profound female companionship, a man almost totally oriented toward the company of women, and attempt to go out into the world of men, indeed even dominate the world of men so that he might find balance there. For his mind was possessed of that intolerable masculine pressure to command which develops in sons outrageously beloved of their mothers. To be the equal of a woman at twelve or six or any early age which reaches equilibrium between the will of the son and the will of the mother, strong love to strong love, is all but to guarantee the making of a future tyrant, for the sense of where to find one's inner health has been generated by the early years of that equilibrium – its substitute will not be easy to create in maturity.

I see Lawrence's fiction as in part a series of attempts (some of them indeed nightmarish) to balance that soul and to find some sort of equilibrium between its male and female aspects. The passion to be masculine must be seen as part of the passion to understand and define the relations between male and female, between men and women.

In his fiction Lawrence tried out various masculine roles in order to arrive at an idea or ideal of manliness, some more successful than others. Below I explore what I find to be the three most important: the mother's son; the man's man; and the phallus.

2
The mother's son

For most of us, whether we are male or female, our mother is the first love of our lives. She is the one with whom we have our first physical relationship, our first intimacy, and all our subsequent physical relationships, all our intimacies, will be coloured – though not, I believe, determined – by those experiences. She is the one who first defines relationship for us and, whether positively or by default, defines love. As she handles our bodies, so will we handle them, whether with respect or contempt, whether indulgently or punitively. As she feeds us, so will we deal with our hunger, regarding all our appetites as undemanding, overweening or unproblematic accordingly. As she comforts us, so will we deal with our discomfort and our pain, seeing them either as capable of assuagement or as interminable and unendurable. As she talks to us, so do we value language and communication. As she respects our capabilities, our effectiveness, our integrity, so ultimately will we.

Our first relationship, whether we are boys or girls, is with a(nother) woman, and our first experience of the world is one of what may be called the world of women. This phrase is not intended prescriptively, but as a straightforward description of the way things generally are today and certainly were in the 1880s and 1890s of Lawrence's childhood. It refers to the everyday domestic world of the family and family relationships, and to the community which is their immediate context. It is a world of order, routine and attention to detail. It is a world of warmth and closeness and often of passionately enmeshed emotions, a private world which at the same time allows little in the way of individual privacy. It is a world, especially in working-class homes, where women are the teachers, the managers, the bosses. If we are female, we may if we wish remain in that world for the rest of our lives. If we are male, the wider world expects us to escape from and outgrow it as we approach maturity. The extent to which we accomplish this task has long been regarded, in the absence of any formal puberty rites, as the badge of manhood.

David Herbert Richards Lawrence was born at Eastwood, Nottinghamshire, in 1885, the fourth child and second son of Arthur Lawrence and Lydia, née Beardsall. His father was a miner and his mother had formerly been a schoolteacher. The difference in social standing indicates a love-match, and at first the marriage seems to have been happy enough. But as the children started to arrive, as money became tighter, as Arthur Lawrence started to drink, and as Lydia withdrew emotionally from him (impossible to tell cause from effect in all this) the marriage deteriorated rapidly. By the time Lawrence was born there were constant rows as well as the occasional scene of outright violence.

According to Achsah Brewster's account of what Lawrence had told her of his childhood, the mother

> would gather the children in a row, and they would sit quaking, waiting for their father to return while she would picture his shortcomings blacker and blacker to their childish horror. At last the father would come in softly, taking off his shoes, hoping to escape unnoticed to bed, but that was never allowed him. She would burst out upon him, reviling him for a drunken sot, a good-for-nothing father. She would turn to the whimpering children and ask them if they were not disgusted with such a father. He would look at the row of frightened children and say, 'Never mind, my duckies, you needna be afraid of me. I'll do ye na harm.'

This is a rather more sympathetic portrait of the father as well as a less sympathetic portrait of the mother than those drawn by Lawrence in his avowedly autobiographical novel, *Sons and Lovers*. But the general situation is much the same in both accounts.

The hero Paul Morel is rather a 'delicate boy, subject to bronchitis', and so from an early age the especial object of his mother's attention. From the start,

> she felt strangely towards the infant. Her heart was heavy because of the child, almost as if it were unhealthy or malformed. Yet it seemed quite well. But she noticed the peculiar knitting of the baby's brows, and the peculiar heaviness of its eyes, as if it were trying to understand something that was pain.

Because she no longer loves her husband she has not wanted this child. But there it is: fragile, sensitive, alive and somehow special. In spite of herself, she is moved by it.

A wave of hot love went over her to the infant. She held it close to her face and breast. With all her force, with all her soul, she would make up to it for having brought it into the world unloved. She would love it all the more now that it was here; carry it in her love. Its clear knowing eyes gave her pain and fear. Did it know all about her? When it lay under her heart had it been listening?

Communication between mother and infant is instant and intuitive, founded in love, but also in fear and pain.

The suggestion is that Paul has indeed been listening to his parents, and he continues to do so throughout his childhood. Often he wakes up at night, hearing thuds and shouting downstairs and he waits, sleepless, terrified that his father will hit his mother yet again.

There was a feeling of horror, a kind of bristling in the darkness, and a sense of blood. [The children] lay with their hearts in the grip of an intense anguish ... And then came the horror of the sudden silence, silence everywhere, outside and downstairs. What was it? Was it a silence of blood? What had he [the father] done?

Small wonder that young Paul suffers from fits of depression, even at the age of three or four. These fits cast a shadow on his mother's heart, and, again, 'her treatment of Paul was different from that of the other children.'

Paul does not know what is causing his depression, but it is of course his mother's pain. He not only shares his mother's pain, but internalizes it as his own. And she in turn internalizes what has become his pain as her own again. This blurring of the boundaries between two individuals in the assumption of one another's suffering constitutes a very strong bonding, one of the strongest and most basic there is. Like many another son (and indeed daughter) of an unhappy mother before and since, Paul Morel feels towards his own mother a kind of mother-love, that is, a love which is protective, tender, fierce and possessive, a love which contains both fear and pain. As a boy, he possesses the emotions of a mature but anxiety-ridden woman.

But the young Paul is also internalizing his father's pain, his bewilderment and resentment. Because the central relationship between mother and son is so powerfully realized in *Sons and Lovers*, it is easy to overlook or underplay the fact that Paul is also his father's son. In a sense Lawrence underplayed it himself, and the father–son relationship remained unfinished business to be worked through in later novels. Achsah Brewster tells us that Lawrence later felt

he had not done justice to his father in *Sons and Lovers* and felt like rewriting it. When children they accepted the dictum of their mother that their father was a drunkard, therefore was contemptible, but that as Lawrence had grown older, he had come to see him in a different light; to see his unquenchable fire and relish for living. Now he blamed his mother for her self-righteousness, her invulnerably Christian virtue within which she was entrenched. She had brought down terrible scenes of vituperation upon their heads from which she might have protected them.

Mothers should use their power to protect rather than absorb their children. But, although there is hardly a hint of any such criticism of Mrs Morel in the novel, the portrait of Walter Morel is not altogether unsympathetic.

Morel gets on well with his workmates and the neighbours, being 'so ready and so pleasant with everybody'. He whistles cheerfully or sings hymns as he works in the garden or mends the family's shoes. There is much emphasis on his physical presence and the details of his daily behaviour, as if the author were fascinated by the actions and appearance of this strange creature, an adult male, 'happy in his man's fashion'. Sometimes in the Morel household, in between the rows, 'everything felt free of care and anxiety'. There are festive occasions when 'everybody was mad with happiness in the family. Home was home, and they lived it with a passion of love, whatever the suffering had been.' Early in the novel Lawrence describes Morel's nature as 'purely sensuous', adding that Mrs Morel 'strove to make him moral, religious. She tried to force him to face things. He could not endure it – it drove him out of his mind.' And Lawrence is capable of seeing that 'the pity was, she was too much his opposite. She could not be content with the little he might be; she would have him the much that he ought to be. So, in seeking to make him nobler than he could be, she destroyed him.' Lawrence, if not Paul, is enough of the father's son to understand the plight of Walter Morel.

Morel is often described as a boor or a brute, and 'all the children, but particularly Paul, were peculiarly *against* their father, along with their mother.' They loathe him and, as they approach adolescence, he takes a perverse pleasure in provoking their loathing. Paul has a private religion and prays very often, 'Let my father die.' But when his father fails to come home from the pit at tea-time, he prays, 'Let him not be killed at pit,' and shares his mother's anxiety over the father's non-appearance. In short, he shares his mother's ambivalent attitude towards the father. Although she refers to him as 'the nuisance', she is also capable of recalling their early days together with nostalgic affection. And she still sleeps with him.

An early chapter describes how the mother transfers her primary emotional allegiance from father to son (William, the eldest) but it is by no means written in a tone of Oedipal triumph. As his wife turns 'for life and love to the children', Morel becomes 'more or less a husk' but 'he half-acquiesced, as so many men do, yielding their place to the children.' This is a theme to which Lawrence was to return again and again with increasing sympathy for the man. In the story 'England, My England' Egbert, a very different character from Walter Morel, becomes similarly acquiescent and, as a consequence, loses his manhood and hence his will to love. In *Sons and Lovers* the Oedipal victory is compounded with an Oedipal guilt which subsequently takes a lifetime of reparation. Paul cannot entirely hate his father; he is flesh of his flesh, much as he would like to deny it.

In *The White Peacock* (which prefigures both *Sons and Lovers* and *Lady Chatterley's Lover*) parent–child relationships are very much in the background. The narrator is a rather wet young man called Cyril Beardsall (Mrs Lawrence's original surname) who stands apart from the action, and the story is mainly concerned with the doings of his peer group. But a comparison between the Beardsall and the Morel households is both interesting and significant. The Beardsall household is rather like the Morel household without the pain (and therefore without the power and the passion). Although Mrs Beardsall, no less than Gertrude Morel, is a recognizable portrait of Lydia Lawrence, all is sweetness and light, and there is no special relationship between her and her son. The Beardsalls are a rung or two above the Morels in the social scale and (quite unrealistically) never feel the pinch of poverty. The young people talk books, painting and music, quoting the classics with ease and discussing their feelings minutely in long and finely modulated speeches. There is no Mr Beardsall, no father.

Or rather, there is a Mr Beardsall and there are two fathers, each of whom comes to an untimely end. Beardsall calls himself Carlin and drifts around from job to job, often sleeping rough and slowly drinking himself to death. He deserted his family when the children were young (as does Aaron Sissons in *Aaron's Rod* – but he is exonerated) and they believe him to be dead. Early in the novel he does die – of drink and in a cheap lodging house. 'Poor old Carlin' is described as 'a jolly decent fellow – generous, open-handed' but also as 'close' and unfathomable. He is clearly as unfathomable to the author as he is to the characters in the novel. His life remains a mystery and his death, though pitiable, is unmourned, even by his stoical widow whose regret is focused, rather, on her children. 'You might have had a father – ' she tells her son. His reply is, 'We're thankful that we hadn't, mother. You spared us that.'

Carlin is given short shrift compared to Walter Morel, with whom he has much in common. The parental conflict has been avoided (indeed, evaded) and apparently dismissed. But there is another character in *The White Peacock* who has much in common with Walter Morel – and more with Arthur Lawrence. This is Annable the gamekeeper, a prefiguring of Parkin/Mellors: at once the embodiment of natural man and one of nature's gentlemen. According to William Hopkin, an early friend of Lawrence's, 'Arthur Lawrence was not of the material to mould into his wife's idea of a gentleman. He was one naturally.' According to Frieda

Lawrence, all these gamekeeper portraits constitute a tribute to Lawrence's father. It seems to me that, whereas Carlin is the portrait of a father drawn by a mother's son, Annable is a portrait drawn by a father's son.

Annable is the idealized working-class hero: a bit of a brute, maybe, especially in his behaviour towards women and children, but independent, emotionally self-sufficient and, above all, physically strong and healthy with an animal pride in his own body. In a word, manly. In another few words, everything the young Lawrence was not and knew himself poignantly not to be. Annable, like Parkin/Mellors, feels bitterly towards women, his former wife in particular. Like Birkin in *Women In Love* and Lilly in *Aaron's Rod*, he tends to rant on about the state of the world and, in particular, the state of relations between men and women. None of this is explored in any depth in *The White Peacock* but the germs of the Lawrentian hero whom women love to hate are already evident. So are the makings of the inadequately internalized father, the inadequately internalized adult male forever trying to find its rightful place within the Lawrentian psyche, forever the object of reparation, forever the unattainable self-image. Halfway through the novel Annable is killed by a fall of stones in a quarry. A double Oedipal murder, then? Yes, I think so. But the deaths of the two men also indicate Lawrence's ambivalence towards adult maleness and his inability to reconcile, for the moment, his conflicting feelings.

Paul Morel, then, internalizes the pain of both his parents, although the internalization is different in kind and degree for mother and father. Overtly taking his mother's part, he covertly internalizes both the pain and the passion of the parental marriage. Because he is a child, he cannot properly understand what he has internalized. Because what he has internalized forces him, in a profound sense, to think and feel as an adult, he cannot properly be a child. For Paul, for any child in a similar position, this must be an almost intolerable burden. How does he cope?

Although Lawrence emphasizes Paul's sweetness and often describes him as lovable, it is probable that Paul appears to his contemporaries, as did Lawrence to his, as a bit of a sissy.

Lawrence's sister Ada wrote that as a child Lawrence 'preferred the company of girls', and William Hopkin revealed in a radio interview that Lawrence's schoolfellows called him '"mardy", which is a term used to signify a sort of babyish disposition.' At the age of fourteen Paul Morel, 'a rather small and rather finely-made boy,' is looking reluctantly for work. Lawrence tells us that 'he suffered very much from the first contact with anything' and that his school learning has given him 'nothing of commercial value'. Although he secretly yearns to be a painter, 'his ambition as far as this world's gear went, was quietly to earn his thirty or thirty-five shillings a week somewhere near home, and then, when his father died, have a cottage with his mother and live happy ever after.' A sweet ambition for a seven-year-old, perhaps, but hardly likely to be acceptable to Paul's peers, many of whom are by now working down the pits. It is 'a bitter humiliation and anguish to him' to look through the job advertisements in the columns of the local newspaper. But eventually he is called for an interview at Thos. Jordan, Manufacturer of Surgical Appliances. It looks as though Paul, however ill equipped he may be for it, is about to enter the world of commerce, the world of men.

His mother accompanies him to Nottingham for the interview, she 'gay like a sweetheart', and he 'with something screwed up tight inside him'. It is from her that he takes whatever little courage he possesses for the ordeal. He watches her buy the train tickets and 'as he saw her hands in their old black kid gloves getting the silver out of the worn purse, his heart contracted with pain of love for her.' The pain of loving her has now become the pain of leaving her, at least partially, and of forgoing her maternal protection in the larger world which is outside her sphere. The interview is excruciating, but Paul is engaged as a spiral clerk at eight shillings a week.

Paul is now the only child of the family living at home. So, 'Mrs Morel now clung to Paul.' And he in turn clings to his mother.

Everything he did was for her. She waited for his coming home in the evening, and then she unburdened herself of all she had pondered, or of all that had occurred to her during the day. He sat and listened with earnestness. The two shared lives.

Is there really anything so strange about this? I think not – or at least, not yet. The situation has developed inevitably and has not yet become insupportable. At this stage in the story Mrs Morel comes across as a rather narrow-minded but industrious woman who takes the job of mothering seriously. She also comes across as a lonely, frustrated and slightly embittered woman who has no choice but to live her life through her children, her main source of joy and strength.

Given the apparently bleak circumstances of her past and present life, Mrs Morel has created in her own family something fruitful and a gift for the future. Emotional sustenance must come from somewhere and most of us find it where we can. A woman who has never had or who has abandoned the opportunity to work outside the home is likely to find it in her family. Mrs Morel is a pathetically brave woman, if rather lacking in foresight. The ultimate problem with devoting your life to your children is, as every sensible mother knows, that they grow up and leave you. And then where are you, what have you got? Mrs Morel seems to accept in theory that her children will leave her, but in practice she is not so stoic. Like most women in her position, she does not seem to understand the extent of her own power. When the crisis comes, her self-confidence wavers until it approaches desperation and she contracts cancer.

The crisis is twofold: first comes the death of her eldest son, William; then the arrival on the scene of Miriam, Paul's first sweetheart. William is the strong and handsome son, the one who was to do big things in the big wide world, things which his mother could experience vicariously and for which she could take some of the credit. He is barely twenty when he dies of pneumonia in his London lodgings, his mother arriving too late to save him. Always she addresses him, alive or dead, not by name but as 'my son!' This whole episode makes sombrely painful reading: the blind and all-consuming grief of Mrs Morel; Paul's futile attempts to comfort her; his feeling of being emotionally distanced from her for the first time in his life; and his own grief being swallowed up in her larger grief, uncomprehendingly assuming its maternal depths and dimensions.

Paul cannot tell whose pain belongs to whom: if it is his mother's, then it must be his also. It seems as if the bond which was made at his birth, the bond which dissolved the boundaries between Paul and his mother, is now being renewed. But this time his mother is not implicated, does not respond according to the old patterns, and seems unaware of her younger son's existence. It is only when Paul too becomes dangerously ill with pneumonia and Mrs Morel has to nurse him back to health, often lying in bed with him in the process, that she seems to recognize him and call him, like William, 'my son, my son!' Paul has now become Paul-and-William to Mrs Morel, The Son who has been resurrected and restored to her by a miracle of good fortune helped along by her own loving care. The old bond has been renewed now more firmly than ever. From now on Paul has to bear the burden of his mother's concern and ambition not only for the Paul-he-is but also for the William-who-might-have-been.

The renewal seems to have come at exactly the wrong time, that is, around puberty when the boy is beginning to become aware of the 'sex necessity', as Lawrence calls it in *Fantasia of the Unconscious*. There, by means of an extraordinarily elaborate systematization, Lawrence evolves an alternative strategy for making sense of the events of his early life. Briefly: the human body is divided into upper and lower sympathetic centres, front and back. The upper centres govern the intellect and idealism, the lower the passions and sensuality. The front stands for everything that is soft, vulnerable and approachable, the back all that is adamant and self-protective. In each case some sort of balance must be struck between the two in the interests of psychic health.

It is idealism, lodged in the upper sympathetic centres, which 'recognizes as the highest earthly love, the love between mother and child.' What, asks Lawrence, does this mean?

It means, for every delicately brought-up child, indeed for all children who matter, a steady and persistent pressure upon the upper sympathetic centres, and a steady and persistent starving of the lower centres, particularly the great voluntary centre of the lower body. The centre of manly independence, of exultation in the sturdy, defiant self, wilfulness, masterfulness and pride, is steadily suppressed. The warm, swift sensual self is steadily and persistently denied, dampened, weakened, throughout all the period of childhood . . . Life must always be refined and superior. Love and happiness must be the watchword . . . Vile, bullying forbearance.

This is a long way from Paul's concept of mother-love, but it is quite consistent with the views of later Lawrentian heroes on motherhood – and indeed womanhood. The warm, tender qualities as well as the aggressive, independent ones have been arrogated to the male, while the female is left in sole possession of the territory of idealism, morality, sentiment. In Lawrence's own terms, Paul, with his sweet sensitive conscience, is firmly locked into the world of women.

Lawrence's following description of the typical recipient of mother-love could well be one of the hero of *Sons and Lovers*:

Then we have exaggerated sensitiveness, alternating with a sort of helpless fury: and we have delicate, frail children with nerves or with strange whims. And we have the strange cold obstinacy of spiritual will, cold as hell, fixed in a child.

Then the one parent, usually the mother, is the object of blind devotion, whilst the other parent, usually the father, is an object of resistance. The child is taught, however, that both parents should be loved, and only loved: and that love, gentleness, pity, charity, and all higher emotions, these alone are genuine feelings; all the rest are false, to be rejected.

The result is that

a painfully false relation grows up: a relation of two adults, either of two pure lovers or of two love-appearing people who are really bullying one another. Instead of leaving the child with its own limited but deep and incomprehensible feelings, the parent, hopelessly involved in the mode of selfless love, and spiritual love-will, stimulates the child into a consciousness which does not belong to it, on the one plane, and robs it of its own spontaneous consciousness and freedom on the other.

Such action amounts to 'fatality', 'irreparable disaster', and even 'a holy obscenity'. Strong words indeed, and full of all the unreasoning bitterness of one who feels himself to have been wronged but has only just realized the extent of the damage.

Elsewhere in *Fantasia of the Unconscious* there is a speech which neither the adolescent nor the adult Paul ever delivers to his mother:

The hour of sex strikes. But there is your child, bound, helpless. You have already aroused in it the dynamic response to your own insatiable love-will. You have got your child as sure as if you had woven its flesh with your own. You have done what it is vicious for any parent to do: you have established between yourself and your child the bond of adult love . . . All your tenderness, your cherishing, will not excuse you. It only deepens your guilt.

Lawrence's later characters are quite capable of delivering such brutal speeches to one another with no apparent qualms. But part of the power of *Sons and Lovers* lies in the fact that its characters are equally frail and uncertain, and that no one knows better than anyone else. The confusions of adolescence are portrayed as confusions and the dawning of sexuality, whether dim or suddenly demanding, is depicted as something which cannot be fully understood. It is nevertheless clear that Paul's bond with his mother can no longer be construed as belonging to the innocence of childhood.

The term incest is never used in *Sons and Lovers*, but in *Fantasia of the Unconscious* Lawrence attempts to bring it out into the open. The 'bond of sympathy' described above is then defined as 'a sort of incest. It is dynamic, *spiritual* incest, more dangerous than sensual incest, because it is more intangible and less instinctively repugnant.' This assertion seems to me questionable, to say the least, and Lawrence goes on to modify it a couple of paragraphs later. 'Our psyche is so framed that activity aroused on one plane produces activity on the corresponding plane. So the intense, *pure* love-relationship inevitably arouses the lower centres in the child, the centres of sex.' Which is to say that, if a mother treats her adolescent son as her nearest and dearest spiritual love, she will inevitably arouse in him some form of sexual response. This is surely what happens in *Sons and Lovers*, although I think that the exclusively spiritual quality of Mrs Morel's love is open to question from the start.

No sooner does Lawrence reach his conclusion than he shies away from it again.

Now the deeper sensual centres, once aroused, should find some response from the body of some other, some friend or lover. The response is impossible between parent and child. Myself, I believe that biologically there is a radical sex-aversion between parent and child at the deeper sensual centres.

We have, on the one hand, spiritual incest, which is the more repugnant because the more insidious form; and on the other hand, sensual incest, which is also repugnant but, although the desire for it is a logical outcome of the spiritual form, is in any event impossible. This tortuous division reads like a case of protesting too much.

Later, in the section on sleep and dreams, Lawrence makes a further modification.

I may develop a profound and passionate love for my mother, in my days of adolescence. This starts, willy-nilly, the whole activity of adult love at the lower centres. But admission is made only of the upper, spiritual love, the love dynamically polarized at the upper centres. Nevertheless, whether admission is made or not, once establish the circuit in the upper or spiritual centres of adult love, and you will get a corresponding activity in the lower, passional centres of adult love.

The activity at the lower centres, however, is denied in the daytime. There is a repression. The friction of the night-flow liberates the repressed psychic activity explosively. And then the image of the mother figures in passionate, disturbing, soul-rending dreams.

Sensual incest is no longer impossible, merely unadmitted or repressed. But does the boy who dreams incestuously of his mother actually harbour 'a repressed incest desire'? On the contrary, says Lawrence. Such a boy is dreaming not of what he desires but what he fears, in much the same way as 'if you secretly wished your enemy dead, and feared he might flourish, the dream would present you with his wedding.' There is of course some truth in this line of argument, but what Lawrence fails doggedly to see is that the desire and the fear are inseparable: they may appear to be in opposition, but they are in fact identical, and the presence of one cannot lead us to suppose the absence of the other.

In *Sons and Lovers* it is when Paul meets his first sweetheart that the sensually-incestuous tension between himself and his mother, hinted at after the death of William, begins to be openly expressed. It is Miriam rather than the now semi-vanquished Walter Morel who is the real threat to the bond. Miriam lives at nearby Willey Farm with her parents and her unsympathetic, rather bullying brothers. It is a household in which 'her great companion was her mother. They were both brown-eyed and inclined to be mystical, such women as treasure religion inside them, breathe it in their nostrils, and see the whole of life in a mist thereof.' Miriam's beauty is that of 'a shy, wild, quiveringly sensitive thing, and she feels keenly the difference between herself and her coarser brothers. Paul she sees at once as a potential kindred spirit and 'the boy's poor morsel of learning exalted him almost sky-high in her esteem.' He teaches her algebra and gives her books to read, and they discuss both literature and nature much in the manner of the young people in *The White Peacock*. Miriam thinks the world of Paul; he is attracted to her, sometimes fascinated by her, but he has his doubts.

These doubts are fed by the now failing Mrs Morel, who frets and stays up late, and gets angry when Paul spends his evenings with Miriam. Her reaction to the girl, which she at first keeps to herself, is that 'she is one of those who will want to suck a man's soul out till he had none of his own left . . . She will never let him become a man.' At this point, and perhaps in the novel altogether, there is no evidence for Mrs Morel's strange assumption. But she sticks to it and cries in her heart after Paul has gone, 'She's not like an ordinary woman, who can leave me my share in him . . . She wants to draw him out and absorb him till there is nothing left of him, even for himself. He will never be a man on his own feet – ' Mrs Morel's accusations against Miriam sound very much like Lawrence's accusations against the spiritually-incestuous parent in *Fantasia of the Unconscious*, that is, they embody a description of Mrs Morel herself.

Miriam is repeatedly described as 'spiritual', and there is a great deal of emphasis on her soul as well as on her passivity and her suffering. Her relationship with Paul is intense and intensely intimate. According to Lawrence's own arguments in the *Fantasia*, Paul's lower sympathetic centres must by now be in a state of arousal: he must be feeling sexual desire for Miriam. As indeed he does. And yet at the same time he does not. The basis for his desire is obvious. The basis for his lack of desire he attributes to Miriam's excessive spirituality.

But is Miriam really so terribly spiritual? She seems rather to be shy, inexperienced and unusually sensitive. Her mother has told her that there is one dreadful thing in marriage which must be borne: sex. But at the same time her feeling for Paul is undeniably composed in part of physical attraction. Girls don't always heed what their mothers tell them. It is Mrs Morel who insists on seeing Miriam as a voracious soul rather than as a seductive young body. Mrs Morel has consciously prepared herself for the advent of young, female bodies in the life of her son: a young, female body, she can argue, is precisely what she herself can't give him. Bodies are, therefore, not particularly important. If she were to admit that they were, she would also have to admit that she and Miriam are sexual rivals – which is to think the unthinkable – and moreover that they are rivals in a struggle which Mrs Morel is bound to lose.

There is a great deal of self-deception going on here, as later events prove. As she sees it now, what Mrs Morel has not prepared herself for is a young woman who will poach and encroach on what she considers to be *her* territory. William's fiancée was a flighty, empty-headed creature of whom Mrs Morel could sourly disapprove while recognizing that she herself would still be allowed access to her son's emotional depths. But Miriam, says Mrs Morel, is different. What she means is that her feeling for Paul is different: it is deeper and more passionate than her feeling for William. Mrs Morel sees something of herself in Miriam. And so, eventually and fundamentally, does Paul. As ever his feelings find their level when they are inseparable from his mother's. In the end he sees in Miriam only what it suits Mrs Morel that he should see.

But for a long time he is torn between the two women. He loves Miriam; he loves his mother; he hates Miriam for causing his mother pain; he hates himself for causing his mother pain in loving Miriam; but he never consciously hates his mother. We are back to that first bond formed in fear and pain as much as in love. Paul is 'bound in by [his] own virginity', like 'many of the nicest men' he knows.

> They were so sensitive to their women that they would go without them for ever rather than do them a hurt, an injustice. Being the sons of mothers whose husbands had blundered brutally through their feminine sanctities, they themselves were too diffident and shy. They could easier deny themselves than incur any reproach from a woman; for a woman was like their mother, and they were full of the sense of their mother.

Here are alternative grounds to Miriam's excessive spirituality for Paul's failing to act upon his desires. And yet, in failing to act and follow through, he does Miriam another sort of hurt, another sort of injustice. He rejects her repeatedly in all sorts of ways so that she never knows where she is with him. And he hates her bitterly whenever he hurts her, just as Walter Morel hates his wife because his violence has made her suffer. Just as the young Paul, even then his father's as well as his mother's son, hates his sister's doll because he has broken it, and afterwards makes a sacrifice of it by burning it.

When Paul and Miriam eventually make love, she too is like a 'sacrifice'. Paul is at first blind with her beauty, 'the most beautiful body he had ever imagined', and he is 'unable to speak or move, looking at her, his face half-smiling with wonder'. Her body is there for him, but 'the look at the back of her eyes, like a creature awaiting immolation, arrested him, and all his blood fell back.' If Miriam is going to be immolated, then he himself must be the immolator, and the thought is enough to make him lose his erection. The mother's son sees male sexuality as essentially cruel. But mother's sons are not cruel. It is as if Paul were saying to himself, if mother knew what I was up to, she would find out that I am not her sweet, loving little boy, but a brute, just like my father. It is here that his burgeoning image of himself as a man, an adult male sexual being, comes crashing into conflict with his image of himself as his mother's son. The chapter is entitled 'The Test on Miriam', but it actually describes the 'test on Paul'.

The incident comes roughly three-quarters of the way through the novel, and we have been well-prepared for it, especially by an

episode in the chapter entitled 'Strife in Love', which is one of the
most powerful and most painfully explicit in the whole story. Paul
is telling his mother for the umpteenth time that he does not love
Miriam, but she continues to be accusatory and sarcastic. 'Mrs
Morel was so intense that Paul began to pant.' Having done his
best to reassure her verbally, he stoops to kiss his mother good-
night, but

she threw her arms round his neck, hid her face on his shoulder, and
cried in a whimpering voice so unlike her own that he writhed in agony:
  'I can't bear it. I could let another woman – but not her. She'd leave me
no room, not a bit of room . . .'
  And immediately he hated Miriam bitterly.
  'And I've never – you know, Paul – I've never had a husband – not
really – '
  He stroked his mother's hair and his mouth was on her throat.
  'And she exults in taking you away from me – she's not like ordinary
girls.'
  'Well, I don't love her, mother,' he murmured, bowing his head and
hiding his eyes on her shoulder in misery. His mother kissed him a long,
fervent kiss.
  'My boy!' she said, in a voice trembling with passionate love.

Mrs Morel tells lies about Miriam; she assumes that it is her
business to 'let' another woman enter into a relationship with her
son; the fact that she has never had a husband (if, indeed, it is a
fact) is of no relevance to her son's love-life, yet she sees it as
crucially relevant; but her actions, especially that 'long fervent kiss'
speak louder than any words.

   This is where Mrs Morel forfeits my sympathy. As the mother
of two grown-up sons myself, I find her conduct inexcusable.
Every mother, Mrs Morel included, knows better than to be able
knowingly to confuse and distress her children. Once she has taken
her son into a loverlike embrace and he has responded in passionate
kind, she is prepared to be generous. 'Perhaps I'm selfish,' she
concedes. 'If you want her, take her, my boy.' Now that she has
put the primary bond between herself and her son to the test and it
has withstood, she is prepared to 'let' Paul have what she knows he
doesn't want. Her manipulation of Paul is altogether conscious and

deliberate. She is playing games here, dangerous and destructive games. But, then, the stakes are of the highest.

So much then for Mrs Morel's tacit protestations of spirituality with regard to herself and Miriam. Her own love for Paul has never been spiritual, but deeply and heavily emotional. Now it is revealed as overtly sexual. Small wonder that, after making love with Miriam (and, in the circumstances, it is surprising that he manages to do so at all) Paul feels 'always the sense of failure and death'. He has betrayed his mother twice over: as the tender, protective son and as the unattainable lover. In becoming Miriam's lover he is killing his mother's son (or growing up) and also his mother's fantasy lover. And he cannot go on doing so: it would be tantamount to suicide. Not only suicide, but a double suicide: the death of Paul and the death of the internalized mother; the death of the bond.

The scene in the 'Strife in Love' chapter is interrupted by the entrance of Walter Morel, returning home drunk from the pub. His comment on seeing mother and son together is, 'At your mischief again?' Lawrence describes this comment as 'venomous', but we can take it as we may. A quarrel over money ensues, and father and son nearly come to blows. At this point Mrs Morel faints (rather like Lady Macbeth – is this a faint or a feint?) and the two men are thus diverted. Paul ministers to his mother, 'the tears hopping down his face', while the father stumbles off to bed. Paul urges his mother not to sleep with his father, but she protests, 'I'll sleep in my own bed.' On the landing he kisses her 'close' and in bed is in 'a fury of misery'. 'And yet somewhere in his soul he was at peace because he still loved his mother best. It was the bitter peace of resignation.'

In one short episode both Morel, who has now fought his last fight in that home, and Miriam have been, to use Lawrence's own word, 'defeated'. But this is not the end of the matter as far as Miriam is concerned. Paul, being young and almost despite himself a sexual being, is not quite as resigned as he imagines to being solely his mother's son. It is only after Paul's relationship with Miriam has become a sexual one, that is, after they have both tried every possible method of making it work, that he can finally reject her, can finally admit that the primary bond with Mrs Morel is the strongest in his life and the one which must not be broken on pain of death.

And indeed it is only death that can end it: the death of Mrs Morel. It is while she is dying slowly of cancer that Paul can enter into a sexual relationship with another woman, Clara Dawes, who differs from both Mrs Morel and Miriam in that she is independent, self-confident, unashamedly sensual, and holds decidedly feminist views. In the affair with Clara (this chapter is entitled 'Passion') Paul begins to shed some of the attributes of sonhood and to grow up. But again the process remains incomplete, arrested, and he has to come up with all sorts of excuses for finding Clara wanting. He is not now under the same sort of daily pressure from Mrs Morel, whose illness has robbed her of the strength to fight. At the same time she now represents a stronger adversary than ever, in that her son's grief and concern for her renders him incapable of giving himself wholeheartedly to any other relationship. In consequence, Clara is made to suffer, perhaps less than Miriam (such things are difficult to quantify) but in the same sort of way.

Paul Morel's story is by no means an uncommon one, even today when women theoretically have more emotional resources available to them than had Mrs Morel, and are less inclined to endure unsatisfactory marriages. 'Mother-damaged' men are a menace to other women no less than to themselves. Should we blame mothers? Not entirely. It is important to distinguish, as always, between causation and blame. The ultimate cause of Mrs Morel's frustration and bitterness is, after all, the traditional role of motherhood that men have assigned to women.

Mrs Morel takes a long time to die and in doing so draws out her son's suffering as well as her own. It then rebounds upon the other women in his life. The situation becomes unbearable and Paul, plotting with his sister, administers a fatal dose of morphine, ostensibly to shorten his mother's anguish, but in reality and by admission also to shorten his own. Mrs Morel is now the baby, Paul the controlling mother-figure, but whereas she gave him life, he deals her death. Rationally speaking, his action is a merciful one, but rationality has never been a characteristic of his relationship with his mother, and the murder (if such it can be called) comes as a bit of a shock. There is an element of revenge in it. The chapter in which this episode occurs is entitled 'The Release': a release for both Paul and Mrs Morel, but also a release from the primary bond formed in fear, pain and love.

As might be expected, Paul is devastated by the death of his mother: it is, after all, partially the death of himself, the death of a mother's son. He feels lost, confused, and even contemplates suicide, 'wanting to go after her'. The weeks go on. 'Always alone, his soul oscillated, first on the side of death, then on the side of life, doggedly. The real agony was that he had nowhere to go, nothing to do, nothing to say, and *was* nothing in himself.' Neither Miriam, nor Clara, who has now returned to her husband, can afford him any solace. Like most men, he has no male friends to whom he can turn. But at the end of the novel there is a kind of hope, the hope that out of nothingness new life can be born. The death of the mother may mean the death of the son, but it may also (and this is only a scarcely-glimpsed possibility) be the birth of the man. The hope is not founded on any insight about the future, much less any clear plan of action, but simply and tentatively on the fact of life itself.

Frieda worked very closely with Lawrence on *Sons and Lovers*, working through the conflicts with him, and supplying him with some of its most cogent material. In her *Memoirs and Correspondence* she writes, 'I lived and suffered that book, and wrote bits of it when he would ask me, "What do you think my mother felt then?"' On the page of the manuscript which describes Mrs Morel's death, she wrote in the margin, 'Poor devil – now at last you are free.' And it would seem that it was not until he had written *Sons and Lovers* that Lawrence was in any sense 'free' of his mother. 'One sheds one's sickness in books,' he wrote in a letter to Edward Garnett. Well, not entirely. If that were so, writers would be the healthiest and happiest people alive – a manifest untruth – and would soon give up writing. But the purpose of writing *Sons and Lovers* does seem to have been largely therapeutic. Except in a few short stories, and then in scathing, satirical terms, Lawrence never wrote again about the relationship between mother and son. It is almost as though a ghost had been laid to rest – the ghost of the son as well as that of the mother.

However, there is a passage at the end of *Sons and Lovers* which suggests otherwise. Paul argues thus with himself: ' "You're alive." "She's not." "She is – in you." ' Something of his mother will remain in Paul, and something of him will remain in her world, the world of women. To some extent Paul's consciousness will remain that of his mother, that of a woman. In his brilliant book *The Von Richthofen Sisters*, Martin Green suggests that Lawrence too remained at least in part in the world of women, making increasingly extensive forays into the world of men, only to return, disillusioned and defeated, to base. It seems to me that Lawrence writes more convincingly – more movingly and more powerfully – about the world of women than he writes about the world of men. The extraordinary thing about Lawrence's fiction (in this context) is not that he writes well about women, but that he writes so badly and ineptly about men.

Apart from Paul Morel, all Lawrence's leading male characters are to me imperfectly realized and therefore, in varying degrees, unsympathetic. I would contract an instant diplomatic illness in order to avoid Birkin or Mellors or the equally unattractive Aaron and Lilly. They are all such self-conceited bullies that it could be supposed that there is not a mother's son among them. But in fact their misogyny and their allegiance to notions of male supremacy both spring directly from their despised mother's sonhood. They are all trying very hard indeed to become men's men.

3
The man's man

In the writing of *Sons and Lovers* Lawrence struggled, with Frieda's help, to understand himself, the nature of family relationships and the nature of love. Once he had met and married Frieda, Lawrence was soon to come to the conclusion that 'the relationship between man and woman is the central fact in actual human life.' The quotation is taken from the essay 'We Need One Another', but it could equally well have come from any of perhaps another hundred sources throughout Lawrence's writing. In the same essay he goes on to make a point which is also frequently reiterated. 'Next comes the relationship of man to man. And, a long way after that, all the other relationships, fatherhood, motherhood, sister, brother, friend.' Precedence has been given to the sort of relationship which was considered only briefly in *Sons and Lovers*; motherhood (and with it sonhood) has been downgraded; and the relationship of woman to woman is not even mentioned. This constitutes a pretty fair summary of Lawrence's scale of values for interpersonal relationships from *Women In Love* onwards, although it often seems in the course of that novel and others of Lawrence's middle period that the relationship of man to man is threatening to take precedence over the relationship between man and woman.

Norman Mailer sees Lawrence as a man who 'had lifted himself out of his natural destiny, which was probably to have the sexual life of a woman,' someone who 'had become a man by an act of will, he was bone and blood of the classic stuff out of which homosexuals are made.' And there is a great deal of homoeroticism in Lawrence's work, ranging from the overtly (though never sexually consummated) erotic, through blood-brotherhood, to the schoolboy-crush relationship between leader and follower who together will do great things in the world of men. For Lawrence, the relationship of man to man was never unproblematic and sometimes bitterly disappointing. In essence, he wanted men to

love him as much as he loved them but, despite repeated assertions
to the contrary in his fiction, they never did. And he wanted to love
and be loved by a man while retaining his hard-won heterosexual
identity, but in practice this proved impossible.

Comptom Mackenzie claims that Lawrence once told him, 'I
believe the nearest I've ever come to perfect love was with a
young coal miner when I was sixteen.' And there is an apparent
substantiation of this claim in *The White Peacock* where Cyril, the
weedy narrator, sees himself in contrast to the robust and energetic
George Saxton, son of a local farmer. This is a typically Lawrentian
pairing between man and man, echoing that first pairing between
male and male: father and son.

After the two men have been swimming in an icily cold pond,

We stood and looked at each other as we rubbed ourselves dry. He was
well-proportioned, and naturally of handsome physique, heavily limbed.
He laughed at me, telling me I was like one of Aubrey Beardsley's long,
lean, ugly fellows. I referred him to many classic examples of slenderness,
declaring myself more exquisite than his grossness, which amused him.

Beardsleyesque indeed. And the chapter title has a *fin de siècle*,
Yellow Book ring to it: 'A Poem of Friendship'. But there is no
doubt as to who is the more manly of the two.

I had to give in, and bow to him, and he took on an indulgent, gentle
manner. I laughed and submitted. For he knew how I admired the fair
fruitfulness of his form . . ., He polished his arm, holding it out straight
and solid; he rubbed his hair into curls, while I watched the deep muscles
of his shoulders, and the bands stand out in his neck as he held it firm . . .

Faced with the dazzling spectacle of male beauty, Cyril reacts,
much as Connie Chatterley does to Mellors, by submitting in awe.
He finds himself thinking of the gamekeeper Annable, who had
such pride in his own body. Now lost in wonder, Cyril invites
further domination from George.

He saw that I had forgotten to continue my rubbing, and laughing he took
hold of me as if I were a child, or rather, a woman he loved and did not
fear. I left myself quite limply in his hands, and, to get a better grip of me,
he put his arm around me and pressed me against him, and the sweetness

of the touch of our naked bodies, one against the other, was superb. It satisfied in some measure the vague, indecipherable yearning of my soul; and it was the same with him. When he had rubbed me all warm, he let me go, and we looked at each other with eyes of still laughter, and our love was perfect for a moment, more perfect than any love I have known since, either for man or woman.

The love between man and man is based in physical attraction and entails the willing submission of the weaker to the stronger. It is also a love without fear or pain, but sweet, superb, satisfying and imbued with laughter.

This episode prefigures two similar scenes in Lawrence's later fiction and contains elements of both: the famous wrestling scene between Birkin and Gerald in *Women In Love*, and the episode in *Aaron's Rod* where Lilly rubs oil all over the sick and failing Aaron. And yet all three scenes are very different in tone and emphasis. *The White Peacock* episode belongs to the innocence of boyhood and is almost nostalgic already in the telling. The *Women In Love* episode is thick with the tension of otherwise unexpressed emotion and verges on the sadistic. In *Aaron's Rod* the relationship between the physically weaker and stronger is reversed, and the closeness between the two men is beginning to shade from the openly homoerotic into the concept of leader and follower. Taken together, the three episodes demonstrate the progression of Lawrence's thought and feeling about man-to-man relationships.

Women In Love is not one of my favourite novels, and to my mind makes a disappointing sequel to the beautifully accomplished *The Rainbow*, of which it was at first intended to be a part. The milieu is mainly upper-to-middle-class Bohemia, a world in which Lawrence is, in more senses than one, out of his class. Unlike Aldous Huxley, who wrote so brittly and brilliantly of this very same milieu (and often of the very same people), Lawrence was not of their number, and could never entirely allow himself to become so. In 'An Autobiographical Sketch' he writes: 'As a man from the working class, I feel that the middle class cut off some of my vital vibration when I am with them. I admit them charming and educated and good people often enough. *But they just stop some part of me from working.*' This seems to me true of both Lawrence and his hero/surrogate Birkin in *Women In Love*.

Birkin fails to understand the people around him and, instead of trying to do so, goes into a state of defensive loathing and rage against them. Consequently the tone of the novel is often bilious. That is, when it is not hysterical – the two often merge. I find the hysteria, with its hints of underlying sadism, more difficult to cope with than the bile. People seem to hate and loathe each other again and again for no good reason, and often intensely or even insanely. Lawrence's hate-words like 'will', 'mind', 'know', or 'understand' tend to be heavily underlined (i.e. italicized) in the text, and repeatedly qualified by such terms as 'insane' (again), 'hellish', or 'diabolic'. The overall impression is that of a tortured and self-torturing authorial presence, and an authorial mind which is badly, perhaps disastrously, out of control. The result is disturbing, bewildering and, finally, alienating.

Women In Love reads like the novel in which Lawrence tried to work through the problem of his own homosexuality, while never quite admitting it, never quite coming to terms with it. There are four main characters: the Brangwen sisters, Ursula and Gudrun, whom we have already met in *The Rainbow*; Gerald Crich (always referred to as Gerald) who is son and heir to a local mine-owning family; and Rupert Birkin (always referred to by his surname, as was Lawrence himself) who is a schools inspector. The novel is thrown off balance immediately because, although we know a lot about the backgrounds of the other three, about Birkin we know next to nothing. He seems to have no antecedents, just a rather unlikely circle of friends. Perhaps this is how Lawrence wanted to see himself at the time: Birkin is certainly his mouthpiece. Lawrence seems to believe that no further information is necessary, and yet we readers are supposed to sympathize and participate in the deadly conflicts taking place in the psyche of this shadowy and far from attractive figure.

Lawrence has either loaded the dice against himself or is being arrogant enough to assume that Birkin and his views are both self-evidently admirable. I think he is being arrogant, whether from pride ('I am not going to beg for your sympathy, dear reader') or from perversity ('This is the way it is, dear reader, and you can take it or leave it') it is impossible to say: probably a mixture of the two. But I also think he is being evasive. He does not want us to know too much about Birkin's family, especially his relationship with his mother, because then both he and we should have to confront the problem of Birkin's homosexuality head on. The underlying assumption is that the reader will not be in sympathy with Birkin's plight. Given that the novel was first published in 1921, this assumption is surely not without foundation.

Birkin is torn between loving men and loving women or, rather, between loving Gerald and loving Ursula. The mother's son, who wistfully and worshipfully admires the male physique, is in conflict with the father's son, who wishes to possess and dominate a woman while fearing, as the son of both mother and father, that this is exactly what she will do to him. Gerald is in part the magnificent male animal who appears so often in Lawrence's fiction: 'fair, good-looking, healthy, with a great reserve of energy. He was erect and complete, there was a strange stealth glistening through his amiable, almost happy appearance.' But he is also Cain, a boy who, albeit accidentally, killed his brother. Which is to say that Gerald is, like homosexuality itself, unnatural, dangerous and accursed.

At first it seems both arbitrary and melodramatic that he should be so – after all, he seems a nice enough fellow – but the evidence soon begins to pile up. First, there is the episode in which Ursula and Gudrun watch Gerald deliberately expose his mare to terror in the form of a noisily shunting train.

A sharpened look came on Gerald's face. He bit himself down on the mare like a keen edge biting home, and *forced* her round. She reared as she breathed, her nostrils were two wide hot holes, her mouth was apart, her eyes frenzied. It was a repulsive sight. But he held on her unrelaxed, with an almost mechanical relentlessness, keen as a sword pressing into her. Both man and horse were sweating with violence. Yet he seemed calm as a ray of cold sunshine.

The sexual connotations are unmistakable, the male part in the proceedings being revealed here as both cruel and destructive. As such it is an extension of Paul Morel's feelings about sexuality in relation to Miriam.

Gerald's bright Nordic beauty is also cold and obdurate, his behaviour less than fully human but at the same time human indeed, which makes it all the more horrifying. When Ursula later rebukes Gerald for his behaviour, he protests that, in controlling and mastering his mare, he was only doing what was 'natural', and Birkin chips in to reprove her for her sentimentality: a horse does not have the same feelings as a man. Ursula argues her case at length and the argument ends in an apparent impasse between male and female attitudes towards the natural world. It seems to me that Lawrence is ambivalent here about whether or not the human male is a natural destroyer and, by extension, whether or not male sexuality is necessarily cruel and destructive. For Birkin, caught between the world of men and the world of women, this is a problem indeed.

The picture becomes somewhat clearer with the description of Gerald as an industrial magnate. Like Clifford Chatterley, Gerald is intent on running the pits (which he has now inherited from his father) on economically rational lines, laying off old hands with the necessary pensions, replacing other men by machines, and bettering the lot of his new, improved workforce. He has a paternalistic social conscience and aims to create a perfect system, a perfect machine, for the benefit of all concerned.

He had a fight to fight with Matter, with the earth and the coal it enclosed. This was the sole idea, to turn upon the inanimate matter of the underground, and reduce it to his will. And for this fight with matter, one must have perfect instruments in perfect organization, a mechanism so subtle and harmonious in its workings that it represents the single mind of man and by its relentless repetition of given movement, will accomplish a purpose, irresistibly, inhumanly. It was this inhuman principle that inspired Gerald with an almost Godlike exaltation. He, the man, could impose a perfect, changeless, godlike medium between himself and the matter he had to subjugate ... a great and perfect machine, a system, pure mechanical repetition ad infinitum, eternal and infinite.

This highly significant passage, which goes on in much the same vein for another page and a half, contains many of Lawrence's hate-words: will, mechanism, machine, repetition, inhuman, eternal, infinite. And here everything Lawrence hates is connected specifically with the male principle, the principle which seeks to dominate not only women and horses, but the whole of natural creation, to its own relentless will. It is both inhuman and malely human.

It is Hermione Roddice, the aristocratic hostess, who is rebuked most often and consistently for the exercise of her will. She and Birkin accuse one another of forcing themselves on other people in the manner of an insensitive child (or a botanist) who forces the bud of a flower apart to see what is inside, to see how the object functions. The accusations levelled against Hermione by both Birkin and Lawrence are vituperative in the extreme: often they can only be described as hysterical. The male destructive principle is hateful enough in men, but it is even more hateful in women because it is not natural to them. As in the discussion of the mare episode, the concept of the essentially destructive male principle is at once rejected (for what it is) and accepted (as a characteristic more natural to the male than to the female). But it is never quite endorsed.

The concept of man (and I do mean man rather than woman) as a triumphant conqueror of nature is a familiar one. In the expansionist nineteenth century it was closely tied to the concept of progress and generally endorsed in industrial countries by both Church and State (though not by novelists such as George Eliot or Elizabeth Gaskell) as an essential part of the human race's belief in itself. It is only comparatively recently that the idea has fallen into disrepute, being analysed most cogently and exhaustively by Erich Fromm in his *The Anatomy of Human Destructiveness* (1974). Many of his ideas have since been taken up by the women's movement, most notably by Susan Griffin: it is interesting to see her and her followers assume what is essentially a Lawrentian position, designating the female as a natural and the male as a cultural agent. Although Lawrence was later to advocate natural agency as a characteristic of the male as well as the female principle, in *Women In Love* he is still deeply and painfully enmeshed in coming to terms with maleness as it seems to exist in both social and sexual life. And in the persona of Birkin he is caught and torn between love of it and hate of it.

Birkin is both attracted and repelled by Gerald. Early on in the novel, when Birkin has been doing his best to bully Gerald into admitting that he is unhappy and afraid of himself,

There was a pause of strange enmity between the two men, that was very near to love. It was always the same between them; always their talk brought them into a deadly nearness of contact, a strange, perilous intimacy which was either love or hate or both.

But at this stage, although 'the heart of each burned for the other', they do not admit as much, preferring to keep their relationship a 'casual free-and-easy friendship'. Neither of them is

going to be so unmanly and unnatural as to allow any heart-burning between them. They had not the faintest belief in deep relationship between men and men, and their disbelief prevented any development of their powerful but suppressed friendliness.

This is disingenuous: it becomes obvious very quickly that Birkin – but not Gerald – does have such a belief; that he hates Gerald for his disbelief; and that what is being suppressed amounts to rather more than friendliness.

Gerald loves Birkin, after his fashion, but does not take him seriously. So Lawrence tells us at least twice. This seems to me the root of the matter, and the root of the problem. Other statements which suggest that Gerald is more deeply implicated read like wish-fulfilling hypotheses on the part of either Birkin or Lawrence. When Birkin is ill, Gerald comes to see him (this is a recurring Lawrentian situation) and gets lectured for his pains. He looks at Birkin 'with subtle eyes of knowledge', seeing in him

the amazing attractive godliness of his eyes, a young spontaneous goodness that attracted the other man infinitely, yet filled him with bitter chagrin because he mistrusted it so much. He knew Birkin could do without him – could forget and not suffer.

In the light of the outcome of the novel, it seems to me that those feelings have been misattributed: it is surely Birkin who is feeling both strongly attracted and bitter about it, Birkin who knows that Gerald can do without him. At the same time

Quite other things were going through Birkin's mind. Suddenly he saw himself confronted with ... the problem of love and conjunction between two men. Of course this was necessary – it had been a necessity inside himself all his life – to love a man purely and fully. Of course he had been loving Gerald all along, and all along denying it.

Because Birkin loves Gerald and has been denying it, Lawrence manages to persuade himself that Gerald loves Birkin in the same way, and has been similarly denying it. It is rather more difficult to persuade the reader because Gerald's subsequent actions are not consistent with such an attribution. When Birkin continues to cling to it, he appears to the reader who, like Ursula, knows better, as simply deluded.

According to Frieda, the model for Gerald was in part the writer John Middleton Murry (as was his wife Katherine Mansfield for Gudrun) to whom Lawrence was indeed intensely attached. That Murry failed to recognize himself may indicate that the portrait is a partial one, but it may also be a further indication that Lawrence has misattributed homoerotic feelings to Gerald. The conversations between Gerald and Birkin closely resemble those between Murry and Lawrence in 1916 when the two men were living as neighbours in Cornwall. In his biography of Lawrence, *The Priest of Love*, Harry T. Moore tells us that 'Murry's greatest difficulty that spring was with Lawrence's proposal of *Blut bruderschaft*.' And, in the sickroom scene in *Women In Love*, blood-brotherhood is exactly what Birkin goes on to propose to Gerald. Lawrence and Murry quarrelled over this – and on many subsequent occasions. Again and again in his letters Lawrence reviles Murray with all the bitterness of a disappointed and rejected lover, the sort of bitterness which informs *Women In Love* and points the way to Gerald's ultimate destruction. Hell knows no fury like a man scorned.

Women In Love is a novel full of blood – Gerald's spurs in the mare's flank and the rabbit which draws blood from Gudrun's arm are both dwelt on in fascinated detail – and emotional violence. It is a novel written by a man struggling with violent passions. The wrestling match between Gerald and Birkin is not, as Harry T. Moore would have it, just innocent manly sport but, as the chapter heading 'Gladiatorial' indicates, deadly combat. 'They seemed to drive their white flesh deeper and deeper against each other, as if they would break into a oneness.' Birkin is a man fighting not only with another loved and hated man, but with a demon within. He 'seemed to penetrate into Gerald's more solid, more diffuse bulk, to interfuse his body through the other, as if to bring it into subjection.' And 'they wrestled swiftly, rapturously, intent and mindless at last.' Enter, penetrate, potency, union, oneness, physical junction: the sexually connotable words multiply as the match draws nearer its climax. Again, this is male sexuality unmistakably connected with violence, but here the dynamism of the violence comes from suppressed sexuality itself. When the bout is over, they are both 'spent' and 'waited dimly, in a sort of non-being, for many uncounted, unknown minutes'. Although Gerald is the stronger, Birkin is declared the winner because his strength has been 'almost supernatural'. We are supposed to believe that his moral superiority has somehow won the day.

The physically weaker man is no longer, as in *The White Peacock*, in thrall to the stronger, but has made himself an equal, perhaps even the superior he so often proves in Lawrence's later fiction. And he has become so, not by sheer physical force but by force of intellect and of something indefinable which amounts approximately to purity of soul. Although the 'wrestling had some deep meaning for them', it is 'an unfinished meaning', for Birkin at least. He must now attempt to put what has happened into words – a medium in which he is also Gerald's superior – and thus press his victory home. 'We are mentally, spiritually intimate,' he tells Gerald, 'therefore we should be more or less physically intimate – it is more whole.' Gerald agrees with a 'pleasant laugh', stretching out his arms 'handsomely'. Birkin tells him how beautiful he is, that he has a 'northern beauty like light refracted from snow – and a beautiful plastic form', and tries to persuade him that the wrestling match constitutes some sort of 'pledge' between them. Gerald laughs again and evades him, going off to fetch his dressing-gown and leaving Birkin alone.

At once Birkin's thoughts revert to Ursula. Even when Gerald returns, resplendent in his Bokharan kaftan, 'really it was Ursula, it was the woman, who was gaining ascendancy over Birkin's being at this moment. Gerald was becoming dim again, lapsing out of him.' At this point Birkin tells Gerald that he has proposed marriage to Ursula and the two men proceed to discuss women and love. It would seem that the wrestling match has been a sort of homoerotic stag night for Birkin, perhaps even a sort of exorcism. But it would be a mistake to assume that Birkin has wrestled with the demon of his homosexuality and brought it entirely into subjection. The meaning of the match, the meaning of the intimacy between the two men, remains unfinished business for the rest of the novel.

When Gerald skis off to die in the snow which mirrors his icy and dazzling beauty, Birkin is at first numb and can even look at the body dispassionately.

But when he went again at evening, to look at Gerald between the candles, because of his heart's hunger, suddenly his heart contracted, his own candle all but fell from his hand, as, with a strange whimpering cry, the tears broke out . . . he sat with sunken head and body convulsively shaken, making a strange horrible sound of tears.

He tells Ursula who has followed him and is looking at him in some horror, 'I didn't want it to be like this.' But, having calmed himself,

Then suddenly he lifted his head and looked at Ursula with dark, almost vengeful eyes.
'He should have loved me,' he said. 'I offered him.'
She, afraid, white, with mute lips, answered:
'What difference would it have made!'
'It would!' he said. 'It would!'

He remembers how he and Gerald clasped hands after the wrestling match 'with a warm, momentous grip of final love'. If Gerald

had kept true to that clasp, death would not have mattered. Those who die, and dying still can love, still believe, do not die. They live still in the beloved. Gerald might still have been living in the spirit with Birkin, even after death. He might have lived with his friend, a further life.

Well, perhaps. But it is also clear that even Gerald's bodily death is not sufficient punishment for his having failed to reciprocate Birkin's love: he must also be killed in the spirit, that is, killed completely and forever. Not even hell, it would seem, is bad enough for him.

But the matter does not and cannot end so easily and cleanly. Birkin continues to brood over Gerald's death and in doing so holds himself apart from his wife, Ursula. Eventually she challenges him, asking him why he needs Gerald, why she is not enough for him. She doesn't need anyone else but him: why isn't it the same for Birkin? His reply is,

'Having you, I can live all my life without anybody else, any other sheer intimacy. But to make it complete, really happy, I wanted eternal union with a man too: another kind of love.'
  'I don't believe it,' she said. 'It's an obstinacy, a theory, a perversity.'
  'Well – ' he said.
  'You can't have two kinds of love. Why should you!'
  'It seems I can't,' he said. 'Yet I wanted it.'
  'You can't have it because it's false, impossible,' she said.
  'I don't believe that,' he answered.

How hesitant this is: Birkin is not being entirely honest with Ursula. The novel ends on his disbelief, but it is Ursula who speaks with the voice of common sense: love too is the art of the possible.

Murry later claimed that Lawrence was fifteen per cent homosexual and eighty-five per cent heterosexual. How on earth it is possible to quantify such matters so precisely I don't know, but it seems to me that at this point of his life, his early thirties, there was a large proportion of homosexuality in Lawrence's psychological make-up. Frieda denied as much during Lawrence's lifetime, but after his death told Richard Aldington in a 1949 letter that Lawrence had at this time 'a passionate attachment for a Cornish farmer', adding somewhat ambiguously that 'of course it was a failure', and that she had put up a fight for her husband's affections. The prologue to the American edition of *Women In Love* (which interestingly enough was almost immediately suppressed by

Lawrence himself and never published in his lifetime) sheds some light on the matter. Writing about Birkin, Lawrence explains:

All the time he recognized that, although he was drawn to women, feeling more at home with a woman than with men, yet it was for men that he felt the hot, flushing, roused attraction which a man is supposed to feel for the other sex ... In the street it was the men who roused him by their flesh and their manly vigorous movement ... It was the man's physique which held the passion and the mystery to him ... He loved his friend, the beauty of whose manly limbs made him tremble with pleasure. He wanted to caress him ...

This surely needs no further comment from me.

Lawrence goes on to describe 'a strange Cornish type of man', and says that in his presence, 'again Birkin would feel the desire spring up in him, the desire to know this man, to have him, as it were to eat him, to take the very substance of him.' Birkin's homosexuality is voracious, then, and rooted in primitive oral fantasies of domination and submission. There is in it an element of rage and revenge against the loved object, as there is in the baby's love for the mother who can thwart but can never be possessed completely. Such feelings are totally consistent not so much with Birkin's as with Lawrence's treatment of Gerald. It is, after all, Lawrence and not Birkin who sends Gerald to his untimely death amid the northern snows.

Homosexuality cannot be admitted openly, for whatever reasons, either by Birkin or by Lawrence during the course of the novel itself. Maybe, after the banning of *The Rainbow*, the risk was too great. Maybe contemporary taboos against homosexuality prevented such matters from being thoroughly and honestly discussed in private, let alone in public, and so Lawrence was discouraged from being thoroughly honest with himself. Maybe (and there are various passages in the essays to support such a supposition) Lawrence basically believed homosexuality to be unnatural and therefore suspect, perhaps even wicked. Maybe he felt that Birkin's nature was not totally homosexual and that therefore homosexuality should not be emphasized. Maybe (and this is what I believe to be true) Lawrence was painfully and hopelessly confused about his own sexuality.

The Prologue goes on to describe Birkin's predicament in terms which indicate as much:

And then in his soul would succeed a sort of despair, because this passion for a man had recurred in him. It was a deep misery to him. And it would seem as if he had always loved men, always and only loved them ... 'I should not feel like this,' and 'It is the ultimate mark of my own deficiency that I feel like this.'

Birkin's homosexuality makes him feel guilty and inadequate, less of a man than he might otherwise be. 'He never accepted the desire and received it as part of himself.' We must suppose that Birkin is tormented. No wonder *Women In Love* is full of shrieks of agony, full of blood and darkness. No wonder it is permeated with hatred and loathing: they are Lawrence's own self-hatred and self-loathing.

I don't think I am going too far in thus identifying Lawrence and Birkin. I really don't believe that anyone who never or even rarely had doubts as to the nature of his own sexuality would or could write as Lawrence does in the suppressed Prologue. It seems to me that, after writing *Women In Love*, Lawrence had finished with overt homoeroticism in much the same way as he had finished with the mother–son relationship after writing *Sons and Lovers*. At any rate, the erotic element in the relation of man to man is played down in the immediately succeeding novels until it disappears entirely as foregrounded subject-matter. The eroticism inherent in such relationships is sublimated into something more high-minded, something for which Lawrence can offer either political or religious justification. But it is never treated without anxiety.

Aaron's Rod, which next takes up the theme of man-to-man relationships, seems to have been written by a man who hates women. But it is more than a misogynist tract in that it is also written by a man who needs women – or, more accurately, by a man who needs a woman and intermittently hates himself (and her) for doing so. Martin Green has suggested, I think convincingly, that all Lawrence's most misogynistic utterances were written during his many separations from Frieda, or after some quarrel with her which seemed at the time to be irreparable. Much of

Aaron's Rod was written while Lawrence was in Italy and Frieda in London visiting her children from her former marriage to Ernest Weekley.

The two main characters are Aaron Sissons, a miner and a amateur flute player, and Rawdon Lilly, a writer. Aaron has walked out on his wife and two young daughters for no apparent reason, beyond that he is fed up with being a husband and a father. Lilly is married too, but for significant portions of the action his wife Tanny is away in Norway visiting her family. Lilly resembles Lawrence, not only in his profession but, rather than the more manly working-class Aaron, also in his physique. He is generally considered to be the author's mouthpiece, but it would be truer to say that Aaron and Lilly represent different aspects of the Lawrentian psyche and express correspondingly intermeshed views on the ever-vexed question of the relations between men and women. In doing so, and in discussing such relations at length, they both explore and exemplify relations between man and man.

Like many another Lawrentian hero, Aaron is exceedingly bitter about women and seems to have no regard whatsoever for his children. That he is justified in leaving his wife (for such is the implication) and that he loves her (for such is his repeated avowal) seems at first to be equally improbable. Aaron's wanderings appear to be motiveless, his bitterness and depression without foundation. He has two affairs with other women, one in London with an artist called Josephine and another in Italy with a musical Marchesa. After the first he becomes ill and attributes his attack of flu to his having given in to Josephine, to having been unable to resist her. After the second, which is as unemotional as the first but is based on Aaron's 'unalloyed desire', he hates the Marchesa and finds her 'deadly'.

Kate Millett finds arrant misogyny here, but this is at best a half-truth. It is quite clear that in each case Aaron is torturing himself because he has been unfaithful to his wife, Lottie. After the affair with Josephine, he tells Lilly, 'I cried, thinking of Lottie and the children. I felt my heart break, you know. And that's what did it.' That is, it is the breaking of his heart which has led to the breakdown of his body in the form of flu. With the Marchesa he constantly feels that she is 'not his woman'. Elsewhere we are told that he has had other affairs 'out of spite or defiance or curiosity. They meant nothing. He and Lottie loved one another.'

Spite and defiance are interesting motives for extra-marital affairs, and there is an element of each, as well as of curiosity, in Aaron's relationships with Josephine and the Marchesa. Spite implies revenge, paying the other person back in kind. In the present context it suggests that Lottie has been unfaithful to Aaron, and yet there is no evidence to confirm any such suggestion. It seems to me that Lawrence has skewed things round here, perhaps in order to divert attention from the true state of affairs between himself and Frieda. As things stand, there is no cause for Aaron to feel spiteful. Defiance implies making a statement in opposition to another statement. Here it means that Aaron needs Lottie, but is forced, for whatever reasons, to assert otherwise. His attempts at infidelity end in miserable failure and he succeeds only in hurting and bewildering himself. Like Lawrence, Aaron is basically monogamous and suffers whenever he departs from his belief in marital fidelity.

When Aaron has flu it is Lilly, temporarily living apart from his wife and alone, who looks after him, nursing him, cooking for him and even washing and darning his socks, 'as efficient and unobtrusive a housewife as any woman'. The two men discuss marriage and agree that they hate married people, 'stuck together like two jujube lozenges'. Aaron agrees with Lilly when he says that 'everybody ought to stand by themselves in the first place – men and women. They can come together in the second place, if they like. But nothing is any good unless each one stands alone intrinsically.' Standing alone is what Aaron has been trying to do – and with scant success. Lilly, by contrast, is claiming both in words and by his self-sufficient domestic behaviour that he has learned how to stand alone. At this stage he is still presenting his separation from Tanny as amicable and non-problematic. In doing so, he is reassuring Aaron that what *he* has done in separating himself from *his* wife is necessary and altogether justified in the name of individual (note, not manly) independence. Superficially it all sounds very sensible, but in fact what the two men have in common

is their desperate need for their women and their equally desperate
need to deny the existence of any such needs. Unlike the pact
between Gerald and Birkin, the pact between Aaron and Lilly
depends heavily on this denial.

As Aaron's condition worsens, the relationship between the two
men deepens. Lilly is calmly in control of the situation, the
physically weaker man with the stronger at his mercy. But here
there is no note of triumph. Aaron being so weakened, it is hardly
necessary, and Lilly tends him as a mother would her child. He
decides to administer a physiological-cum-psychological aid to
recovery and rub his patient with camphorated oil 'as mothers do
their babies whose bowels don't work'. Aaron would rather be left
alone, but Lilly is firm with him.

Quickly he uncovered the blond lower body of his patient, and began to
rub the abdomen with oil, using a slow, rhythmic circulating motion, a
sort of massage. For a long time he rubbed finely and steadily, then went
over the whole of the lower body, mindless, as if in a sort of incantation.
He rubbed every speck of the man's lower body – the abdomen, the
buttocks, the thighs and knees, down to the feet, rubbed it all warm and
glowing . . . till he was almost exhausted.

There is of course a strong element of the erotic in Lilly's actions,
but it is quite without the fervour and indeed the perfervid sadism
of the eroticism in *Women In Love*. On the contrary, it is avowedly
maternal, the weaker man becoming the stronger but sick man's
mother, and thus in a position to exert total but tender control.
Even the language – 'every speck', 'all warm and glowing' – is
rather motherly, which is to say, babyish. The massage is a success
and Aaron perks up. A man has done a mother's job as well as any
woman. Who needs women?

It is only at the end of the chapter that Lilly mentions the man-
to-man relationship, and then it arises directly out of a discussion
of men–women relations. Neither man likes the idea of being a
father or, rather, of being the husband of a mother. 'Sacred
children and sacred motherhood,' Lilly declares, 'I'm fed stiff by
it.' Aaron agrees and replies out of what he clearly believes to be
bitter experience, 'When a woman's got her children, by God,

she's a bitch in a manger.' Then, as he turns 'excitedly in the bed', he expounds what later becomes a well-worn Lawrentian theme:

They look on a man as if he was nothing but an instrument to get and rear children. If you have anything to do with a woman, she thinks it's because you want to get children by her. And I'm damned if it is. I want my own pleasure or nothing: and children be damned . . . Be damned and blasted to women and all their importances . . . They want to get you under, and children is their chief weapon.

The solution, says Lilly, is for men to cultivate male solidarity and together stand up to women, forcing them to admit that men are more important than children, 'But the rotten whiners, they're all grovelling before a baby's napkin and a woman's petticoat.' All except himself and Aaron.

What a pair of manly babies they are themselves! But Lawrence, if neither Aaron nor Lilly, has his reasons for the puerile belief that an adult male must be in rivalry with his own children for a woman's attention. Lilly becomes more and more bitter, and his final speech is,

And can you find two men to stick together, without feeling criminal, and without cringing, and without betraying one another? You can't. One is sure to go fawning round some female, and they both enjoy giving each other away, and doing a new grovel before a woman again.

Cringing, fawning, grovelling, some female: the vehemence of the words is out of all proportion to Lilly's own situation as described in the novel. This is the bitterness of a man who has been badly hurt by a woman, and feels both betrayed and humiliated by the suspicion that the woman loves her children more than she loves him. Even as a suspicion, it cannot be applied to Lilly's childless wife. But rather more than a suspicion can be applied to Mrs Morel. And it is clear from Lawrence's many utterances on the subject, especially in his letters, that he imagined the same could be applied to Frieda.

It is tempting to speculate that the Lawrentian hero has renounced homoerotic man-to-man relationship, only to discover that heterosexuality is not the easier, less painful option after all, and that women, ungrateful beasts that they are, remain stubbornly oblivious to the enormous sacrifice he has made in committing himself erotically to them. Be that as it may, at this stage in his career it is heterosexual relationship which is now the more threatening to his manliness, and man-to-man relationship which can provide him, through a sense of male solidarity, with some sort of reassurance that he is a man.

In this new man-to-man relationship men are no longer bonded primarily by mutual attraction but by their shared difference from and apparent ill-treatment at the hands of women. To call this misogyny is to oversimplify. When Aaron takes Lilly's advice he does so in defiance and denial of his own needs. He needs Lottie desperately but is damned if he is going to admit it. She needs him too, but concludes that she is better off without him – which she probably is. Despite appearances to the contrary – the wretched wife abandoned with her children – it is clear that he needs her more than she needs him. This, for Aaron, is what hurts. This is why he cannot forgive Lottie. To have the greater need is to be the weaker and so be rendered less of a man.

It is often said that Lawrence never forgave his mother for loving him. If the behaviour of the Lawrentian hero is anything to go by, it would be truer to say that he never forgave himself for loving her, for having been so sensitive and susceptible to her, for not having been manly enough to resist her. Male novelists often exemplify manliness as the ability to win, conquer or subdue women – an easily-accomplished task in which there is much self-congratulation. But for the Lawrentian hero the task is never easy: often it is well-nigh impossible. The best he can manage in the search for manliness is to resist women, either by overt rejection or by refusing to give of himself emotionally. Kate Millett calls such behaviour 'male frigidity', and considers it solely as a misogynist weapon. Again, this is a half-truth. The behaviour must be seen essentially as a self-protective, self-defining strategy.

Aaron returns to Lilly in search of male solidarity, but finds himself being lectured instead on 'healthy, individual authority'. Lilly tells him that he must give up his 'love-urge' and his 'love-whooshing' – that is, his needs for sexual passion and for a loving relationship with a woman. Only then can Aaron unfold his own destiny 'as a dandelion unfolds into a dandelion and not a stick of celery'. Only then can the love-mode be replaced by the more significant power-mode.

We *must* either love or rule. And once the love-mode changes, as change it must, for we are worn out and becoming evil in its persistence, then the other mode will take place in us. And there will be profound, profound obedience in place of this love-crying, obedience to the incalculable power-urge. And men must submit to the greater soul in a man, for guidance: and women must submit to the positive power-soul in man, for their being.

Aaron is sceptical about these grandiose plans. 'You'll never get it,' he says more than once. He is especially sceptical when Lilly says that 'woman will submit', adding, 'Anything else will happen, but not that.' Meanwhile, to whom must Aaron submit? 'Your soul will tell you,' is Lilly's enigmatic reply. The implication is that it is Lilly himself, but Lawrence seems to have lost the nerve to say so. If the notion were not so absurd, this would be a chilling and ominous end to the novel.

It is, however, chilling enough. Lilly's hatred is not directed solely against women, but takes in the masses, the mob, democracy, Buddhism, Christianity, 'folks who teem by the million, like the Chinese and Japs and Orientals altogether', and the 'craven' Europeans, Asiatics and Africans. Like Birkin he purports to hate humanity – or most of it. But, to a greater extent than Birkin, he is full of zeal to reform it – for its own good, of course. Lilly hates practically everything and everyone except the strong, manly male, and such is the basis of his bond with Aaron. What they both hate and fear more than anything else is their own weakness, which they see as a lack of manliness. Lilly hopes to find manliness by converting love-relations into power-relations. But Aaron cannot go thus far. In a benumbed emotional state after his affair with the Marchesa, Aaron writes a letter to his elderly benefactor, Sir William Franks, telling him that he does not want kindness or love, does not believe in harmony or in people loving one another.

I believe in the fight and in nothing else. I believe in the fight which is everything. And if it is a question of women, I believe in the fight of love, even if it blinds me. And if it is a question of the world, I believe in fighting it and having it hate me, even if it breaks my legs. I want the world to hate me because I can't bear the thought that it might love me. Of all things love is most deadly to me.

These are the words of someone who knows (or thinks he knows) what a dangerous business it is to love and be loved by someone else: how can one become softened and therefore unmanned by love, can become absorbed in and by the other to the detriment of one's individual identity. But they are also the words of someone who believes in duality/polarity and, by implication, in the possibility of a balance (if not yet a reconciliation) between the two. They are not the words of a man who, like Lilly, purely worships power.

After he has quoted Aaron's letter Lawrence goes on to comment, more in his own persona than Aaron's,

Well, here was a letter for a poor old man to receive. But, in the dryness of his mind Aaron got it out of himself. When a man writes a letter to himself, it is a pity to post it to someone else. Perhaps the same is true of a book.

Perhaps, indeed. This is one of many of Lawrence's naïvely transparent pieces of self-revelation. And I think this is the way to look at *Aaron's Rod*: a letter which Lawrence is writing to himself. It is really a book about the horrifying discovery that men need women, and about the concomitant, even more horrifying suspicion that men need women more than women need men. Male bonding is a strategy for dispelling such suspicions and for denying the need. But, if male bonding is to be effective, it must take place not in the world of women and children, but in the wider world which is the world of men, the world of politics.

Kangaroo takes up the themes of love and power, of the opposition between the world of women and the world of men. It is an extraordinary novel, much underrated, and utterly different in tone from either *Women In Love* or *Aaron's Rod*. Not only are the descriptions of the Australian landscape and seascape dazzlingly well-written, brimmingly alive, but the authorial attitude to the human race is capable of both compassion and good humour. It is an apparently disjointed novel, but is really a sort of improvisation on many Lawrentian themes, disparate and oblique, but nevertheless coherent in that it follows the thought-processes of a writer struggling towards greatness as well as those of a man striving towards wholeness. In his essays Lawrence tends to present the results of such processes in dogmatic form, often over-stating himself. In *Kangaroo*, the perspective shifting constantly against an unfamiliar background, all dogma is examined, qualified and finally opposed.

Richard Lovat Somers is a poet and essayist who has come to Australia with his wife Harriet, much as did Lawrence and Frieda, in a spirit of quest, experiment and adventure. They rent a bungalow, 'Torestin', in a suburb of Sydney next door to Jack and Victoria Callcott's bungalow, 'Wyewurk'. It is through Jack that Somers comes to meet the charismatic Ben Cooley, otherwise known as Kangaroo. Jack and Kangaroo both belong firmly in the world of men, not only because they are engaged in political activity *per se*, but because their own peculiar brand of politics is based in man-to-man relationships and – in the true Australian fashion of mateship – excludes women altogether. Like the Freemasons, that other monument to male bonding, the Diggers are organized in lodges and operate in secrecy. But their aim is revolution and the seizure of power. They claim to be above or beyond party politics, but they are in fact a right-wing quasi-military group, mainly composed of veterans (the year is 1922) of the 1914–18 war. They have a taste for blood as well as an exaggerated respect for discipline and authority.

Their leader Kangaroo is, however, no field-marshal: he sees himself as the saviour of 'his' people and, in the manner of saviours, preaches universal love. In him power and love are reconciled, the love of power being sold in elaborate rhetoric as the power of love. It is difficult to see very much beyond rhetoric in the Diggers' philosophy – if such it can be called – or to believe that its theoretical basis carries the same importance as either its hierarchical structure, its insistence on secrecy or its desire for power. It is those attributes, rather than its gospel, which render it a strictly male preserve.

Jack can be taken as a typical adherent of the movement, an ex-soldier and a man's man. From the moment they meet he and Somers, opposing types, are wary of one another rather than, like Gerald and Birkin, being caught between love and hate. It is a wariness based in class as much as in nationality and, more than either, an intuitive recognition of difference. Somers knows 'pretty well Jack's estimation of him', sensing the modicum of contempt for the male who is not a man of action, but 'a brilliant little fellow'. And he sees that Jack 'felt just a bit uneasy because the same little fellow laughed at his "manliness", knowing that it didn't go right through. It takes more than "manliness" to make a man.'

Does it, indeed? This is not the sort of sentiment we have come to expect from the Lawrentian hero. Somers knows, moreover, what it is Jack wants from him; 'which was that they should talk together as man to man – as pals, you know, with a little difference. But Somers would never be pals with any man. It wasn't in his nature.' Unmoved as he seems to be by the appearance of manliness and the prospect of male bonding alike, is Somers, then, a new breed of Lawrentian hero?

Well, yes and no. Somers is more self-aware than either Birkin, Aaron or Lilly and knows very well that he is 'struggling with the problem of himself and calling it Australia'. Unlike any of them, he can be quite objective about himself and even laugh at or mock his own pretensions – accomplishments all fostered in part by the lovingly critical Harriet. Although he is often described by both Harriet and himself as bad-tempered, he comes across as the mellowest of Lawrence's hero/surrogates, and any bitterness he expresses is not only thoroughly explained but made to seem justified. Like all Lawrentian heroes, Somers has to go through his own dark night of the soul, but he has the self-confidence and experience to be able to handle it, question its necessity, be earnest and rueful by turn and eventually come through, if not exactly smiling, then at least in a state of relative calm. In short, the Lawrentian hero has in some measure grown up and evolved at least in part into what he himself can call a man.

The man-to-man relationship is still at first a lure to Somers. He is caught, pulled this way and that, between the world of women and the world of men. He wants to do something, be active, in the world of men and to find a prominent place there, to be a leader. For this ambition he is mocked by Harriet, representing the world of women, and sometimes by himself. As a writer, he works alone 'without any connection whatever with the world of men'. Even the war has not involved him 'as a man among men', because he was rejected on health grounds for military service. The war has in fact embittered him, and the chapters describing the Somers's wartime experiences make painful reading. These chapters are an exact and impassioned account of what happened to Lawrence and Frieda during the war: accused of being spies, hounded out of Cornwall, they lived in a state of persecution and intermittent paranoia, trying not to feel like criminals or pariahs. Those were the years, so Somers claims,

when the world lost its real manhood. Not for lack of courage to face death. Plenty of superb courage to face death. But no courage in any man to face his own isolated soul and abide by its decisions. Easier to sacrifice oneself. So much easier!

The world of man-to-man relationships is also the world of war. Although it offers prospects of action, comradeship and male solidarity, it can also be soul-destroying. So Somers is at first cautious, though tempted, when the Diggers approach him in the hope that he will lend intellectual respectability to their cause.

The first approach comes from Jack whose enthusiastic insistence that fate has brought them together makes Somers uncomfortable. When Jack repeatedly asks Somers if he can trust him, his eyes are 'dark, dilated, glowing'. When Somers says, after some hesitation, that he trusts Jack, Jack embraces him. 'And on his face was a strange light of purpose and of passion, at once exalted and dangerous.' Lawrence often describes man-to-man relationships as dangerous, the danger being compounded with mutual attraction, but here it is clear that Jack's fervour, the very same fervour which is rampant in *Women In Love*, is inappropriate, way over the top. Instead of responding in kind, Somers is simply bewildered.

However, it may be himself quite as much as Jack, whom he cannot really trust.

When, on a later occasion, Jack proposes a special bond between the two of them, suggesting 'cautiously and intensely' as befits a member of a secret society that 'if you and me was mates, we could put any damn mortal thing through,' Somers is in a quandary.

He liked the man. But what about the cause? What about the mistrust and reluctancy he felt? And at the same time, the thrill of desire. What was offered? He wanted so much. To be mates with Jack in this cause. Life and death mates. And yet he felt he couldn't. Not quite. Something stopped him.

He is tactfully evasive with Jack, saying he is not sure that he is 'a mating man', and the question is left open.

Somers is left to analyse the reasons for his reluctance – which has in fact taken him by surprise. His conclusion that 'he didn't want a friend, he didn't want loving affection, he didn't want comradeship,' surprises him further. No wonder. This is a complete turnaround for the Lawrentian hero, and the paragraph in which it is summed up is worth quoting almost in full:

It took Lovat Somers some time before he would really admit and accept this new fact. Not until he had striven hard with his soul did he come to see the angel in the way; not till his soul, like Balaam's Ass, had spoken more than once. And then, when forced to admit it, it was a revolution in his mind. He had all his life had this craving for an absolute friend, a David to his Jonathan, Pylades to his Orestes; a blood-brother. All his life he had secretly grieved over his friendlessness. And now at last when it really offered . . . he didn't want it, and he realized that in his innermost soul he had never wanted it.

The implication is that the Lawrentian hero has, in growing up, outgrown his need for homosexual or quasi-homosexual relationships. This is not an inference which will please homosexuals, but I think it is one that must be taken.

It is not, however, the whole story. Somers still wants '*some* living fellowship with other men' rather than the isolation which is forced upon him by his profession, a profession which has also cut him off from the men of the working class to which he originally belonged. He doesn't know what sort of form this fellowship might or should take, and can only come up with

the mystery of lordship. The mystery of innate, natural, sacred priority. The other mystic relationship between men, which democracy and equality try to deny and obliterate. Not any arbitrary caste or birth aristocracy. But the mystic recognition of difference and innate priority, the joy of obedience, the sacred responsibility of authority.

Even in context this is a bit of a jump from David and Jonathan. But it is interesting to note in passing that Frieda's erstwhile lover, Otto Gross, designated the German militaristic state as essentially homosexual because it was made up of men placed one on top of the other, to the exclusion of women. Although it is difficult to believe in the sensitive Somers so easily assuming the mantle of what was later to become Fascism, it is rather easier to believe that Lawrence, the special and sensitive scholarship boy, needs must be a supporter of meritocracy. And as later events prove, Somers is only trying the garment on for size. At this stage he is preparing himself, as Lawrence is preparing us, for the meeting with Kangaroo.

Ben Cooley is another of Lawrence's attractive-repulsive males. Physically he resembles the animal after which he is named. 'His face was long and lean and pendulous, with eyes set close together behind his pince-nez, and his body was stout but firm.' Much is made of his stoutness, his thick thighs and, especially, his large belly. Kangaroo is no Gerald-like Adonis: apart from anything else, he is too old. 'He was a man of forty or so, hard to tell, swarthy, with short-cropped dark hair and a smallish head carried forward on his large but sensitive, almost shy body ... He was really tall but his way of dropping his head took away from his height.' He is 'really ugly', but when he smiles, takes on 'an exceedingly sweet charm' and is momentarily 'like a flower'. At their first meeting, Somers surmises more than once that Kangaroo has 'Jewish blood'.

The very best that is in the Jewish blood: a faculty for pure disinterested-ness, and warm, physically warm, love, that seems to make the corpuscles of the blood glow . . . his heart was pure in kindness. An extraordinary man. This pure kindness had something Jehovah-like in it . . . He was not angry or indignant. He was more like a real Jehovah. He had only to turn on all the levers and forces of his clever, almost fiendishly subtle will, and he would triumph.

The 'wicked' thought comes into Somers's mind that Kangaroo resembles 'the lamb of god grown into a sheep'. This is hardly the manly hero which we have been led to expect.

And yet hero Kangaroo undoubtedly is. He is a leader, an orator with 'a beautiful voice' and eyes that shine 'with a queer holy light'. Somers is 'abashed' before 'the steady loveliness of this man's warm, wise heart'. Such descriptions imply that Kangaroo is a suitably charismatic leader for the Diggers, but at the same time that he is altogether too douce to appeal to their militaristic idealism. However, the connection soon becomes clear. The kernel of Kangaroo's message is that 'man again needs a father, who uses his authority in the name of living life, and who is absolutely stern against anti-life.' Kangaroo sees himself as a benevolent tyrant: he is a father in much the same way as Hitler's Germany was a Fatherland.

Somers sees Kangaroo's rhetoric as a latter-day Judaeo-Christian mode. A kindly, authoritative father . . . the idea appeals to him even as he is being mesmerized by its embodiment: 'even his body had become beautiful to Somers – one might love it intensely, every one of its contours, its roundness and downward dropping heaviness. . . . Beautiful, beautiful, as some half-tropical, bulging flower.' Kangaroo is like a Chinese Buddha, and it is evident from the worshipful description that we are not in the realms of politics at all, but in the realms of religion. Such indeed is the whole tendency of the novel. It looks as though the Lawrentian hero may at last have found himself a credible role model: the father, the inadequately-internalized father of Paul Morel; and the role which Aaron and Lilly were both unable to assume.

However, I don't think so. For one thing, Lawrence drops enough hints throughout his description of that first meeting – not least his reference to Kangaroo's fiendishly subtle will – to prepare us for Somers's ultimate rejection of all that Kangaroo stands for. For another, Kangaroo is a very odd father indeed.

Kangaroo is a father without a complementary mother, and his fatherhood constitutes a male mirror-image of parthenogenesis. Long before Somers has met Kangaroo, Jack tells him, 'Kangaroo could never have a mate . . . No, there's no female kangaroo of his species.' And, just as there is no female fit to be his mate, in the sense of 'spouse', so there is no male fit to be his mate in the sense of 'buddy'. (Jack uses the word 'mate' in both senses throughout this conversation, and there is never a flicker of recognition from either him or Somers – who notices and comments on all sorts of minutiae – that there is anything significant in this usage.) In the act of fatherhood Kangaroo is neither fertilizing sperm nor fertile ovum, but something bigger and more complete than either, something which nourishes and shelters and seems to bring forth of its own accord. He is, in short, a womb. Or rather, he exemplifies a male fantasy of womanhood, a fantasy which is based on unadmitted envy and is more narcissistic than it is homosexual. As such, it is neither the first nor the last instance of male wish-fulfilment in Lawrence's work.

In spite of the emphasis on the firmness of his flesh, there is something feminine in Kangaroo's appearance: his narrow shoulders, broad hips and spreading thighs. But it is in his abdomen that he most resembles a woman, and a pregnant woman at that. 'You felt you were cuddled cosily, like a child, on his breast, in the soft glow of his heart, and that your feet were resting on his ample, beautiful "tummy".' Kangaroo is already a mother, now pregnant again, perhaps permanently so. This is what he has made of himself, arrogating to himself all the qualities of parent-hood, whether or nor it is biologically possible for him to do so. He has little good to say about mother's sons.

Man that is born of woman is sick of himself. Man that is born of woman is tired of his day after day. And woman is like a mother with a tiresome child: what is she to do with him? . . . Man that is born of woman is a slave in the cold, barren corridors of the ant-hill . . . And from this there is no escape. None. Not even the lap of the woman.

He himself was 'once a man born of woman', but he is now 'a son of man', womanless. This is the source and secret of his strength. Why should he need a woman – whether wife or mother – when he has now appropriated for himself all the most worthwhile womanly qualities?

It seems to me that Lawrence is still trying to work through Birkin's problem, though in a subtler and less naked fashion: is it possible to have, to exist in, both the world of women and the world of men? Somers knows that his marriage is and has been of primary importance to him, so he, unlike Kangaroo, cannot reject the world of women altogether. In addressing Harriet as 'woman who is born of man', Kangaroo is paying her a compliment according to his own lights. But his recognition of the world of women is in fact minimal and hypocritical. When he becomes 'loud and passionate' in declaring his love for the mass of men (and he means the male of the species) Somers is alarmed, although he and Harriet are still impressed. Carried away by his own rhetoric, Kangaroo then shouts that he loves Harriet too, and 'I defy you to prevent me.'

Kangaroo loves as the Christian God loves, in defiance of merely human attempts to prevent him. Like God, Kangaroo loves people in spite of themselves. In becoming more than either man or woman (which is not, by the way, a strategy he advocates for his followers – only for himself) Kangaroo has become more than human. But, paradoxically, he has also become less than human, more particularly less than a fully-sexed adult male. Godhead is not perhaps the way to manliness after all and, as the novel proceeds, with Somers and Harriet working through the conflicts in their marriage, the all-embracing love of Kangaroo soon begins to appear like an impossible idealism which cannot be applied to ordinary human life. Ultimately Somers comes to view it as positively destructive to individual integrity for both men and women. And then Kangaroo is rejected with more thoroughness than is the manly Jack.

Somers's involvement with the Diggers' cause remains little more than a flirtation. When he meets the Labour leader, Willie

Stuthers, who is Kangaroo's political opponent, he is again mesmerized – so much so that he is forced to reacknowledge his own working-class roots as well as the identification between a man and his life's work. But really Somers is not much of a political animal, more of a floating voter. He may be a 'thought-adventurer' (which is how he sees man – but not woman) but his thought can be called political only in the most naively idealistic terms, and he ends up more or less where he began: in the plague-on-both-your-houses position. The most important action in the novel is not going on in the political arena at all, but inside Somers himself. In fact, this is the whole point and thrust of the novel: inside oneself is where the most important action is. This is the really sacred arena, in comparison to which political events, however dramatic and immediate, are merely profane.

But profanely dramatic and immediate events are what move the novel on – a circumstance of which Lawrence is avowedly and cheerfully aware. The political climax comes in the form of what is called in a chapter heading, 'A Row in Town'. Although it is subsequently played down by the authorities, this is really rather more than a row: a head-on confrontation between right and left which ends up as a bloody battle. During the fracas Kangaroo is shot and taken to hospital. Somers manages to escape before the going gets too rough, and it is Jack who brings him the news. It is also Jack who now confirms for Somers the real meaning of the Diggers' movement.

As Jack describes the scenes of violence, 'the strangest grin in the world was on his face', and he speaks in 'a hoarse whisper'.

'I settled *three* of 'em – three!' There was an indescribable gloating joy in his tones, like a man telling of the good times he has had with a strange mistress. 'Gawr, but I was lucky. I got one of them iron bars from the windows, and I stirred the brains of a couple of them with it, and I broke the neck of a third . . .'

He reached his face towards Somers with weird, gruesome exaltation, and continued in a hoarse secret voice:

'Cripes, there's *nothing* bucks you up sometimes like killing a man – *nothing* . . . When it comes over you, you know there's nothing else. I never knew till the war . . . Having a woman's something, isn't it? But it's a fleabite, nothing, compared to killing your man when your blood comes up.

Somers, who of course never fought in the war, feels a 'torn feeling in his abdomen'. He simply cannot reply. Jack goes on to say how angelic he feels after killing, and how gentle he then is making love with his wife. 'Killing's natural to a man, you know,' he tells Somers. 'It's just as natural as lying with a woman.' And still Somers cannot reply.

Jack is the apotheosis of the physically manly man in Lawrence's fiction. More than Gerald, he makes plain the connection between sex and violence. Indeed, he himself makes a connection between sex and murder, and leaves us in no doubt as to which he prefers. He embodies all that the Lawrentian hero hates and fears in the male principle as it operates in the contemporary world of men, and at the same time all that he is reluctantly fascinated by. Somers's silence implies that he is disgusted by Jack, but the fact that he does not express his disgust in words – and he a writer, a man who verbalizes compulsively – also implies that some of the fascination remains. The only comment we get from Lawrence comes in the form of an item which Somers coincidentally finds in a local newspaper, describing the Melanesian urge to kill as a moment of atavism which may be overcome by self-control. It is offered to the reader without any gloss from either Somers or Lawrence, and thus is highly ambiguous.

Somers goes to see Kangaroo in hospital, the little man who was too frail to fight in the war visiting the sickbed of the formidable leader now laid low by an assassin's bullet. As Kangaroo's doctrine has become repulsive to Somers, so now too has his person, and he shrinks from being touched by him. The room is already tomb-like, filled with the odours of flowers, and of decay, mortality. Kangaroo is still preaching the 'faithful and fearless love of man for man', 'surpassing the love of women'. But Somers has now seen where this sort of love can lead, and he becomes 'very pale, his face set'. When Kangaroo accuses him of being afraid of love, Somers becomes 'more and more tormented in himself'. In a way, he admits, he does love Kangaroo, but he doesn't want to.

Afterwards, when he has left the hospital, he is

almost blinded with stress and grief and bewilderment. Was it true what
Kangaroo had said? Was it true? Did he, Richard, love Kangaroo, and
deny it? And was the denial just a piece of fear? Was it just fear that held
him back from admitting his love for the other man?

Shades of Birkin. Somers, however, comes to a conclusion which
is very far from Birkin's.

He believed in the God of fear, of darkness, of passion, and of silence, the
God that made a man realize his own sacred aloneness. If Kangaroo could
have realized that too, then Richard felt he would have loved him, in a
dark, separate, other way of love. But never this all-in-all thing.

The all-in-all thing is 'a strain and an unreality', an ideal which
cannot be lived up to, an ideal which leads men away from their
own innermost needs. But once men find their sacred aloneness,
'then one can meet as worshippers, in sacred contact in the dark.'
Somers goes walking by the sea where, after a great struggle, he
finds himself 'soulless and alone by the Southern Ocean in
Australia'. Why, he asks himself, does he wrestle with his soul? 'I
have no soul.' It is in the abnegation of soul or self that he can
glimpse the beginning of freedom, and an end to his torment.

His next and last meeting with Kangaroo is none the less painful
for his discovery. In a sense, it is more painful because he now has
to put his discovery to the test. Kangaroo says that he is dying and
accuses Somers of killing him. Tacitly, Somers disagrees. Kangaroo
then urges Somers, once more, to admit that he loves him. Somers
is at first evasive, then tries out of compassion to say what Kangaroo
wants to hear. But he cannot: he does not love Kangaroo, and the
words just do not come out. It is Jack, appearing suddenly at the
bedside, who loves Kangaroo, Jack who can pledge himself in
the love of man for man. All Somers can express is his 'immense
regard'.

Afterwards, in the street, Jack is disgusted by what he sees as
Somers's meanness. 'If a man can't speak two words of pity for a
man in his state, why, I think there's something wrong with that
man.' But Somers refuses to compromise himself, as he has

refused to be bullied by Kangaroo, and once again remains silent. Later, thinking of Kangaroo, he tells himself, 'I don't love him – I detest him. He can die. I'm glad he's dying. And I don't like Jack either. Not a bit. In fact I like nobody.' When Kangaroo dies, Somers refuses to attend the funeral. Thus must the mother's son protect himself from the threatening prospect of parental love. And thus must the guilty and tormented homoerotic protect himself from the lure of a love whose nature the heterosexual (they are, of course, both the same man) can never entirely endorse.

And yet, when Somers goes to the zoo and watches the animals, especially the kangaroos, 'the tenderness came back'. It is a 'dark, animal tenderness, and another sort of consciousness, deeper than human'. Later Lawrence was to call this 'phallic tenderness', the sort of tenderness which connects us, through the very fact of our being alive, with the whole of the natural world and is the basis of a proper marriage. But is it really 'deeper than human', and can it appropriately be called 'phallic'? I don't think so – on either count. It is the sort of tenderness a pregnant woman feels towards the natural world, of which she is now so intimately a part. It is the sort of tenderness felt by a mother who, in giving birth, realizes both the fragility and the tenaciousness of life. I am not of course saying that all women feel like this; nor am I saying that men cannot. What I am saying is that, in his quest for manliness which leads him at last to the phallus, Lawrence repeatedly distorts biology in order to arrogate for the male all that he values or envies in the female.

4

The phallus

The mother's son and the man's man. Until now the Lawrentian
hero has hardly presented himself as an attractive proposition as
far as women are concerned. Women readers could be forgiven for
exclaiming despairingly: there must be more to men than *this*!
There is indeed more, but whether it is any better is a different
matter. There are glimpses throughout Lawrence's fiction of a
man whom he calls 'the free, proud, single being', but they are
only glimpses, and inevitably the manifestation cannot sustain itself:
the independent male cannot remain independent for long, but
needs must find another man whom he can admire or a woman on
whom he can depend and by whom he is nourished. Lawrence
being Lawrence, some rationale must be found for this type of
behaviour and, what is more, a rationale which must be made to
seem irrefutable. Simple admissions of human weakness, laziness
or imperfection will not do. Global and indeed universal justification is ultimately necessary. The symbol by which Lawrence
chooses to reconcile man in his inviolable individuality with the
needs of both the mother's son and the man's man is the phallus.

The phallus is more than just a penis, as the habitual use of the
definite article implies. It is also rather more than an erect penis,
that is, an instrument for servicing or pleasuring women and for
getting children. It is an achievement in itself, the achievement
of maleness. Norman Mailer castigates feminists for the 'dull
assumption that the sexual force of a man was the luck of his birth,
rather than his final moral product', adding later that 'no wonder
[Lawrence] worshipped the phallus, he above all men knew what
an achievement was its rise from the root, its assertion to stand
proud on a delicate base.' For the frail and sickly Lawrence, penile
erection was a triumphant demonstration of male strength.

Poetic though this may sound, I don't think it is quite the whole
truth about Lawrentian phallicism. John Thomas the phallus may

well be in its profane manifestation, but as a sacred object it is also
the mysterious source of all spontaneous life, indeed *the* primary
source of life itself, and this is what makes it worthy of worship.
The phallus is a sort of First Cause, an original creator throughout
the natural world. That there is not a sane woman alive who could
believe in the male principle alone as the primary source of life
does not seem to have deterred Lawrence from pursuing and
propounding this belief, or from making it the basis of all his later
theorizing on relations between the sexes: the phallus is the prime
creative agent, not because its actions lead to the birth of children,
but because they lead to the rebirth of both man and woman in the
sexual act.

The phallus represents not only man's connection with woman
but his difference and eternal separateness from her. Aaron Sissons
is a musician and his rod is a flute, an overt and somewhat obvious
phallic symbol. It is by virtue of his flute that he stands independent
and alone, able to wander and earn his living as he pleases. (Much,
of course, as Lawrence could by his pen – a connection he himself
makes quite explicitly.) But towards the end of the novel, when an
anarchist's bomb is thrown into a café, the flute gets broken and
Lilly advises Aaron to throw it away, adding the 'pleasant remark'
that Aaron will have to live without a rod meanwhile. The
implication is that Aaron has been deploying his phallic power
wrongly, especially in his affair with the Marchesa who has used
him as a 'magic implement' and caused him to question the whole
concept of 'phallic immortality' in the sexual act. In plain terms
Aaron has discovered that loveless fucking, however technically
accomplished, is also valueless fucking, and an activity which
diminishes his sense of self, his sense of himself as a man. Only
when he has learned to keep himself apart and to use himself
according to the dictates of his own soul will he be able to achieve
manliness and therefore true phallic selfhood.

There is much that is puritanical in Aaron's attitude. One senses
that he feels pretty guilty for having had such a good time with the
Marchesa, and his guilt is compounded by the fact that neither of
them really cares for the other. But there is also the ever-present
Lawrentian suspicion that in the sexual act the woman's is the

better part. If she is getting more of a bargain, then the man is spending, squandering himself to no ultimate avail. 'Give thyself,' is Aaron's conclusion, 'but don't give thyself away.' Virility is something which can be used up, leaving you bankrupt, so don't be too profligate with it, and always make sure you get your money's worth. This eminently Victorian counsel, in which the self is likened to a bank account, is less one of meanness than of careful husbandry. It is, after all, only the rich who can afford meanness: the poverty stricken have no choice but to scrimp and save, and Aaron's are poverty-stricken male sexual anxieties indeed.

In *Kangaroo* Somers can see his neighbour Victoria Callcott, as Aaron saw the Marchesa, as a sort of saced prostitute, a priestess who will use the male in the service of some arcane female rite. He is strongly attracted to Victoria, a pretty young woman, and considers having a fling – though he himself puts it more preten- tiously as a 'sacred moment of bacchus' – in the interests of widening his range of sexual experience. It is his puritanism which ensures that he will resist temptation and, in resisting, furnish an enhanced sense of his own manliness.

But his heart of hearts was stubbornly puritanical. And his innermost soul was dark and sullen, black with a sort of scorn. These moments, bred in the head and born in the eye: he had had enough of them. These flashes of desire for a visual object would no longer carry him into action. He had no use for them.

Now, it has been claimed by many feminists, notably by Andrea Dworkin writing on pornography, that male sexual desire is largely a matter of response to visual stimuli. And certainly a reading of novels written by men tends to bear out such a supposition. The extraordinary thing about the Lawrentian hero (and about Lawrence himself, as is vouched by many of his friends and acquaintances) is that he does not respond to women along such conventional lines.

The Lawrentian hero is no stud, red-bloodedly and competitively roused by the sight of a woman whom he knows to be prized as a sexual object by other men. Such responses are not what phallic consciousness is about. The *Kangaroo* passage carries straight on:

'There was a downslope into Orcus, and a vast, phallic, sacred darkness, where one was enveloped into the greater god as in an Egyptian darkness. He would meet there or nowhere. To the visual travesty he would lend himself no more.' Somers has converted Aaron's rod from an instrument which blossoms in response to sweetness and light, and all that light can visually afford, into an instrument of darkness, invisible, unknowable, and part of some vast, mysterious orchestra.

Throughout the novel Somers can intermittently hear this 'dark god knocking'. He is often reluctant to listen and tempted to dismiss such emanations from the darkness as 'blarney'. When Kangaroo tries to probe him, he becomes unsure of himself and embarrassed but eventually concedes that his is 'the great God who enters us from below, not from above'. Kangaroo becomes snappy with him and asks him to explain further: his own god, the God of Love, is being challenged. Somers explains that his god enters us 'not through the spirit. Enters us from the lower self, the dark self, the phallic self.' Kangaroo doesn't know what he is talking about. To him, the phallic self must mean the self which seeks and embodies human love and connection. Somers shakes his head and explains in 'a slow, remote voice'.

I know your love, Kangaroo. Working everything from the spirit, from the head. You work the lower self as the instrument of spirit. Now it is time for the spirit to leave us again; it is time for the Son of Man to depart, and leave us in the dark, in front of the unspoken God: who is just beyond the dark threshold of the lower self, my lower self.

Love as defined by Kangaroo has become 'trivial' to Somers, who now stubbornly refuses to be seduced by Kangaroo's blandishments. But the struggle leaves him 'queer and cave-like, devoid of emotion'. No wonder. The Lawrentian hero has managed in one short scene to reject both the god of the man's man and the god of the mother's son who is the god of Mrs Morel. He goes out to look at the stars and 'free himself from the cloy of humanity'. He is moving on.

In *Fantasia of the Unconscious* Lawrence devotes a whole chapter to the 'lower self', which is at once a physical and a psychological

Men

entity. 'Below the waist we are sightless' and 'have our being in darkness'. We have 'nice daytime selves' which belong above the waist, but we also have 'night-time selves' which belong to 'darkness and the elemental consciousness of blood'.

Every day the sun sets from the sky and darkness falls, and every day, when this happens, the tide of life turns in us. Instead of flowing upwards and outwards towards mental consciousness and activity, it turns back, to flow downwards. Downwards towards the digestion processes, downwards further to the great sexual conjunctions, downwards to sleep.

There is a duality/polarity between the two selves, both sex and love belonging to the lower self. In 'genuine, passionate love' there is 'no interference of the upper centres. Love is supposed to be blind. Though modern love wears strong spectacles.'

This, then, is the lower self through which Somers can dimly apprehend his dark, phallic gods, and begin to define not only the relationship of man to woman (which is essentially based in sex) but the relationship of man to man (which is based in trust and obedience) as aspects of some 'great communion' in the dark. What this actually means in plain, everyday terms is difficult to say. But then that is the point: Somers is feeling his way towards that which cannot be defined, that which can only be apprehended intuitively.

The starting-point, he decides, is not after all in fellowship, but in 'the man by himself'.

This is the beginning and the end, the alpha and the omega, the one absolute: the man alone by himself, alone with his own soul, alone with his eyes on the darkness, which is the dark god of life. Alone like a pythoness on her tripod, like the oracle above the fissure into the unknown ... the strange words that the oracle must utter. Strange, cruel, pregnant words: the terms of the new consciousness.

How can this darkness, in which a priestess sits alone and then utters strange words which come to her from beyond, be described as 'phallic'? Is this really an image of a man finding his manliness?

It seems to me that it is less an image of a man (as opposed to a woman) than an image of a writer, and a writer very much like

Lawrence himself. The intuitive apprehension of reality, the passive listening, the mediumistic trance: these are all generally (or at least primarily) considered to be properties of the world of women. But they embody qualities which are both characteristic of and necessary to many a writer, yes, novelists as well as poets. They are certainly qualities which are evident in Lawrence's own writing, qualities which often give it its essentially Lawrentian flavour.

Somers/Lawrence is arrogating to the phallus not only that which traditionally belongs to the female, but that which essentially belongs to the writer, whether male or female. In doing so, he is justifying himself as both man and writer. The two are congruent: he is defining and justifying what he is. In a way, his arrogance is astonishingly modest and generous: he makes no great claims for his own talent, but extends its properties to include all men. In another way, it is shameful and brutal, in that it excludes women from what is rightfully theirs on equal terms with men. The phallus often seems like a desperate device for keeping women in their proper place but it is also, like Aaron's misogyny, a self-defining strategy. And it is so in more ways than one.

Somers cannot remain listening alone in the phallic darkness for long. He has to return to base, to Harriet, for some sort of sustenance which will give strength for further thought-adventuring. At such junctures he has to admit to himself

that only the dark god in her fighting with my white idealism has got me so clear: and that only the dark god in her answering the dark god in me has got my soul heavy and fecund with a new sort of infant. But even now I can't bring it forth. I can't bring it forth. I need something else. Some other answer.

This image of a man being made pregnant by his own wife would be very odd indeed, were it not also evident that here is a writer describing the relationship between himself and his muse (women writers don't have muses) and the agonies of a writer's block. Somers does not lack the creative impulse, but he cannot act upon that impulse: he has lost his nerve, or his faith in himself, which is what a writer's block amounts to. He turns first to the 'unutterable dark god', and then to the 'utterable, sometimes very loud dark' of

Harriet, but there is still something which does not quicken as does a child in the womb. He feels – to change the gender of the metaphor – impotent.

In order to function both as man and writer Somers needs a god or gods and a woman, but as yet he cannot reconcile those needs. The only way he can find to link the two relationships so that they form a whole is in a chain of domination and submission with himself at the centre. Harriet is being stubborn and refusing to submit or bow down to him. The Somers's marriage is at sea, and 'you can't have two masters of one ship: neither can you have a ship without a master.' Understandably enough, Harriet thinks this is nonsense, adding that their marriage is a houseboat, not a ship. Somers concludes with some reluctance that before Harriet will accept him as lord and master, he 'must open the doors of his soul and let in a dark Lord and Master for himself . . . Let him once truly submit to the dark majesty . . . and the rest would follow.' The male obsession with hierarchy seems to be unshiftable. Man submits to God and woman submits to man: 'He for God only, she for God in him.' It is a wearisomely banal conclusion to have reached after all that thought-adventuring, the sort of sentiment Somers could have heard expressed any night of the week in the Dog and Duck, without having to go all the way to Australia to discover it. And perhaps, alas, this is the very point: it is the sort of conclusion Walter Morel and his mates might well have reached often over their pints.

There must be more to it than that. And indeed there is another way of looking at it – from, as it were, the other end. Before the gods a man is made or becomes woman. Before the gods a man is allowed to behave like a woman without necessarily losing his manliness. He is allowed to become open, sensitive, inspired, vatic, and so acquire the qualities Somers needs in order to write his poetry. He can become as a woman in the sacred world so long as he retains his manhood in the profane world. This latter is necessary because otherwise he might lose sight of himself as a man altogether. The difference, indeed polarity, between himself and 'his' woman becomes crucial both for his well-being and for his very functioning. In brief, unless Somers can believe in himself as a man, he cannot function as a writer. And where can he find this belief? In the usual place: in a woman. This is of course a circular argument because Somers has already made up his mind as to the proper function of a woman. Instead of questioning the concept of hierarchy (which would break the circuit) he sees the problem as one of making the 'phallic' hierarchy work.

Somers demands submission from Harriet because he cannot get belief. Or rather, and I use Coleridge's phrase deliberately, he cannot get the willing suspension of disbelief. Earlyish in the novel he has a dream in which a composite wife-and-mother figure torments him, and he interprets it as meaning that neither his wife nor his dead mother has ever believed in him. At the height of his rows with Harriet, Somers expects her

to believe in his adventure and deliver herself over to it; she was to believe in his mystic vision of a land beyond this charted world, where new life rose again.
And she just couldn't ... 'Then, believe in *me*,' he said desperately.
'I know you too well,' she replied. And so, it was an impasse.

Believe in me! Again and again, this is what the Lawrentian hero demands of the women in his life. Paul Morel imagines that neither Miriam nor Clara believes in him sufficiently. Birkin wants Ursula to believe in him. And now here is Somers ... Who does the Lawrentian hero think he is? Some kind of god?

Well, yes and no. In Lawrence's next novel, *The Plumed Serpent*, the two leading male characters do indeed set themselves up as gods. And belief is what a god demands from his worshippers rather than what a man should be demanding from a woman. But there is another relationship in which, as Coleridge's phrase implies, belief is crucial: the relationship between reader and writer. Especially when we talk about novels (unless of course we are literary academics – in which case we pretend to be rather more sophisticated) we talk in terms of belief. We believe or don't believe in the characters as 'real' people: either they convince us or they don't. We believe or don't believe in what happens in the novel: it either 'rings true' or 'it just wouldn't have happened like that.' If we do believe, we *are* compelled, we *do* submit. It seems to me that at least part of what Somers is demanding from Harriet is that she should be his ideal reader, the one with whom perfect one-way communication is possible. It is hardly a two-way relationship, but Somers is of course demanding no more from Harriet than most male writers demand from their wives – or mistresses, or mothers.

In keeping Harriet/Frieda so firmly in her place as reader rather than writer, Somers/Lawrence is expressing an old male fear. If women are allowed to become writers, that is, thought-adventurers, inspired, in direct touch with the creative source, they will not stick around to be readers for men. They will become equals and, oh horrors, just like men. Then, because they are also biological mothers, women will have the monopoly of creativity, bringing forth, giving birth. Where does that leave men?

At women's mercy, is the short answer. But to be at a woman's mercy is to be again a mother's son, a fate which is almost worse than death. And as Aaron and Lilly both insist so desperately, to be a man is more than to be a child: otherwise what is the point of growing up? (Maybe this is why so many men never bother.) To become a man's man is one way of insisting that one is a man rather than a child. But it is only a partial solution: men still need women, as they did when they were mother's sons, but the horrifying thing is that women no longer seem to need them in the same way as did their mothers or their childless wives. Women now have their own sons, a circumstance in which men have themselves unwittingly colluded, only to find that they have been robbed of the primary importance due to their manhood. How can men win? How can they ever hope to win? And how, especially, can they win a war the existence of which is not even recognized by women?

Somehow or other men must define themselves in terms which even women will recognize as irrefutably superior. They must find something which they all have in common to the exclusion of women. Such is the thinking behind both Freud's theory of penis envy and Lawrence's theory of phallic supremacy. All creative, innovative and effective action must be concentrated (in Freud's profane version) in the penis, or (in Lawrence's sacred version) in the phallus. It is no coincidence that Freud and Lawrence were both the favourite sons of their mothers.

Writing of Lawrence at the time of *Lady Chatterley's Lover*, Norman Mailer surmises, 'he was ill and his wife was literally killing him every time she failed to worship his most proud and delicate cock.' Well, maybe. It seems to me that, if *Kangaroo* is anything to go by, Lawrence was threatened just as bitterly by his wife's apparent failure to believe in the ideas he expressed as a writer, and to follow him around the world in their pursuit. The two are probably inseparable. Both Lawrence and Mailer tend to confuse sexual potency with creative power. It is not a mistake likely to be made by a woman writer.

The theory of phallic supremacy is taken up and pursued in *The Plumed Serpent*, which is set in Mexico and, like that other monumental novel with a similar background, *Under the Volcano*, has a hypnotic, hallucinatory quality which seems to be peculiarly Mexican. The title refers to Quetzalcoatl, which is at the same time a religion and a god, the feathered snake once worshipped by the Aztecs. Quetzalcoatl, being a bird which flies in the air and comes to us from above as well as a snake which emerges from the earth and comes to us from below, embodies a religion which recognizes duality/polarity and attempts to reconcile opposites. In *Fantasia of the Unconscious* Lawrence posited the opposed upper and lower, daytime and night-time selves; in *The Plumed Serpent* this opposition is made flesh, and the schemata of the essayist put to the test in fiction – and, in the hymns of Quetzalcoatl, in poetry.

The cult of Quetzalcoatl is revived by the charismatic Don Ramon Carrasco and, to a lesser extent, his cohort, General Viedma, known as Don Cipriano. Ramon, whom we see for the most part through the eyes of the forty-year-old protagonist, Kate Leslie, is 'almost horribly handsome', and can compel or subdue by his sheer physical presence.

With the blue sash round his waist, pressing a fold in the flesh, and the thin linen seeming to gleam with the life of his hips and thighs, he emanated a fascination almost like a narcotic, asserting his pure, fine sensuality against her ... He emitted an effluence so powerful, that it seemed to hamper her consciousness, to bind down her limbs ... his terrible aloof beauty, inaccessible, yet so potent.

Descriptions such as these, and there are plenty of them, make me wonder how Lawrence had the nerve to criticize Charlotte Brontë for her portraits of sexually attractive men. There is more than a touch of the bodice-ripper about his own.

With Kate's help, Ramon despatches a couple of would-be assassins, after which feat, 'his trousers on his loins were also sodden with blood, they stuck red to his hips. He did not notice. He was like a pristine being remote in consciousness, and with far, remote sex.' What, you may well ask, does sex have to do with all the bloodshed? Kate shudders over the slaughter, but Ramon is glad that the two men have been killed, and now has a 'pristine, clear brow, like a boy's, a sort of twilight changelessness'. No doubt he feels, as did Jack in *Kangaroo*, like an angel.

It seems to me that what Kate feels for Ramon is that same reluctantly fascinated attraction which Birkin feels for Gerald. As such – and not least in Ramon's remoteness and inaccessibility – it is peculiarly homoerotic. Ramon embodies the male principle, as does Gerald, in obvious physical terms, and in his ability to remain sexually attractive even as he is shedding blood. Further, his capacity for inflicting pain and death actually enhances his sexual attraction while rendering him at the same time less sexually accessible. Male sexuality and male violence are two sides of the same coin, the face and the obverse of manliness.

But, as in *Women In Love*, Lawrence cannot altogether endorse the logical conclusion to such masochistic forms of attraction. Don Cipriano, who is pledged to Ramon as follower to leader, does not share Kate's squeamishness about blood-letting. Indeed he is not averse to killing other human beings himself, whether in the course of his army duties, or when so instructed by Ramon. Such latter occasions are, however, sacred rather than profane. And, just as the bright Gerald is vanquished in the wrestling match by the dark, moral superiority of Birkin, so does Cipriano gradually supplant Ramon in Kate's soul. It is through Cipriano that she begins to apprehend the meaning of phallic consciousness and abandon her propensity for being visually attracted by men.

Compared to the dazzling Ramon, Cipriano is an apparently unassuming character, shorter than Kate, dark and bearded 'like an imperial'. Like Ramon, he is attractive-repulsive, but not in the same way. Ramon stuns with the splendour of his plumage, his aquiline rapacity and his aquiline remoteness. Cipriano is still as a snake and moves with the quiet deftness of a snake.

His face was changeless and intensely serious, serious almost with a touch of childishness. But the curious blackness of his eyelashes lifted with such intense maleness from his eyes, the movement of his hand was odd, quick, light as he ate, so easily a movement of shooting or of flashing a knife into the body of an adversary ... that her heart stood still. There was something undeveloped and intense in him, the intensity and the crudity of the semi-savage. She could well understand the potency of the snake upon the Aztec and Maya imagination.

Although Ramon and Cipriano are both killers, hence men, their manliness is to be apprehended on different levels. Kate shrinks from Cipriano at first, fascinated and with a 'sensation of fear'. And, in a strange but significant conjunction of Quetzalcoatl, 'she felt somewhat as the bird feels when the snake is watching it.'

Cipriano is at first man to Ramon's god, endorsing his leader's claim to godhead in his reincarnation as Quetzalcoatl, and employing his troops to quash rebellions or empty the Catholic churches of their Christian paraphernalia, which are then ceremonially burned. But when he has proved himself in his leader's eyes, he too can achieve godhead and become a reincarnation of Huitzilopochtli, the Aztec god of war, fire and human sacrifice. In assuming such a role, he becomes 'once more the old, dominant male', capable of opening a new world to Kate. It is a world of 'twilight, with the dark, half-visible face of the demon-god Pan, who can never perish, but returns upon mankind from the shadows. The world of shadows and dark prostration, with the phallic wind rushing through the dark.' The prostration, however, is all Kate's. Sensing the 'phallic mystery' in Cipriano, she wants to give in to him and his power completely. She now decides that she prefers him to Ramon, 'who is remote from any woman', and, reader, she marries him.

But Ramon is not remote from any woman: he has two wives during the course of the novel and, when it suits him, he is not remote from either of them. He just doesn't fancy Kate: she is too white, Westernized and rational for him. Or so it would seem. There is something contrived in the way Kate manages to persuade herself that Cipriano is the better bet, and for the rest of the novel she still hankers after Ramon, much as Birkin hankers after Gerald. But it is necessary to the novel that she choose Cipriano, the man who, in bowing down to a lord and master, becomes a lord and master himself. And here *The Plumed Serpent* goes further than *Kangaroo*.

Having proved his manhood satisfactorily, Cipriano must now go on to prove his godhead. After the assassination attempt on Ramon, the surviving plotters are dealt with according to the religion of Quetzalcoatl and, more particularly, according to the requirements of its god, Huitzilopochtli. The 'grey dog' Guillermo has been enticed by the 'grey bitch' Maruca to betray his master, Ramon, and the two of them are ceremonially garrotted in the yard in front of the church by Cipriano's men. Of the four remaining prisoners, who draw lots, one is spared as a concession to the female principle (Kate), and the other three stripped and blind-folded. Cipriano himself takes hold of the dagger.

'The Lords of Life are Masters of Death,' he said in a loud, clear voice.
And swift as lightning he stabbed the blindfolded men to the heart with three swift, heavy stabs. Then he lifted the red dagger and threw it down.
'The Lords of Life are Masters of Death,' he repeated.

In order to be a lord and master, it is necessary to have power over both life and death. In order to be a life-giver, you must also become a life-taker, Quetzalcoatl being a religion which essentially reconciles opposites. It sounds plausible but repulsive. Is this just total, raving megalomania on Lawrence's part?

Perhaps not entirely. In *Of Women Born* Adrienne Rich quotes Frieda Fromm Reichmann's essay, 'On the Denial of Woman's Sexual Pleasure':

... There is a Persian myth of the creation of the world which precedes the Biblical one. In that myth a woman creates the world, and she creates by the act of natural creativity which is hers and cannot be duplicated by men. She gives birth to a great number of sons. The sons, greatly puzzled by this act which they cannot duplicate, become frightened. They think, Who can tell us, that if she can *give* life, she cannot also take life?

It seems to me that Ramon and Cipriano are reacting in the same sort of fear as those Persian mother's sons. Lawrence seems to be attacking this submerged male fear from the other end: he (and it must be he) who takes life must also be he who gives life, the primary creative source.

The bodies are carried into the church and, in a grisly but prettified ceremony from which women are excluded, the men daub themselves with some of the blood and sacrifice the rest to Huitzilopochtli. Blood has now acquired overtly magical (religious) properties, symbolizing both life and death. Ramon, in his Quetzal-coatl persona, acknowledges the bravery of the three slain men (in contrast to the cowardice of Guillermo and Maruca, whose blood has not been shed) and sends their souls into the next world with his blessing. The magic of blood is now contained in its symbolizing the cycle of life, death and rebirth – exactly as the menstrual cycle has always done. It is difficult to resist the suspicion that the men have evolved their own ceremony of blood in rivalry to the women's natural cycle, along the lines set out by Bruno Bettelheim in his *Symbolic Wounds: Puberty Rites and the Envious Male.* Which is why women must be excluded. The women's secret is menstruation, but the men's secret – which no woman must ever be allowed to discover – is that there is no men's secret. Elaborate male rituals in which blood is shed have evolved as a sort of compensation for male inadequacy. The men may be able to fool one another, but because it is in truth women who shed blood and give birth, there is not a woman who would be fooled, and the men would expose themselves to what they dread most: female ridicule. The Diggers' elaborate male rituals can now be seen as the same sort of process at one remove.

It is men rather than women, the Quetzalcoatl religion insists, who are in touch with life's mysteries and therefore have power over life and death. The keyword here is 'power'. It is men rather than women who, in the present context, think in terms of power, because they were once mother's sons, subject to the power of the female. For mother's daughters, life extends the promise of a similar power, and so women take their womanliness for granted, while men spend their lives evolving strategies for proving that their power is now equal to the power of women. Women may have their own mysteries of blood (actually, this is barely conceded in *The Plumed Serpent*) but man is blood plus power.

Later Ramon makes a further bid for the power of male blood when he tells Kate that 'man is a column of blood with a voice in it ... And when that voice is still, and he is only a column of blood, he is better.' Man is better off when he is all phallic power, and doesn't bother to think too much. For Ramon the truest symbol of man is the erect penis now elevated even beyond erection into something which can equal the power of the woman: the godlike phallus. In other words, man is or should be (or, heaven help us, must be) all cock – which seems to me a fair description of the religion of Quetzalcoatl. But then I, like Kate, am 'only a woman'.

Kate is satisfied with her womanhood and at first refuses to become a goddess, saying that such an elevation would make her 'die of shame'. But when Cipriano claims that he cannot become a god unless she is a goddess, she gives in. After the executions he comes to her, 'flickering, flashing and strangely young, as young and boyish as a flame'. His flame is virginal, being eternally renewable, and 'it made her again and again always a virgin girl.' She tells herself,

Why should I judge him? He is of the gods. And when he comes to me, he lays his pure, quick flame to mine ... It leaves me insouciant like a young girl. What do I care if he kills people? His flame is young and clean. He is Huitzilopochtli and I am Malantzi. What do I care what Cipriano Viedma does or doesn't do? Or even what Kate Leslie does or doesn't do?

Cipriano cannot be blamed for murdering people, any more than fire or the sun can be blamed for burning people. Fire would not be fire if it were not also capable of destruction. Fire and the gods are beyond human mortality. Is Lawrence really telling us that we can turn ourselves into gods and get away with murder?

It seems to me that what he intends to tell us is that we should not deny the dark, destructive forces in ourselves but recognize them as the obverse of our creativity. But it also seems to me that he is telling us a great deal more than he intended about male fears and male envy of the female.

Becoming gods and goddesses is not everyone's cup of tea, even if such an infusion were generally available. Kangaroo, the sexless, womanless god-in-man of Judaeo-Christianity, was finally rendered less than man. Being both servants and embodiments of the phallic gods, neither Ramon nor Cipriano is sexless and, if they are womanless, they can neither achieve nor retain their godhead. In becoming phallic gods-in-men they can admit their need for and dependence on women. But not just any women: woman at her womanliest as they are men at their manliest. That is, woman recognizing and submitting to male superiority. The admission is conditional, and there it sticks. Kate Leslie never quite endorses Quetzalcoatl. Not even the blandishment of becoming a goddess – a step in the direction of an equal-but-separate policy – can altogether succeed in producing the woman who can willingly maintain the man in his frail state of maleness.

The phallus seems to mean whatever Lawrence wants it to mean, whatever he feels himself to be or thinks he should be: man as both active and passive, silent and vocal, creator and destroyer. Paradoxically (and it is a paradox rather than a contradiction) there is something androgynous about the phallic male. And there is also something rather childish. Part of him remains rooted in the world of women and children, and stands as an outsider in the conventional world of men. In his quest for manliness, Lawrence often questions its conventional images, softening and feminizing them. But he can never quite exorcize the image of male sexuality as violent and brutal (nor resolve his ambivalence towards such an image) until the novel which started life as *Tenderness* and eventually became *Lady Chatterley's Lover*. I shall return to this novel later. But first it is necessary to examine some of Lawrence's images of women.

PART TWO
Women

1

The cloud of self-responsibility

The Lawrentian hero is a more or less identifiable character, but the Lawrentian heroine (if, indeed, there is such a creature) seems to have rather more facets to her composition than does her male counterpart. The hero is not, as a rule, at home in the world of men, where he tends to become shrilly dogmatic and somewhat desperate. In venturing into the discussion of political or social questions, Lawrence himself is nearly always over-insistent and repetitive, flailing agape like a fish out of water. It is in the world of close emotional and domestic relationships, the world of women, that he seems to be in his true element: on firm ground, but following the thread blindly and intuitively through the labyrinth of the indefinable self. And it is Lawrence's women rather than his sadly incomplete and ineffectual men who compel belief. Rather as Milton wrote so powerfully about hell and Satan, but so tediously about God and heaven, so Lawrence writes with greater conviction and credibility about what he purports to consider the inferior sex. Does this mean that Lawrence was, as Blake considered Milton to be, 'of the devil's party without knowing it'?

A reading of Lawrence's early work, which is largely concerned with the experience of young people growing up, often indicates as much. His young women consistently express feminist or near-feminist views as to their status or their expectations of life. And occasionally even the authorial voice can give vent to similar sentiments. In this context the key word (which rings anachronistically but was an early favourite of Lawrence's) is 'self-responsibility'.

According to Cyril, the narrator of *The White Peacock*, his sister Letty is guilty of a 'shirking ... shuffling of her life'. The fault consists in her unquestioning acceptance of a conventional marriage to a respectable young man who later becomes a Tory MP, a marriage in which only incessant childbearing can alleviate her sense of torpor. When Cyril urges her 'to take some work that she could throw her soul into, she would reply indifferently.' And she seems not to have the courage of the youthful convictions she once held.

Like so many women she seemed to live for the most part contentedly, a small indoor existence with artificial light and padded upholstery. Only occasionally, hearing the winds of life outside, she clamoured to be out in the black, keen storm. She was driven to the door, she looked out and called into the tumult wildly, but feminine caution kept her from stepping over the threshold.

Her situation is made more painful, and at the same time less forgivable, by virtue of her intelligence which is only too capable of recognizing the deficiencies in her chosen way of life.

There is a 'touch of ironical brutality in her' when she describes her occupation or career as 'Mother', and her business as a flourishing one. But, as Cyril notes, she is also being basically truthful.

Having reached that point in a woman's career when most, perhaps all of the things in life seem worthless and insipid, she had determined to put up with it, to ignore her own self, to empty her potentialities into the vessel of another or others, and to live her life at secondhand. This peculiar abnegation of self is the resource for a woman for the escaping of the responsibilities of her own development. Like a nun, she puts over her face a living veil, a sign that the woman no longer exists for herself: she is the servant of God, of some man, of her children, or maybe of some cause. As a servant, she is no longer responsible for herself, which would make her terrified and lonely. Service is light and easy. To be responsible for the good progress of one's life is terrifying. It is the most insufferable form of loneliness and the heaviest of responsibilities.

Like so many women of her generation (and mine) Letty has bartered her self-responsibility for security, comfort and freedom from anxiety.

The most insufferable form of loneliness. Terrifying. The heaviest of responsibilities. There can be no doubt here as to either the difficulty or the necessity of the quest for selfhood. No wonder that Ursula in *The Rainbow* feels the necessity descend on her like a cloud at adolescence. It is not a quest to be undertaken by men only, but one for people of either sex, if they are to be able to call themselves people at all. In order to realize our potential (a task which life demands of us) we must be prepared, whether we are men or women, to be both terrified and lonely and to face both our fears and our isolation courageously again and again. This can hardly be called a sexist message. On the contrary, it is commendably tough on all those women who turn to men to protect them from the rigours of the independent life. It is a message which basically Lawrence never repudiates. But he does vary its terms of reference as he attempts to define and redefine the proper constituents of female selfhood.

The *White Peacock* passage makes no reference to womanliness or femininity, either as an easily observable quality (or set of qualities) or as an idea/ideal to be striven towards. Letty has, on the contrary, been treading a well-worn feminine path which has rendered her less of a person, a self, than she might otherwise have become. The suggestion is that the feminine stereotypes – wife, mother, nun, servant – are at odds with the achievement of selfhood. But, for women, the achievement of selfhood must entail the achievement of womanhood, because we are bodies as well as minds. How is this dilemma to be resolved?

If the quest for manliness involves some sort of separation from the world of women, so then does the quest for a complementary womanliness. The nature of the separation is at first more or less the same for both sexes and amounts in effect to a separation from the parental family – or growing up. In Lawrentian terms, it requires a form of rebirth. And, in a very important sense, the achievement of selfhood remains independent of gender. But, in an equally important sense, it eventually depends very heavily upon gender. Lawrence's bias in defining womanliness is generally towards wifehood (but not motherhood) and away from singleness. But his concept of marriage is supposedly a new one, far removed from Letty's fate, and involving the union of the new man and the new woman.

Given that the new man in the form of the Lawrentian hero has arrogated for himself and manliness all the attributes of the world of women which are either attractive or useful to him, the new womanliness must either be very similar to the new manliness, or else totally redefined so as to complement the new, improved definition of manliness. To me, the former alternative appears as self-evidently true. But Lawrence chose the latter. Why?

It seems to me that Lawrence's choice was made on the basis of a belief in the essential frailty of the male, and a corresponding belief in the essential strength of the female. I happen to share both beliefs but, unlike Lawrence and unsurprisingly enough, I cannot perceive them as any sort of threat, either to myself or to the rest of humanity. If you do perceive what you believe to be true as a threat, both to yourself and to the rest of humanity, you are thereby divided, and your task becomes twofold: in the first place, you must prove your supposition true; in the second, you must prove it both dangerous and destructive. It seems to me that Lawrence often sticks at the point of convincingly demonstrating female strength, without going on to convince that it is necessarily A Bad Thing. Perhaps he was incapable of doing so. And perhaps it was impossible for him to do so: he doesn't have a case.

2

To marry or not to marry

Women In Love begins with the Brangwen sisters, Ursula and Gudrun, discussing what Lawrence sees as the all-important question for young women: to marry or not to marry? Both the sisters and Alvina Houghton in *The Lost Girl* choose at least partical economic independence in the face of parental opposition when each decides to earn her own living. But such independence never quite gains authorial approval as an end in itself: marriage must still be considered sooner or later. Gudrun wonders whether 'one needs the *experience* of having been married', and the conversation continues as follows.

'Do you think it need *be* an experience?' replied Ursula.
   'Bound to be, in some way or other,' said Gudrun coolly. 'Possibly undesirable, but bound to be an experience of some sort.'
   'Not really,' said Ursula. 'More likely to be the end of experience.'

Is marriage necessarily a dead end, as it is for Letty, and an automatic bar to self-realization? Or does it offer an opportunity, perhaps the supreme opportunity, for personal growth? The assumptions in *Women In Love* are, first, that the latter might be true, and then that it *should* be true: the question as to whether or not it *is* true cannot be resolved. Other questions have to be asked first, the most important of which is, personal growth for whom? What sort of woman is likely to gain from what sort of marriage? Sooner or later these questions become focused into a more specific one: what sort of woman is both capable of and ready for marriage to the Lawrentian hero?
   Lawrence's young women are often commended by the author for the extent to which they have achieved selfhood rather than womanhood. But any such achievement must first entail a recognition of what is traditionally a woman's lot. Both Emily in *The White Peacock* and Miriam in *Sons and Lovers* (essentially a

development of the same character) are given to grumbling about the limitations of being a girl. Miriam, who is little more than a servant to her numerous brothers, tells Paul that she does not want to live at home – a fact which he has some difficulty in comprehending.

'What do you want, then?'

'I want to do something. I want a chance, like anybody else. Why should I, because I'm a girl, be kept at home and not allowed to be anything? What chance *have* I?'

'Chance of what?'

'Of knowing anything – of learning, of doing anything. It's not fair, because I'm a woman.'

She seemed very bitter. Paul wondered. In his own home Annie was almost glad to be a girl.

Almost, but not quite? Paul goes on to say, frowning, that surely women ought to be as glad to be women as men are to be men, but Miriam insists that men have got everything going for them. When Paul offers to each her algebra, she hesitates, but he is determined that she shall have whatever chance he can offer, and if necessary to call her bluff. Whether or not Miriam subsequently learns any algebra is not made clear, but she is certainly taught – if in a rather bullying manner. She is not an apt pupil (which, considering that she has never been to school is hardly surprising) and Paul soon becomes impatient with her.

It is not Miriam's slowness which enrages Paul again and again as much as her humility in the face of learning. It is clear to modern readers that Miriam is humble because she has never been taught anything else. But Paul's irritation is not just a piece of youthful cruelty. It is, in an important respect, similar to Cyril's irritation with Letty: to the observing male, both women appear to be wilfully rejecting the opportunity to impose themselves on life and to act upon it with any sense of attack. Paul sees Miriam's failure at algebra as symptomatic of her larger failure to live.

Miriam does lack courage. She moves through life, both physically and mentally, in 'fear and self-mistrust', feeling 'hot pain' when pushed high on a swing, disoriented when climbing a stile and unable to jump from even a small height – the very prospect of which is enough to make her eyes dilate, 'exposed and palpitating'. Paul's mission is to induce her to jump, both literally and metaphorically: to take a leap in the dark. It could be argued that she does as much in falling in love with Paul, and I think Lawrence does in fact argue such a case in *The Plumed Serpent* on behalf of Ramon's second wife, Teresa, whose early biography is in many respects similar to Miriam's. But in *Sons and Lovers* the implication is that Miriam will not, cannot – at any rate, does not – take any sort of leap.

Miriam, however, has more self-confidence than Paul imagines, a womanly self-confidence (so Lawrence suggests) which is beyond his youthful understanding. In a way, she is sure of Paul, sure of her power over him, and of the rightness of their belonging together. She has enough faith in their relationship to suppose that she recognizes what Paul is looking for in his affair with Clara: 'a sort of baptism of fire in passion'. She can 'let' him go to Clara as she 'could let him go to an inn for a glass of whisky', because such toleration will eventually lead to her repossession of Paul. But she does not divulge any such thoughts to him. Both her reasoning and her concealment of it amount to the better part of (traditionally feminine) wisdom, which derives its strength from subterfuge and is thus geared to maintaining the status quo in relationships between men and women. Even her willingness to act as an intellectual foil to Paul is seen as a form of subterfuge, in that she is humouring him to the end of possessing him and thus maintaining her own female power.

Miriam is not a fit bride for Paul because she operates in the old female mode of Mrs Morel, gaining strength from the possession of others rather than the possession of herself, her own soul. Or so Paul would have us believe. Lawrence is not so sure. Despite all authorial directives to the contrary, Miriam does not emerge as a clinging, sexually frigid young woman whose general fear of life renders her fit material for a nunnery. In many ways she is stronger and more worldly-wise than Paul. Perhaps this is what he cannot forgive her.

When, after eight years, the on-off affair comes to an end and

Miriam refuses to go along with Paul's plea that there have been some perfect moments, he is horrified to discover that she has known all along of his attempts to fight her off, to disengage himself from the possibility of being possessed by her.

And she had known. She had known so much, and told him so little. She had known all the time. All the time this was at the bottom of her.

He sat silent in bitterness. At last the whole affair appeared in a cynical aspect to him. She had really played with him, and not he with her. She had hidden all her condemnation from him, had flattered him and despised him.

Miriam's patience with him, her tolerance, and her very niceness are seen as elements of deceit rather than as manifestations of love.

To be known as Miriam knows Paul is to be in a vulnerable position; and to be ignorant that you are thus known weakens your position further. Not only are you being possessed; you are also being duped. This may be a suitable way for a woman to treat a child (and at this point Miriam does call Paul a child of four) but not a man. There is a hint of primitive magic in the notion that one can be so disadvantageously possessed by another, a notion which is at the same time based on the well-founded fears of the mother's son. Lawrence never wants lovers to 'know' each other in the way that Miriam knows Paul, that is, both personally and intellectually, but advocates instead a 'dark' and impersonal knowledge. If a woman knows a man as Miriam knows Paul, as Harriet knows Somers, she will have scant respect for him, be incapable of believing in him, and of course will never truly submit.

Whatever we are told about Miriam in *Sons and Lovers* is geared to one end: to justify Paul's rejection of her. And the same is true, although the reasons are different, of Clara Dawes, the woman with whom Paul first experiences sexual passion. Clara is older than Paul, and married – but separated, and so still asking questions about the value of marriage. She has 'taken up Women's Rights. She was supposed to be clever. It interested Paul.' He is even more interested to discover that she has 'a grudge against men'. Unlike Miriam, Clara represents some sort of challenge. Her eyes are scornful, her speech scathing, and in verbal adroitness she is a match for Paul any day. She has little patience with his flirtatiousness or flippancy, and when he offers to march alongside her in a WSPU demonstration, carrying her banner for her like a mediaeval knight, her reply is cool and devastatingly to the point: 'I have no doubt that you would rather fight for a woman than let her fight for herself.' Her feminism is not an object of scorn, but enhances her attraction.

The problem with feminism is that it has made Clara unhappy. She has been in the women's movement for ten years, and so has 'acquired a fair amount of education', but it has not qualified her for any better work than a job in the spiral department at Jordan's factory, or spinning ('jennying') jobs which can be done at home with her mother and are paid by the piece. When Paul asks her if this latter work is sweated, she replies bitterly, 'More or less. Isn't *all* women's work?' Clara finds her means of earning a living degrading, but she persists in it, refusing to go back to her husband and the economic security of marriage. It would seem that marriage constitutes an even worse degradation.

After five years of marriage and another three years of supporting herself, Clara still shudders at the thought of her husband. 'He – sort of degraded me. He wanted to bully me because he hadn't got me. And then I felt as if I wanted to run, as if I was fastened and bound up.' Dawes has failed to 'waken' her, to get through to her, is 'dirty' and 'brutal': all of which hints at a selfish and insensitive lover. When she fails to respond to him, he finds himself another woman who will, thus providing Clara with an excuse to leave him. Now that she has done so, she professes to find life 'infinitely' happier, and to be satisfied 'so long as I can be free and independent'. But no one, including her mother, really believes her.

Everything about Clara proclaims her freedom and independence. 'She carried her head back, as if she had drawn away in contempt, perhaps from men also.' Her neck, her arms, her chest are all strong and her shoulders curve 'handsomely' under her muslin blouse. But perhaps Clara is too strong, either for her own good or Paul's. She consoles him and becomes his lover because, basically, she feels sorry for him. She 'submits' ('acquiesces' would be a more appropriate term) to 'the hunger and inevitability of his loving her' because

she knew how stark and alone he was, and she felt it was great that he came to her; and she took him simply because his need was bigger than her or him, and her soul was still within her. She did this for him, in his need, even if he left her, because she loved him.

When they make love, they 'included in their meeting the thrust of the manifold grass stems, the cry of the peewit, the wheel of the stars'. Because it has been a moment of the highest passion for Paul, he assumes that it has been the same for Clara, and all his subsequent assumptions about her behaviour are based on this misapprehension.

The moment cannot be recaptured, and Paul imagines that this is what Clara expects from him and that she is 'mad with desire' for him. But later Clara rebukes him, telling him that he knows nothing about her and that, in effect, he is wrong to see her as sexuality incarnate. On the contrary, she cannot see sex as the culmination of their intimacy and has not felt satisfied by their lovemaking. 'A flash of hate for her came up. After all, she was dissatisfied with him even there, where he thought they fulfilled each other.' Clara accuses him of selfishness: 'But is it me you want or is it *It*?' Paul simply cannot understand this question and thinks that she is 'splitting a hair'. He persists in believing that sex is entirely a matter of blind instinct and is spoiled by 'mechanical effort'. Clara is trying to tell him, as kindly and tactfully as possible, that if he had made a bit more mechanical effort in the direction of recognizing her and her needs, she would have been rather more satisfied.

Paul doesn't listen – because he doesn't want to hear. All he can hear, when Clara tells him that at least she always felt her husband wanted her rather than It, is that he is being compared unfavourably to Baxter Dawes. At this moment he decides that Clara must go back to her husband, and he brings the affair to an end. Clara has been beaten – not by Paul, however much he would like to think so – but by economic stringency and the strain of being a social outcast. This seems to me tragic, but Lawrence seems to rejoice slyly in her defeat. Clara has been returned to her rightful place in the scheme of things. Her independence, it has been suggested all along, has been a sham. How can a passionate woman like Clara live without sex? And how can the sexuality of a passionate woman like Clara be contained and channelled into its proper use except in marriage?

Paul, the inadequate lover, persists in this view of Clara as he persisted in his view of Miriam's excessive spirituality, but Lawrence the novelist cannot help but reveal that in neither case is this the whole truth. Just as Miriam is patient and tolerant with Paul, so is Clara. Women are revealed, in spite of Paul, as being capable of enormous generosity in love, a generosity which is all too easily taken for granted by men. Incapable as men are of reciprocity in kind, they fatally misconstrue female generosity as an attack upon their own integrity.

Here in *Sons and Lovers* the web of misunderstanding between men and women is already thoroughly tangled. Whatever women are and do in themselves is devalued; whatever they are and do in relation to men is overemphasized. A woman cannot be divorced from her sexuality – or rather, from a man's sexual apprehension of her. And yet this is exactly what the Lawrentian hero expects of her in the sexual act: that she divorce herself and her individuality from what she is actually doing. Sexuality is something which cannot be acknowledged by consciousness, and all sexual acts should take place in darkness. The trouble with women is that they refuse to recognize the split between the upper and lower selves, and will persist in taking sex personally instead of as an impersonal force of nature. Women are all too palpably *there* whatever they are doing, all too palpably themselves, refusing to become Woman. In short (though this is not of course the inference intended by Lawrence) men are dangerously schizoid, whereas women are whole.

If women are so demonstrably generous and so whole in themselves, what and where is the need for men – for marriage? Inevitably this is a question which Lawrence's young women have to ask themselves. Alvina Houghton comes close to marriage three times before she chooses the darkly handsome Cicio and goes off to live with him in his native Italy. Cicio is altogether unsuitable in conventional terms, being younger, poorer and less well-educated than she is (a typical Lawrentian pairing, this) and the marriage is intended to shock, to reveal a new and superior relationship between men and women. Its superiority consists in the couple's being able to communicate in their lower selves, while their upper selves remain comparatively inarticulate and, literally, do not even speak the same language.

Like Clara, Alvina makes valiant attempts to earn her own living. But nursing turns out to be no more satisfying to her than jennying is to Clara. Like most of Lawrence's young women she has an ambivalent attitude towards marriage. 'She didn't really want to marry anybody. Why should she? She was thankful beyond measure to be by herself. How sick she was of other people and their importunities!' But in practice she cannot resist Cicio and his importuning. When he insists softly and mesmerically (but not of course abjectly) that she accompany him to Italy, she is bewitched by his beauty and loses her will, seeing herself as a sacred prostitute.

She felt extinguished. Cicio talked to her, but only ordinary things. There was no wonderful intimacy of speech, such as she had always imagined and craved for. No. He loved her – but it was in a dark, mesmeric way which did not let her be herself . . . She had to be the quiescent, obscure woman: she felt as if she were veiled. Her thoughts were dim, in the dim, back regions of consciousness – yet, somewhere she almost exulted. Atavism!

Extinguished. Obscure. Dim. Veiled. It would seem that Alvina is, like Letty, shirking the burden of self-responsibility. But there is no doubt that Lawrence endorses her behaviour. She agrees to marry Cicio and to live with him in his poverty-stricken village where, in the Neapolitan fashion, he moves mainly in his man's world, communicating with her only in bed at night.

Lawrence's later fiction reveals that these assumptions as to the passivity and masochism of the female are tenacious indeed. But it also comes gradually to the suspicion that they might constitute a form of male wish-fulfilment. In advocating marriage as the perfect environment for such supposedly female needs, and in presenting us with a heroine so swooningly overwhelmed by the power of male sexuality, *The Lost Girl* comes perilously near to the stock romantic fiction of Mills and Boon. But if all Lawrence's heroines were Alvinas, we should not still be reading his novels today.

The question, to marry or not to marry, is explored at its fullest and deepest in *The Rainbow* and its sequel *Women In Love* through the personae of Ursula and Gudrun Brangwen. Gudrun appears only briefly in *The Rainbow*, the major part of which is concerned with Ursula's growing up. The first third or so of the novel chronicles the history of the Brangwens in the two generations immediately preceding Ursula's. They are farmers in a Midlands area increasingly being claimed by the mining industry, their lives progressing cyclically according to the rhythms of the seasons and the calendar of the Christian church, and untouched by the sort of mechanization so eagerly pursued by Gerald in *Women In Love*. These pages are probably the most beautiful ever written by Lawrence – unsurpassed, perhaps even unsurpassable.

It is into this idyllic setting that Ursula is born, the eldest of (eventually) nine children. Her mother, Anna, is always most occupied and absorbed by the latest of her babies and so, early on, Ursula becomes her father's child. She resents her mother's 'superficial authority', and despises her 'trance of motherhood'.

When she saw, later, a Rubens picture with storms of naked babies, and found that this was called 'Fecundity', she shuddered, and the word became abhorrent to her. She knew as a child what it was to live amid storms of babies, in the heat and swelter of fecundity. And as a child she was against her mother, passionately against her mother, she craved for some spirituality and stateliness.

Ursula's sisters and brothers, 'fiendish, ubiquitous', are healthy and noisy, a torment to her adolescent soul. She has always found being the eldest 'burdensome', and resents being pressed into any role approximating to that of mother or caretaker to the younger ones.

All this is beautifully, poignantly done, and it looks as though

Ursula Brangwen is the stuff of which strong, independent women are made. So, in many ways, it proves. But first she has to go through all the painful processes of adolescence: to reconcile her sensitivity with the growing demands of the impinging world; her sense of her own individuality with the chastening recognition that she is only one among many; her self-respect with the demoralizing sensation of being utterly lost; her expansive yearnings with the contractive environment of her home and her own limitations. As she grows up, the 'cloud of self-responsibility' gathers, the awareness that 'she must go somewhere, she must become something.' Like Letty, she is afraid.

Why, oh why, must one grow up, why must one inherit this heavy, numbing responsibility of living an undiscovered life? Out of nothingness and the undifferentiated mass, to make something of herself! But what? In the obscurity and pathlessness to take a direction! But whither? How even take one step? And yet, how stand still? This was torment, indeed, to inherit the responsibility of one's own life.

But, unlike Letty, she recognizes that self-responsibility is largely a matter of self-creation: the self must be created as the life is being discovered. And, again unlike Letty, Ursula will neither shirk nor shuffle.

As the means towards selfhood Ursula tries both love and work. Her first love affair is with Anton Skrebensky, a young soldier who brings with him a sense of the vast outside world. She is drawn magnetically to him, while being hurt by the attraction. But during the relationship she blossoms, her face 'like a flower in the sun', her mind opened to a fascinating new 'world of passion and lawlessness'. Like the Sleeping Beauty, she has been waiting for that first kiss, after which 'she went to bed feeling all warm with electric warmth, as if the gush of dawn were within her, upholding her. And she slept deeply, sweetly, oh so sweetly. In the morning she felt sound as an ear of wheat, fragrant and firm and full.' It is through Skrebensky that she comes to some sense of her ripeness, her fullness as a woman, but throughout the affair there is an intimation that the recognition comes primarily from Ursula herself, and that Skrebensky is merely accidental. The passion she feels is less for him than a passion to know her own maximum self, limited and so defined against him. She could limit and define herself against him, the male, she could be her maximum self, female, oh female, triumphant for one moment in exquisite assertion against the male, in supreme contradistinction to the male.

In asserting her 'indomitable, gorgeous female self', she embraces Skrebensky, seeming to feel right through his body, 'so exquisitely subject and under her control'. Ursula is realizing the power of her own sexuality, but she has yet to learn that sexuality is not only a matter of power.

On a moonlit night she is inspired with the wish: 'Oh, for the cold liberty to be herself, to do entirely as she liked. She wanted to get right away. She felt like bright metal weighed down by dark, impure magnetism.' Not for her the dim succumbing of Alvina to Cicio. For Ursula, sexuality is now an imposition from without, and one which threatens to erode the boundaries of self, to violate the hard-won fragile self. When Skrebensky attempts to make love to her, she becomes 'hard and fierce and burning corrosive as the moonlight', where he has expected her to be tender and yielding, opening herself to him like a flower. He is destroyed and annihilated, while Ursula triumphs, the sense of her own female power confirmed.

But at the same time she too is shaken: she has always thought of herself as a good and loving person and now, in glimpsing the destructive potential of sexuality, she is pushed towards altering that self-image along lines which could prove fatal to her self-esteem. At once she reverts to being 'nice', like all good little girls, becoming winning with her Anton. But it is too late. He cannot respond in kind, and when Ursula gets home she has to admit that 'she had hurt herself as if she had bruised herself, in annihilating him. She covered up her two young breasts with her hands, covering them to herself, and covering herself with herself, she crouched in bed to sleep.' Ursula is not ready, at sixteen, for adult heterosexuality and cannot yet unloose her dark, passional self. She and Anton can be lovers only 'in a young, romantic, almost fantastic way'. When he goes back to join his regiment, she becomes depressed, 'cold and unliving', but at the same time 'morbidly sensitive'. Her sexuality has been aroused but, having found no satisfactory or fulfilling outlet, flames 'into a kind of disease within her'.

The disease manifests itself in homosexuality, and takes the form of a relationship with Winifred Inger, a teacher at Ursula's school and a woman some twelve years older than herself. To Ursula, Winifred is 'proud and free as a man, but exquisite as a woman'. As their intimacy develops, so Ursula too develops, with Winifred delighting in 'filling and enriching her life'. Winifred herself is interested in the Women's Movement and criticizes men for being inane idealists and therefore impotent. When the long vacation arrives and Winifred goes back to London, Ursula is left isolated, and 'a terrible, outcast, almost poisonous despair possessed her'. She can feel herself disintegrating, 'yet within all the attack of disintegration upon her, she remained herself. It was the terrible core of all her suffering, that she was always herself.'

Ursula has not yet arrived at the loss of self or soul which Somers experiences in Australia. As in the relationship with Skrebensky, she has allowed a certain part of herself to develop, only to have it arrested abruptly. The arrest in each case is occasioned not only by the outward circumstances of physical separation, but by the inward fact of Ursula's own separateness, a circumstance which she herself controls and needs to control because she is still in the process of growing up and separating herself from the parental family. But, whereas in the relationship with Skrebensky she came to some realization of her own adult female self, in the relationship with Winifred it is the loss of this very same self which leads to disillusionment. She still loves Winifred,

but a heavy, clogged sense of deadness began to gather upon her, from the other woman's contact. And sometimes she thought Winifred was ugly, clayey. Her female hips seemed big and earthy, her ankles and her arms were too thick. She wanted some fine intensity instead of this heavy cleaving of moist clay, that cleaves because it has no life of its own.

So she begins to reject Winifred and can 'consent no more to mingle with the perverted life of the older woman'.

Lawrence chooses to grant Ursula a homoerotic affair, only to reject it in bitterly misogynistic terms. The relationship itself is described tenderly, made to seem both passionate and beautiful, as if Lawrence cannot but admit that women, just like men, experience strong homoerotic feelings. While it is in progress, there is no hint from him that the love between Ursula and Winifred is at all unusual, let alone perverted. It is only when the affair has run its course that Ursula begins to express feelings of disgust, which are also those of self-disgust – and both rather more vehement than is warranted in context. On the one hand, Lawrence seems to be saying that homoerotic relationships are a normal and necessary part of growing up for women no less than they are for men. On the other hand, he is saying quite clearly that it is the rejection of such relationships between women which constitutes real growth. It is difficult to resist the conclusion that strong relationships between women (whether erotic or not) constitute a threat because they demonstrate that women can do nicely, thank you, without men.

But I don't think that Lawrence's rejection of the relationship between Ursula and Winifred is only a matter of sour-grapeish male insecurity. It seems to me that the affair is initially portrayed as one of sweetness and light – and indeed enlightenment – because Lawrence sees all such relationships, belonging as they do to the world of women which sets niceness at a premium, as less than honest, and therefore doomed. The honesty is not a matter of openness and frankness between partners, but of being true to oneself and, in particular, to one's lower or night-time self which has its allegiance to darkness. Although Ursula has her dark moments of self-surrender with both Skrebensky and Winifred, the metallic and virginal power of the moonlight in the first instance, and in the second the revelatory power of enlightenment, ensure that neither relationship can be of any real meaning. There is also a hint in the latter instance that what goes on sexually between women must be willed and mechanistic rather than instinctual, complementary, and therefore natural.

Each relationship has engaged only a part of Ursula. Her self-image as a totally loving young creature has been destroyed, but she concludes that it has been so only as an illusion is destroyed: it existed only in her imagination. She is seventeen years old and feels that she has lost the capacity to love or desire. In doing so she wonders whether she has actually ever possessed it. From now on, she decides, she will have no lover, neither will any lover ever want her. She must do something else with her life. But what?

When she decides to become a schoolteacher Ursula, no less than Paul Morel, is daunted by the prospect of entering the world of men. But 'her mother's contempt and her father's harshness had made her raw at the quick, she knew the ignominy of being a hanger-on, she felt the festering thorn of her mother's animal estimation.' Although her father is prepared to support her until such time as she marries, it is a matter of pride with her that she earn her own living. Her parents' opposition, which denigrates rather than forbids, only hardens her resolve, and she steels herself to apply for a job in a school. Eventually she is offered a place in a primary school in a rough area of the neighbouring town of Ilkeston.

Ursula's inward and outward struggles against being beaten or brutalized by the world of men make poignant reading (and, when I first read *The Rainbow*, succeeded in putting me off teaching for life). Ursula is no longer Ursula Brangwen, a teenage girl, but Miss Brangwen the Standard Five teacher. She tells no one that teaching is a torture to her, but perseveres, knowing that she must: it is not only a matter of pride but of self-responsibility.

She did not believe that she could ever teach that great brutish class, in that brutal school; ever, ever. And yet, if she failed, she must in some way go under. She must admit that the man's world was too strong for her, she could not take her place in it . . . And all her life henceforth she must go on, never having freed herself of the man's world, never having achieved the freedom of the great world of responsible work.

In persevering she is proving herself her mother's superior and her father's equal. She is creating herself in her own and not the parental image.

She succeeds by bullying and caning a particularly troublesome boy, only to discover, when his mother visits the school the next day, that he has a heart condition. She shrinks from the brutality and the scandal of what she has done. But she has won: her class now treat her with more respect, and she recognizes that 'nothing but a thrashing would settle some of the big louts who wanted to play cat and mouse with her.' When provoked, 'she seized the cane and slashed the boy who was insolent to her, over head and ears and hands.' In the world of men fear is a more effective weapon than love, and an impersonal hierarchy of teacher and pupils the natural order of things. This is a shattering lesson to Ursula.

But she paid a great price out of her own soul, to do this. It seemed as if a great flame had gone through her and burnt her sensitive tissue. She who shrank from the thought of physical suffering in any form had been forced to fight and beat with a cane and rouse all her instincts to hurt. And afterwards she had been forced to endure the sound of their blubbering and desolation.

The world of men cauterizes and is soul-destroying. It is no place for a young girl.

It would seem that in *The Rainbow* Lawrence sets no great store by the world of men. Ursula's teaching experiences are based on his own as an uncertificated teacher and at the same sort of age. But here they are given added point and power in being allotted to a girl: a girl set in solitary opposition to the massed brute world of men and work. Because Ursula is a woman her struggles to find and keep a place in a man's world are rendered more than usually courageous. They also have the effect of making her seem stronger than other women who remain in the world of women. But this is double-edged: she is also becoming more unwomanly than those other women in choosing to become a schoolteacher, like Winifred, rather than a mother, like her own mother.

And so it is that Ursula is no longer a young girl. To a greater extent than her relationships with either Skrebensky or Winifred, her teaching experience has forced her into the adult world, and she becomes 'isolated now from the life of her childhood, a foreigner in a new life of work and mechanical consideration'. But is this all the adult world consists of? The partial freedom she has gained by her 'strong, cruel move' to become independent of her parents has served to make her aware of further freedoms still beyond her reach and, most of all, 'the big want' to which she cannot put a name. She certainly does not, at this stage, call it marriage. On the contrary, she now goes into some kind of belated adolescent moratorium, and reverts to becoming a Sleeping Beauty once more. Another sort of growth is taking place. 'Her real, individual self drew together and became more coherent during those two years of teaching ... It was always a prison to her, the school. But it was a prison in which her wild, chaotic soul became hard and independent.' By the time she is twenty-two and Skrebensky reappears, she is just about ready for him.

Their love affair is renewed and at first, the two of them being 'enemies in a truce', all promises well. Skrebensky too has grown up and both are excited by the prospect of adult passion. Ursula is particularly excited by the prospect of exercising her female power which Skrebensky's warmth and male beauty have reawakened. 'She was no more Ursula Brangwen. She was Woman, she was the whole of Woman in the human order. All-containing, universal, how should she be limited to individuality?' That she becomes once again like a flower is a good sign: whenever Lawrence compares Ursula to a flower (as he often does in *Women In Love* as well as *The Rainbow*) he is endorsing her behaviour. But there is also a warning note sounded early on in this reunion.

In his dark, male soul, he was kneeling before her, darkly exposing himself. She quivered, the dark flame ran over. He was waiting at her feet. He was helpless, at her mercy. She could take or reject him. If she rejected him, something would die in him. For him, it was life or death.

A man kneeling before a woman is never a good prognostic sign in Lawrence's fiction. A man who puts himself at a woman's mercy, as Gerald later does in relation to Gudrun, is asking to be destroyed. If a woman is given such an opportunity, sooner or later she will take it.

At first Ursula shows little inclination to do so. Achieving their 'superb consummation' when they make love beneath an oak tree on a stormy night, she and Skrebensky reach 'an eternal changeless place' together, and she enters 'the dark fields of immortality', at one with the night. To her, Skrebensky is not a man but 'a dark powerful vibration that encompassed her'. Ursula is now strong and free and has 'never been more herself'; but 'it could not occur to her that anybody, not even the young man of the world, Skrebensky, could have anything to do with her permanent self.' When he suggests marriage, she refuses because marriage would entail the assumption of their 'temporal, social' selves to the detriment of the vivid, passional selves they now so supremely embody.

During the Easter vacation, which they spend together in London and Paris, the relationship begins to fall apart. It becomes clear that, although the affair has given Ursula strength and freedom, it has rendered Skrebensky dependent on her, and that his passion amounts to a form of addiction.

But it all contained a developing germ of death. After each contact her anguished desire for him or for that which she never had from him was stronger, her love more hopeless. After each contact his mad dependence on her was deepened, his hope of standing strong and taking her in his own strength was weakened. He felt himself a mere attribute of her.

Because Ursula is stronger than he is, neither of them can be happy. He becomes tense and constrained, afraid of her body; when they make love now, her eyes are open, looking at the stars. Whatever the big want in Ursula's soul, Skrebensky cannot supply it.

And yet, wondering if she is perhaps expecting too much of life, she now agrees to marry him: it seems slightly preferable to be Baroness Skrebensky than 'Ursula Brangwen, spinster and school-teacher'. But she cannot go through with it, and in the evenings 'a yearning for something unknown came over her'. On another moonlit night, when she is 'like metal' and her voice ringing and metallic 'like the voice of a harpy', she kisses him with a 'fierce, beaked harpy's kiss' from which he shrinks in fear, and their love-making becomes a fight: 'the struggle for consummation was terrible.' Once again she has destroyed him, but now she has destroyed herself as well, and 'all within her was cold, dead, inert.' The relationship is at an end.

There is a great deal of cruelty in this relationship, a cruelty which Lawrence seems to condone. In her egocentricity and indecision, Ursula behaves destructively towards Skrebensky much as Paul does towards Miriam. Lawrence finds their behaviour justifiable because in each case the lover has not found his/her true complement, has not found fulfilment. It would seem that Skrebensky's weakness and dependence bring out the unwomanliness in Ursula as a matter of course, and that therefore she is not to blame for this only too natural train of events. That she is not compelled by Skrebensky is a sign of his inadequacy rather than her excessive idealism. That he does not lead her into the unknown is a sign of his nullity rather than the grandiosity of her yearnings.

But Lawrence is not altogether on Ursula's side, on the side of the woman. In making her womanly fulfilment entirely dependent on the strength of a man, Lawrence is allotting her a secondary place in the relationship. In his essay on Nathaniel Hawthorne, the same sort of argument appears.

Woman is a strange and rather terrible phenomenon to man. When the subconscious soul of woman recoils from its creative union with man, it becomes a destructive force. It exerts, willy-nilly, an invisible destructive influence . . . She doesn't know it. She can't even help it. But she does it. The devil is in her.

But her recoil is the fault of the man who, if he had but sufficient belief in himself, would be able to hold her. Thus, 'woman is the nemesis of doubting man. She can't help it.' It is Skrebensky's lack of belief in himself which leads to his addictive, helpless behaviour and in turn to his destruction. Skrebensky has been asking for it, Ursula only acting according to the obverse side of her womanliness in response.

Unknown to Ursula, Skrebensky marries his colonel's daughter before setting off for India. But Ursula is pregnant. At first the coming child seems like 'the seal set on her own nullity', but later she is 'glad in her flesh', and begins to value living from day to day 'in the body, rich, peaceful, complete, with no beyond, no further trouble, no further complication'. Perhaps she has been arrogant in wanting more than she had with Skrebensky.

Suddenly she saw her mother in a just and true light. Her mother was simple and radically true. She had taken the life that was given. She had not, in her arrogant conceit, insisted on creating life to fit herself. Her mother was right, profoundly right, and she herself had been false, trashy, conceited.

This is a rare and not altogether credible moment of humility for Ursula; Lawrence makes it clear that she has argued herself into it as a means of accepting her pregnancy. She writes to Skrebensky, asking his forgiveness and offering to become his dutiful wife for the sake of their child. Expecting to hear from him within a month, she now has nothing to do but wait. 'For what had a woman but to submit? What was her flesh for but for childbearing, her strength for her children and her husband, the giver of life? At last she was a woman.'

But this is no happy ending. Ursula becomes ill with pneumonia and miscarries. During her delirium, she is aware of Skrebensky as a gnawing ache and her bond with him as a falsity which could not exist, were it not for the child. 'But why, why did it bind her to Skrebensky? Could she not have a child of herself? Was not the child her own affair? all her own affair? What had it to do with him?' Ursula is still a long way from becoming her mother's daughter, and her thinking is more in keeping with that of her latterday descendants than with that of her forebears. By the time the cablegram arrives from Skrebensky, she knows that she would not have gone to him, but kept the child for herself. This is hardly a decision which would have gained public approval in 1915 when *The Rainbow* was first published – and almost immediately banned.

During her illness Ursula has cast off the past, realizing that she belongs neither to Skrebensky nor to her parents, but nowhere and to no one. Her decision to take on single parenthood arises from her repudiation of parenthood. And in losing the child, she can also repudiate her relationship with Skrebensky.

He was as he was. It was good that he was as he was. Who was she to have a man according to her own desire? It was not for her to create but to recognize a man created by God. The man should come from the infinite and she should hail him . . . The man would come out of eternity to which she herself belonged.

Her delirium has taken her to the core of her individuality, to that
essential part of herself which is, in the midst of destruction,
incapable of being destroyed. It is not so much that she has been
reborn as that she is now ready for some sort of rebirth. But in
spite of all Ursula's brave and often lonely struggles, Lawrence
makes it plain that she cannot be reborn without a man.

Ursula's quest now becomes at once more and less easily
definable. It is more so because she now recognizes that it is not a
matter of proving herself either in a man's world or in relation to a
man. It is less so because it has become a matter of waiting,
accepting, ceasing to fight. It has become a matter of trusting
herself to recognize what is right and what wrong for her and the
good progress of her life. In many ways she has come to that loss
of self which marks the finding of a new and naked self. But, at the
same time, it seems to me that Ursula is still living in a fairytale,
still seeing herself as the very special princess for whom the very
special prince will arrive at the appointed time and make everything
all right with his liberating and irresistible kiss.

Although they have much in common and often arrive at similar
conclusions independently in the manner of true blood-sisters,
Ursula and Gudrun are more often emblematically contrasted
throughout *Women In Love*. Ursula's relationship with Birkin
constitutes the prototype of the ideal male–female relationship in
Lawrentian terms. Gudrun's relationship with Gerald is basically
similar to Ursula's with Skrebensky, in that each involves a strongly
independent woman and a man whose nullity leads him to addictive
worship, thence to his own destruction. But Gudrun is depicted
as irredeemably destructive and Lawrence's attitude to her is
correspondingly vindictive.

Gudrun and Gerald both belong to the bright world of the
upper self, and rarely touch the dark depths of which Ursula and
Skrebensky were sometimes capable. When Gudrun first sets eyes
on Gerald, she

lighted on him at once. There was something northern about him which
magnetized her. In his clear northern flesh and his fair hair was a glisten
like sunshine refracted through crystals of ice. And he looked so new,
unbroached, pure as an arctic thing.

As Ursula was by Skrebensky, so Gudrun is magnetized by Gerald; as Ursula found Skrebensky dazzling, so Gudrun does Gerald. These are bad signs. But Gudrun is not dazzled enough to be blinded to something wolflike and sinister in Gerald's bearing. On the contrary, his wolfishness is a large part of his attraction.

And then she experienced a keen paroxysm, a transport, as if she had made some incredible discovery, known to nobody else on earth. A strange transport took possession of her, all her veins were in a paroxysm of violent sensation ... She was tortured with desire to see him again, a nostalgia, a necessity to see him again, to make sure she was not deluding herself, that she really felt this strange and overwhelming sensation.

Gudrun's violent reaction bodes ill for her, in that it illustrates the modern woman's instant susceptibility to sensation. But what is more telling is the unreliability of such sensation, extreme though it may be. Gudrun cannot recognize, let alone trust, her own feelings – which she wants to test and put to the proof immediately. She is not trusting to her own dark self, but to visual impression and response (which is partly why Gudrun has to be an artist) lodged in the upper self and capable of rationalization. If you can argue yourself into something, you can also argue yourself out of it.

Another point in Gudrun's disfavour is that she is not content with, and therefore undervalues, her own femininity. Lawrence repeatedly tells us that although Gudrun is the more beautiful of the two sisters, Ursula is in some mysterious way the more 'womanly'. When the sisters watch Gerald swimming in Willey Water, Gudrun envies him 'almost painfully'.

'God, what it is to be a man!' she cried.
'What?' Ursula exclaimed in surprise.
'The freedom, the liberty, the mobility!' cried Gudrun, strangely flushed and brilliant. 'You're a man, you want to do a thing, you do it. You don't have the *thousand* obstacles a woman has in front of her.'
Ursula wondered what was in Gudrun's mind to occasion such an outburst. She could not understand.

Gudrun wants to act, but action is for men; in being an artist, she is acting as may befit a man, but not a woman. In being an artist, she is not only visual but manual, touching Gerald's face with 'subtle artist's fingers' which, according to Birkin's perception, carry death. When she caresses Gerald, she feels 'her hands so strong, as if she could tear the world asunder'. Here the feeling (or illusion) of omnipotence which is the necessary concomitant of artistic creation is made to seem destructive, and a form of what Winnicott calls 'false male doing'. Gudrun's appearance and actions are both manifestations of the artist rather than of the woman: her stunning good looks and her will to passion, being products of the upper self, are both a form of artifice, are both what is wrought like her own miniature sculptures rather than what grows naturally like a flower.

The cornerstone of Gudrun's repudiation of femininity lies in her repudiation of marriage. She mocks Birkin's ideas about marriage, and he in turn describes her to Ursula as a 'born mistress' rather than a wife. Gudrun herself admits to the newly-married Ursula,

marriage is just impossible. There may be and there *are* thousands of women who want it and could conceive of nothing else. But the very thought of it sends me *mad*. One must be free, above all, one must be free. One may forfeit everything else, but one must be free – one must not be 7 Pinchbeck Street or Somerset Drive or Shortlands. No man will suffice to make that good – no man!

Gudrun has the temerity to think herself above or too good for marriage. Like a true Amazon she would rather have a comrade-in-arms: husbands are so ordinary.

Gudrun sounds so strong, so sure of herself. And yet, only two pages later, Lawrence is at pains to tell us that she is unsure of herself, feels 'a want within herself', and that 'when she compared herself to Ursula, already her soul was jealous, unsatisfied.' Like Ursula before her, she is conscious of the 'big want', but unlike Ursula who has learned to wait and let things happen to her, she immediately tries to analyse and define it.

What was she short of now? It was marriage – it was the wonderful stability of marriage. She did want it, let her say what she might. She had been lying. The old idea of marriage was right even now – marriage and the home.

As with Clara in *Sons and Lovers* it would seem that Lawrence has listened with some attention and not a little sympathy to what might loosely be called feminist sentiments, only to discard them because he simply cannot believe them. And if he cannot believe them, surely those who utter them cannot believe them either: they are being wilful, deceiving themselves.

Which, we are led to assume, is exactly what Gudrun goes on to do:

. . . marriage and the home. Yet her mouth gave a little grimace at the words. She thought of Gerald and Shortlands – marriage and home! Ah well, let it rest! He meant a great deal to her – but – ! Perhaps it was not in her to marry. She was one of life's outcasts, one of the drifting lives that have no root. No, no, – it could not be so.

She conjures up a fantasy picture of herself in a firelit room with a handsome man, cynically concluding that its title is 'Home' and that 'it would have done for the Royal Academy'. Once more the artist, the specially-talented person who rejects the ordinary, the detached visual observer who sees a study in grey rather than Whistler's mother, has gained ascendance over the woman.

As the novel and the affair with Gerald progress, Gudrun becomes more and more resplendent. When the four protagonists are on holiday together in Switzerland and Gudrun appears in a vivid, daring gown, 'she was really brilliantly beautiful, and everyone noticed her.' She and Gerald are both larger than life, 'both with a strange other-world look on their faces, and with a glow in their eyes'. But when Gudrun sees Ursula and Birkin waiting for them, it is she who feels inferior. ' "How good and simple they look together," Gudrun thought jealously. She envied them some spontaneity, a childish sufficiency to which she herself could never approach.' Against all the odds it is the beautiful, brilliant artist who envies her sister, the ex-botany teacher, now wife.

Why should Gudrun envy Ursula? The answer, in simple terms, is: because Ursula has Birkin. But what is so wonderful about

Birkin? Alas, nothing. This is the central flaw of the novel, and one
to which I have already alluded: Birkin fails to convince. Gudrun,
on the contrary, is totally convincing. Whenever she apears on the
page, the other characters fade into insignificance. Her self-doubt,
her sharpness, the cynicism with which she protests her sensitive
female self, and the honesty with which she analyses her own
feelings, cannot but be attractive to (at least) most modern women
readers, whereas Birkin's bile is merely alienating. Lawrence has
defeated his own ends and in doing so has written better (in
depicting Gudrun) than he probably knew: of the devil's party
indeed. We are not supposed to admire and respect Gudrun; and
yet I do, finding that what she repudiates is less her own femininity
than a false male idea of femininity. We are supposed, like Gudrun
herself, to admire and envy Ursula; and yet I can't.

Ursula wants to be loved, so much so that Birkin can with
justification describe her repeated question, 'Do you love me?' as
her war cry. For her, love is the greatest thing and there is nothing
beyond it. When Birkin refuses to say not only that he loves her,
but that he finds her attractive or even good-looking, she is hurt
and becomes biting, mocking him. Birkin does not want to meet
and mingle on the emotional plane, but to meet (only) on some
impersonal plane 'where there is no speech and no terms of
agreement', no obligation, no standard for action, but where one is
asked for nothing and gives nothing, 'only each taking according to
primal desire'. This is his plane 'beyond love'. Ursula finds his
blueprint selfish and Birkin himself conceited. Her aim at this
point seems to be to wring some oblique confession of love from
him – an aim in which she succeeds while finding him ridiculous
and commonplace in his earnestness.

Birkin wants a conjunction in equilibrium, 'a pure balance of
two single beings: – as the stars balance each other'. Ursula's
reaction is, 'Why drag in the stars?' Her scepticism is not that of
the sophisticate who, like Gudrun, has moved in artistic and
Bohemian circles, but that of a woman (or Woman) for whom love
is self-evidently everything. In Lawrentian terms she is behaving as
a woman should, displaying an intuitive confidence in herself as
both womanly and lovable. She is also, woman that she is, being

manipulative. What she wants now is a direct rather than an oblique confession of love from Birkin, and she is determined to have it. Interestingly enough, her attitude towards him is much like Lawrence's own towards Gudrun: because she doesn't believe what Birkin is saying, she is sure that he cannot believe it himself. She knows better.

Eventually Birkin admits 'grimly' that he does love her, but that he wants it to be something else, because they can go one better.

'No, we can't,' she said in a strong voluptuous voice of yielding. 'We can only love each other. Say "my love" to me, say it, say it.'

She put her arms around his neck. He enfolded her, and kissed her subtly, murmuring in a subtle voice of love and irony and submission:

'Yes – my love, yes – my love.'

Game, set and match, then, to the wily Ursula, but as the subtlety and the irony indicate, the match is by no means played out, and the same moves are repeated by each of the players as the novel moves towards their marriage.

Within each couple there is a struggle for supremacy, but the struggles are not taking place on the same plane. Ursula and Birkin are saying to each other: accept my view of the world, or I'm not playing. This is a struggle which is capable of equilibrium as well as compromise in that each partner is allowed his/her complementary separateness and singleness. The relationship between Gudrun and Gerald allows of no separateness but insists on fusion-in-passion, in which each demands all of and gives all to the other. The struggle becomes the life-or-death fight for individual identity which can only be achieved by one partner reducing the other to dependence and, eventually, to destruction. Both partners, enmeshed as they are, are under threat of multiple loss: the loss of the self in passion; the loss (through habituation) of passion itself; and the loss of the mystery which properly belongs to sexual relations. The relationship cannot endure because both Gerald and Gudrun are expecting at once too much (everlasting romantic passion) and too little (neither is interested in peace or simplicity) from one another. It is not capable of equilibrium.

Or so Lawrence would have us believe. The relationship between

Ursula and Birkin is consistently depicted as good and natural, for all their quarrels, and as evidence of their superiority as human beings. That between Gudrun and Gerald is consistently depicted as bad and perverted. It is difficult to see why – not because Lawrence fails to spell it out for us, but because it is so often impossible to accept his terms of reference as meaningful criteria.

Gudrun and Gerald find each other physically beautiful, and say so. At the beginning of their affair,

her fingers went over the mould of his face, over his features. How perfect and foreign he was – ah, how dangerous! . . . She kissed him, putting her fingers over his face, his eyes, his nostrils, over his brows and his ears, to his neck, to know him, to gather him in by touch . . . He was such an unutterable enemy, yet glistening with uncanny white fire. She wanted to touch him and touch him and touch him, till she had him all in her hands, till she had strained him into her knowledge. Ah, if only she could have the precious *knowledge* of him, she would be filled . . .

Her hands are 'eager, greedy for knowledge' like Eve's reaching for the forbidden fruit, and evoke in Gerald a 'fathomless, fathomless desire' which is deeper than death. What passes then from him to her is the 'exquisite shock of his invisible fluid lightning'.

Some twenty pages earlier Ursula too is caressing her lover with her hands, but she is kneeling before him with her face against his thighs.

Unconsciously with her sensitive finger-tips, she was tracing the back of his thighs, following some mysterious life-flow there. She had discovered something, something more wonderful, more wonderful than life itself. It was the strange mystery of his life-motion, there, at the back of the thighs, down the flanks . . . It was here she discovered him one of the sons of God such as were in the beginning of the world, not a man, something more.

She is correspondingly 'beyond womanhood', 'a marvellous flower opening at his knees', and has established 'a new current of passional electric energy between the two of them, released from the darkest poles of the body and established in perfect circuit. It was a dark fire of electricity that rushed from him to her, and flooded them both with rich peace, satisfaction.' What follows, as they remain in this posture, is 'a perfect passing away for both of them'.

Each sister is experiencing and expressing sexual desire through the touch of her hands, but whereas Ursula uses her finger-tips like blind antennae, Gudrun's eyes are open, her larger hands seeking to know and to mould. Whereas Gudrun touches Gerald's face and neck, reaching only his upper self, Ursula touches Birkin in his lower self, arriving at his real and mysterious centre. Gudrun consciously, eagerly, wants to know Gerald; Ursula unconsciously knows all she needs to know of Birkin. Each woman evokes an electrical response in the man, which then passes back to her: for Ursula and Birkin, it takes the form of a perfect circuit; for Gudrun it is like being struck by lightning, too much to bear. She has to postpone consummation, believing as does Gerald that 'to desire is better than to possess'; but Ursula feels 'the marvellous fullness of immediate gratification, overwhelming, out flooding from the source of the deepest life-force'. Ursula finds peace in surrender, but Gudrun holds back in fear from the surrender of the self as subject: she remains Gudrun, whereas Ursula passes beyond individuality. The connection between Ursula and Birkin is rooted in the life-force; that between Gudrun and Gerald is based in death and destruction, devoid of spontaneity.

Well, I envy Lawrence his certainties. Here are two contrasted expressions of female sexual desire, one clearly presented as superior to the other. In Gudrun and Gerald, Lawrence is attacking the concept of romantic love: the *coup de foudre*; the violent, unbearable physical attraction; and the all-or-nothing fusion whose theme-tune is the *Liebestod*. Of course there is something inherently absurd about romantic love, but is it really so destructive and deadly? Some people enjoy it, thrive on it. And why shouldn't they? Lawrence has described Gudrun's emotional state with such understanding and precision: why must he condemn her? He must because romantic love is no sound basis for marriage, and he believes equilibriated monogamy to be the epitome of all heterosexual relations. He cannot allow either us or his characters a plurality of vision.

Similar contrasts prevail and are underlined when each couple make love. Ursula and Birkin drive into Sherwood Forest where it is 'pure night', and they sit for a while in 'stillness and mindless silence' before throwing off their clothes and somehow achieving

the maximum of unspeakable communication in touch, dark, subtle, positively silent, a magnificent gift and give again, a perfect acceptance and yielding, a mystery, the reality of that which can never be known, vital, sensual reality that can never be transmuted into mind content, but remains outside ... She had her desire fulfilled. He had his desire fulfilled. For she was to him what he was to her, the immemorial magnificence of mystic, palpable, real otherness.

Although the night is chilly, they spend it under the hood of the car in 'unbroken sleep'. Whatever happens (and it is far from explicitly described) happens by mutual, unspoken consent and the result is mutual gratification, followed by sleep.

Gerald comes to the Brangwen house by stealth when Gudrun is asleep. He needs her desperately – for relief and to make himself whole, to give himself life. To him it is like a miracle that she can heal him, like the sun, with her 'creative strength', and he worships her as 'mother and substance of all life', cleaving intensely to her like a child at the breast, afraid of being denied gratification. 'Now as the healing lymph of her effluence flowed through him, he knew how destroyed he was, like a plant whose tissue is burst from inwards by a frost.' For her part, Gudrun makes a point of lighting a candle before receiving him 'as a vessel filled with his bitter potion of death. She had no power at this crisis to resist. The terrible frictional violence of death filled her, and she received it in an ecstasy of subjection, in throes of acute, violent sensation.' Friction, sensation, ecstasy: according to Lawrence, those are the products of the will and cannot lead to transcendence.

Afterwards Gudrun cannot sleep, but 'lay wide awake, destroyed into perfect consciousness', while Gerald sleeps like a child with his arms round her. She feels tender towards Gerald, but at the same time jealous of his ability to be satisfied and to sleep. Despite the ecstasy, there is no mutuality in this relationship. Wearied, exhausted, Gudrun passes then into a state of superconsciousness during which she recalls all sorts of incidents from her childhood, understanding them as never before. The night seems like eternity and Gerald 'beautiful, far off and perfected. They would never be together. Ah, this awful inhuman distance between her and the other being!' In the morning she wakes him early, wanting him gone. Only then can she nestle down in the warm groove left by his body, and fall into 'a deep, heavy sleep'.

For Ursula and Birkin, sex is an ineffable and transcendent experience, during which individuality is obliterated. For Gudrun and Gerald, sex is something desperate and frantic, a struggle towards a consummation which neither is capable of reaching in his/her lower self. They remain individuals and hence apart. The problem with this dichotomy is that Ursula and Birkin, capable as they are of attaining perfection, become much less interesting human beings than Gudrun and Gerald. In the novel, as in life, we can never quite believe in perfection, and our sympathies flow towards those who, like ourselves, are imperfect. Wakeful, alienated, hyperconscious Gudrun, particular and individual as she remains, is more recognizable as a fellow creature than are the generalized more-than-man Birkin and more-than-woman Ursula. But, as a medium, the novel cannot bear very much more-than-human: its strength and credibility both come from its basis in a stubbornly human scale.

As an individual, Gudrun is a continuum, remembering and trying to understand her past. As such, she exemplifies for me, but clearly not for Lawrence, the integrity of the self. He approves rather of Ursula, who repudiates her past, her parents and her profession, knowing herself now to be 'new and unbegotten, she had no father, no mother, no anterior connections, she was herself pure and silvery, she belonged only to the oneness with Birkin, a oneness that struck deeper notes, sounding to the heart of the universe, the heart of reality, where she had never existed before.' Such is her marriage to Birkin. But she cannot explain as much to Gudrun, who seems to threaten her, being both more sceptical and more articulate. As far as Gudrun is concerned, 'to isolate oneself with one person isn't to find a new world at all, but only to secure oneself in one's illusions'.

Gudrun is right and Ursula is wrong: the past cannot be

repudiated. Any relationship which is based on such a misapprehension is built on shaky and spurious foundations. We are all now everything we have ever been. Human life is surely a constant process of accretion, rejection and modification, all of which takes place subtly and gradually rather than in a series of metamorphoses: we are not insects. I can see why the miner's son who became a writer might find such a repudiation necessary, but it seems to me that here Lawrence is contradicting himself. The repudiation can only be made as an act of will proceeding from the upper self, and we may be sure that the unconscious will sooner or later exact its own fitting revenge.

It is both good and necessary to have Gudrun's scepticism because it is ours (well, mine) as well. 'One is of the world if one lives in it,' she says, acknowledging the continuity of the self in the world, while claiming that it is an illusion to suppose that one can get out of it and into a new world. She can neither accept nor fully understand Ursula's belief (derived of course from Birkin) in 'something inhuman, of which love is only a little part'. She can only believe in what is human, accessible to consciousness. Ursula's somewhat defensive reaction is to tell herself that Gudrun cannot get beyond love because she has never loved. This is a recurrent Lawrentian theme, but Ursula is not confident enough to voice it, and it is not explored any further.

Once Ursula and Birkin are married and embarked upon their quest for a new world, there is little more, in the context of the novel, which can be said about them. Gudrun and Gerald must now assume centre stage and take over the action. Gerald has to carry the greater blame for the failure of the relationship, much as Skrebensky was accorded greater blame than Ursula. Men should know better than to let themselves become dependent on women; women cannot know better than to take advantage of such masculine failures. If men will not be men, then women will become men instead: strong, independent and dominant. Just like Gudrun. And what will they do with their newfound strength? Why, destroy men, of course. Just like Gudrun.

This is tortuous, twisted and paranoid thinking, full of all sorts of mistaken and contradictory assumptions. There is something called manliness which consists in being strong, independent and dominant. Nature has ordained this state as one belonging exclusively to the male of the species – and yet it is difficult to attain and must be fought for. But, strangely enough, women seem to have no difficulty in attaining it. There is a fixed amount of strength available in the world: men have it and women want it; if women get it, there will be all the less to go round for men. If men want to keep their strength, they must use it wisely in being stronger than women; otherwise women will steal it and use it unwisely, destructively, in being stronger than men.

You don't have to be feminist to find this nonsensical. It does not seem to occur to Lawrence that a woman might well prefer being strong and independent to being weak and dependent for her own sake – nothing to do with men. Nor can he see that a woman might have other purposes for her strength than the destruction of men: if she is strong, male strength is not thereby diminished, but might well be enhanced. Again and again this is a sticking point for Lawrence. He is often prepared to grant a woman the desire for strength and independence; sometimes he even allows her to achieve them both; but he never allows her the ability to cope successfully with them. For him, a strong, independent woman is always 'cocksure' rather than, as she should be, 'hensure'.

In his essay, 'Cocksure Women and Hensure Men', Lawrence asserts that modern men are 'timid, tremulous, rather soft and submissive . . . So the women step forth with a loud *cock-a-doodle-doo*!' But instead of entering the world of men in the appropriate spirit of competition, listening after her crow 'to hear if some other wretch of a cock dare crow defiance, challenge', the cocksure woman

puts all her passion and energy and years of her life into some effort or assertion, without ever listening for the denial which she ought to take into account. She is cocksure, but she is a hen all the time. Frightened of her own henny self, she rushes to mad lengths about votes, or welfare, or sports, or business: she is marvellous, out-manning the man. But alas, it is all fundamentally disconnected . . . suddenly, because she is a hen and not a cock, all she has done will turn to pure nothingness for her.

The cocksure woman changes the ground rules for operating in the world of men, and in doing so displays more singleness of purpose than the man is capable of. Why these thrusting activities should lead to nothingness for women, and not for men, is by no means clear. And yet Lawrence expects us to believe as much in his portrayal of Gudrun.

Or does he? It seems to me that many of Gudrun's thoughts and actions are justifiable to Lawrence and justified by him. But he then goes on to posit that they are the inevitable outcome of what Gerald is and does. The portrait is one of the alienated modern woman struggling to come to terms with herself, her work and her sexuality. As such, it is not unsympathetic: on the contrary, it is minutely and often devastatingly accurate. It is the forced moral conclusions which are false.

After a few months with Gerald, Gudrun begins to feel destroyed and violated by him. He has come to her for repose, but she can find in him none of the 'pure, deep healing rest' she longs for. There is only the friction of his unbroken will against hers, and all he does is to make 'the burden for her greater, the burden of her sleep was more intolerable when he was there'. His demands for the succour of her femaleness have become excessive.

What then! Was she his mother? Had she asked for a child whom she must nurse through the nights, for her lover. She despised him, she despised him, she hardened her heart. An infant crying in the night, this Don Juan.
Ooh, but how she hated the infant crying in the night. She would murder it gladly.

There is nothing henny in Gudrun's murderous impulses. But they arise from Gerald's treatment of her as the eternally-available female body. He is treating her not only as a wife but as a mother, and this latter attitude indicates in Lawrentian terms the ultimate perversion of the man–woman relationship.

Gerald's use of Gudrun throws their relationship off balance, out of equilibrium. His blithe male insensitivity leads her to ask herself who Gerald thinks he is, to reduce and condemn her to a state in which she becomes, like him, a mechanical thing going repetitively through the same wearing, exhausting motion. 'His maleness bores me. Nothing is so boring, so inherently stupid and stupidly conceited. Really, the fathomless conceit of these men, it is ridiculous – the little strutters.' According to Gudrun, Gerald should be a cockerel, strutting 'before fifty females, all his subjects'. When she thinks of marriage, the mines, Shortlands, she is sick at heart.

What *have* I to do with it – and him thinking he can be a lover to a woman! One might as well ask it of a self-satisfied lamp-post. Those men with their eternal jobs – and their eternal mills of God that keep grinding on at nothing! It is too boring, just boring. However did I come to take him seriously at all?

The very thought of the world of men, with its 'mechanical succession of day following day, day following day, ad infinitum', is enough to make her 'heart palpitate with a real approach to madness'. Gerald's manly prowess in the world of men and his childishness as a lover are all of a piece.

Lawrence too has little sympathy for Gerald's world; and he cannot condemn Gudrun for rejecting it and its maddening, monotonous tick-tock. Gerald has nothing to offer 'a woman like Gudrun', a woman of uncommon intelligence and sensitivity. But Gudrun does not stop at rejecting Gerald and his world: she must reject all men as being her inferiors. The implication is that Gudrun, being, like Ursula, a very special sort of woman (though misguided) needs a very special sort of man, like Birkin. Her wilfulness arises from not recognizing as much, and consequently being led into false suppositions about herself, her work and her sexuality.

When Ursula and Birkin leave Gudrun and Gerald in Switzerland, Gudrun becomes friendly with Loerke, a fellow-guest at the resort and a fellow-artist. They talk together for hours in English, his native German and French – a smattering of which they have in common. Wearied by Gerald's physicality, Gudrun finds it 'a real physical pleasure to make this thread of conversation out of the different-coloured strands of three languages'. The manipulation of language, the process of communicating in words, is comparable to

sexual pleasure and – at least as far as sex with Gerald is concerned
– somewhat superior. This is not a comparison of which Lawrence
could have approved in general terms, but Gudrun is allowed her
justification: she picked the wrong man.

Loerke is no male beauty but subtler, more clever and more
talented than Gerald. He is a man who, in Gudrun's words, 'has
some understanding of a woman.' He finds her a remarkable
woman, 'and it was a relief to her to be acknowledged extraordinary.
Then she need not fret about the common standards.' He admits,
when pressed, to finding her beautiful, but what is more important
to him are her wit, her understanding and her ability to match his
own particular intelligence. They are kindred spirits. 'Women and
love,' he tells her, 'there is no greater tedium.' At first she is
slightly offended. 'And yet this was her own basic feeling. Men
and love – there was no greater tedium.' It is mutual understanding,
rather than sensuality and passion, which matters most in relations
between men and women. A compact is made between them and
Gerald's fate too is sealed.

Gudrun and Loerke communicate on a plane of 'subtle inter-
suggestivity', which is incomprehensible to Gerald. For the two
artists, 'Art and Life were ... the Reality and Unreality.' For
Gudrun, 'life doesn't *really* matter – it is one's art which is central.'
For Loerke, 'what one does in one's art, that is the breath of one's
being. What one does in one's life, that is a bagatelle for the
outsiders to fuss about.' In Lawrentian terms they are both
committing the cardinal sin, the sin which Paul Morel warned his
mother against: that of finding life a paltry or insignificant thing.
Lawrence seems to be allowing Gudrun, as a woman, to be an
artist and think like an artist on equal terms with Loerke. But he
does so only by allowing them a sort of parity-in-immorality.

Loerke has made a statuette of a girl seated on a horse, and he
admits that he often slapped his model, reducing her to tears, in
order to get her to sit still. It becomes clear that he has been in the
habit of bullying and exploiting young girls in the interests of his
art, 'his work, the all-important to him'. Gudrun concludes that
love is 'one of the temporal things in her life, except in so far as
she was an artist'. She thinks of Cleopatra, Mary Stuart, the

actress Rachel as 'the exoteric exponents of love'. The purpose of
the lover is to act as 'fuel for the transport of this subtle knowledge,
for a female art, the art of pure, perfect knowledge in sensuous
understanding'. Just as Loerke uses adolescent girls to inspire him,
so Gudrun will use men, seducing them and using them up. This,
then, is the art of the self-conscious artist. But what Gudrun
practises is a *female* art, reconciling understanding and sexuality –
an impossibility in Lawrentian terms. Loerke's behaviour may be
nasty, but there is no hint from Lawrence that it is unmanly.
Gudrun's projected behaviour is unwomanly in that it apes male
behaviour. In claiming parity with Loerke, the female of the artistic
species becomes more deadly than the male.

Woman and artist that she is, Gudrun is both deadly and
invincible. Gerald is afraid that she is complete and self-sufficient,
and he wants to kill her. When he tries to strangle her, he gets
satisfaction from 'watching the unconsciousness come into her
swollen face, watching the eyes roll back. How ugly she was!' But
he cannot succeed in his attempt to desecrate and destroy her, and
it is he who dies, driven to death by his own nullity as much as by
the monster he has engendered in Gudrun. After his death, she is
incapable of shedding a tear, 'emotionless and barren'. Her one
motive is to 'avoid actual contact with the events', so she sends for
Ursula and Birkin, knowing contemptuously that he will take over,
'since he was so *good* at looking after other people'.

Frozen as she is, Gudrun will survive. It is not that she is
incapable of suffering – on the contrary, she spends most of the
novel in a state of mental anguish – but that she has learned to
protect herself, to protect that part of herself which is most
important to her: the subjective self which perceives, analyses and
creates. Whether or not this self is worth protecting and preserving
is left very much in doubt. Lawrence does not tell us directly (he is
too much of an artist himself, for all his protestations) that Gudrun
is mistaken. But it is clear in the context of his work as a whole
that Gudrun represents an Awful Warning: women, don't emulate
her, or you will never be free from self-communing torture; men,
avoid her or you will be destroyed.

Gudrun, the modern woman, is doubly alienated: first, from her

henny self which knows its own gender-based place in the scheme
of things; and second, from her dark, passional self, the self which
can never enter the realm of consciousness. She has no qualms
about functioning successfully on her own merits in the world of
men; and she is all unremitting consciousness – hence her cynicism.
If the dawn of consciousness entails the loss of innocence, then
perceptual consciousness entails perpetual cynicism, irony, doubt –
in short, unhappiness.

But it is not possible for Gudrun to regress into becoming a hen
– if, indeed, she ever was one: she has seen and knows too much.
She cannot be expected to quench her restless intelligence and
creativity in the dark, Lethean waters of sexuality, submitting to
the unknown dark gods through the medium of inarticulate male
power. There is, as Lawrence rightly sees, something satanic in
her refusal or inability (both, I think) to abrogate thought-
adventuring and surrender her intellectual, subjective self. But, as
we all know, Satan is the real hero of *Paradise Lost*. Lawrence
the essayist and moralist would have us believe that Gudrun's
unhappiness is inevitable, and that women like Gudrun must end
in nothingness and despair. Lawrence the novelist stops short –
just – of any such conclusion, and cannot but show Gudrun's
predicament as an important problem, one which is not capable of
easy resolution.

The conclusion to *Women In Love* is patched together, discarding
Gudrun (who disappears abruptly from the action) and Gerald,
and focusing once more on Ursula and Birkin. Gudrun, who
considers herself above such mundane considerations as marriage
and the home, is revealed as not good enough for marriage. Ursula,
being the more womanly of the two sisters, has made a proper, if
very special marriage which befits her own very special status. But,
in down-to-earth terms, she has married a man who wants to cut
her off from her family and friends, does not intend to allow her
any role other than that of being his wife, and is probably
homosexual. Does Lawrence really expect us to believe that she
has made the better choice?

Well, yes, in spite of Ursula's own doubts, he does. Gudrun has
chosen the unnatural state of singleness. Ursula has chosen

wifehood, which is the crown of womanhood. The whole thrust of the novel is towards marriage, towards finding a suitable heterosexual mate. But the matter is not that simple. Marriage is not presented as a happy ending (*Women In Love* is neither comedy nor fairy story) but as a tentative beginning. Its terms have yet to be fully worked out and worked through to the mutual advantage of both partners. And it seems to me that Gudrun is often voicing many of Lawrence's own doubts about marriage, doubts which surface again and again in his portrayals of badly-married women – notably of Lou Witt Carrington in *St Mawr*. The phenomenon of woman as a 'free, proud, single being' who rejects, or comes to reject, marriage has yet to be explored.

3
Odd numbers

Lawrence had a grudging admiration for women alone, the grudge being all the more strong because the admiration was impossible to deny. Mrs Norris, a minor character in *The Plumed Serpent*, is an elderly archaeologist and 'lonely daughter of culture, with a strong mind and a dense will'. The heroine, Kate Leslie, respects her from the first

for her isolation and her dauntlessness. The world is made up of a mass of people and a few individuals. Mrs Norris was one of the individuals. True, she played her social game all the time. But she was an odd number; and all alone, she could give even numbers a hard time.

The portrait is small but exact and – for Lawrence – unusually sympathetic towards the 'odd number' who also happens to be female. The threat posed to even numbers is readily admitted, but because the even numbers present at Mrs Morris's tea-party in Tlacolula are American, uncouth and absurd, her singleness becomes, like Kate's for the moment, a mark of her superiority.

Lawrence is not always so ready to forgive women, even elderly ones, for choosing to be odd numbers: more often, for him, this choice necessarily implies the rejection of men. It is only when he can allow his women to reject men for good reasons, only when he can get past that particular barrier, that he can arrive at a deeper understanding of the motivations for this form of female behaviour. Strangely enough, in view of his professed hatred of Americans and especially the female of the species, he arrives at this breakthrough most surely in the fiction which is set or was written on the American continent.

Alvina's spinsterhood is redeemed by marriage, and Gudrun's desire for singleness is seen as both dangerous and an admission of failure. Lina M'Leod in the story 'The Blue Moccasins' marries a man twenty-three years younger than herself, thus in Lawrentian terms making a pretty good catch. But after the novelty of marriage has worn off, 'she would think, as she had thought in the past, that the highest bliss a human being can experience is perhaps the bliss of being quite alone, quite, quite alone.' Lina is left alone, left by her husband for a woman of his own age, and in a humiliating fashion. As so often in Lawrence's work there is an element of glee in the apparently self-contained woman getting her come-uppance. Again the need for independence is recognized, but not taken seriously, except as a threat to men, a threat which must be obviated by the punishment of the character concerned.

The female odd number is even more of a threat when she is sexually agresssive or predatory. In a cruel little story, 'Monkey Nuts', Joe, a young farmer, is pursued by a woman co-worker in a dogged and rather touching fashion. He allows this to happen without protest and almost without knowing what he is dong, while complaining that she is not the girl for him, not the one he has chosen for himself. His older workmate (and surely there is more than a touch of homosexual jealousy here) denigrates the woman in flagrantly misogynist terms, thus helping Joe to break off the relationship with a piece of childish name-calling. The apparent implication is that male camaraderie is strong enough to withstand feminine wiles. But the subtext reads that it is no such thing, and that it takes two men to vanquish a woman. Miss Stokes disappears, suitably shamed by her sexual rejection, but we are forced to infer that a single woman, as it were on the prowl, is a dangerous object indeed.

Even more cruel – and quite repulsively so – is the fate of Ethel Cane in 'None of That'. Ethel is a rich, energetic and 'very clever' American living alone in Mexico, which to her is 'a land of naughty little boys doing obscene things'. When she is approached by General Isidor Garabay, who expects her 'immediately to become his mistress', she retorts that she is having 'none of that'. The narrator, Colmenares (who shares some of Aaron's more extreme views about women) hates her physically because she seethes against all men, exciting their minds but not their bodies, and thus making them feel small. The reader knows that Ethel has to meet her match.

He arrives in the form of the bullfighter, Cuesta, whom she first sees in action and later invites to her house. The invitation is accepted, and the visits become a regular occurrence. But they never last for more than half an hour, and he is always accompanied by Colmenares, who acts as an interpreter. Ethel is attracted by Cuesta, but she hesitates to make any overt sexual approach. In conversation with Colmenares, the bullfighter is rude and foul-mouthed about Ethel (thus, incidentally, bearing out her estimation of the Mexican male) although he seems unable to stay away from her. When she asks why he never sees her alone, he invites her to his apartment and, having had his way with her, hands her over to his bullfighting chums for similar treatment. After this gang rape, she poisons herself.

What is so horrifying about this story is that Lawrence seems to condone Cuesta's behaviour: he certainly does not condemn it. Ethel has been asking for it. The story is clearly intended as a parable: those who deny the flesh and intellectualize their sexuality shall perish by the flesh because the flesh canot be denied. But if Lawrence thought that this was all there was to this shameful little tale, he was being disingenuous as well as misogynist. To set up an intelligent and independent woman as a figure of fun, and then subject her to mass rape, is not to illustrate the rottenness of white American culture but the cruelty of men (of whatever race) towards women. In connecting male sexuality with cruelty and punishment (always dangerous ground for Lawrence because he cannot make up his mind on this score) the parable misfires badly. It seems to me that Lawrence himself suspected as much: in using Colmenares as the narrator (an unusual device for him) he distances himself from the subject-matter, as if to slant or blur the moral of the story. But he fails, and the moral remains hideously clear.

Ethel Cane's treatment is only an extreme example of what happens in small part to other independent women, especially in the earlier fiction. The vengeful element is all the more noticeable in that such treatment is not meted out to men who choose to become odd numbers. On the contrary, they are admired for their sturdy independence of the female of the species and even hero-worshipped for their self-sufficiency. There is a certain amount of hypocrisy (or shilly-shallying) going on here. It is clear from Lawrence's letters that he was on friendly terms with several odd-numbered women whom he was prepared to treat as equals, in so far as he was capable of thus treating any other human being, and from whom he derived intellectual (and not a little sexual) stimulation. Again, when he can manage to overcome his bile (or, to put it more sympathetically, to wrestle with and so control the unresolved misogynistic elements in his unconscious) he can make cogent statements about Western culture through the medium of a white American woman, without deflecting the moral thrust of his parable.

'The Woman Who Rode Away' was written during the same period as 'None of That', and reworks some of the same themes. Considerably longer, it manages to do justice to the complex moral idea it contains, and it is no accident that here the writing is more confident, more lyrical and attains an almost magical atmospheric intensity. The woman (who is never named) is, like Ethel Cane, an American living in Mexico, but differs from her in that she is married – to a silver mine owner – and has two children. No claims are made for her intellectual prowess, and her longing to be alone springs directly from the circumstances of her marriage and her motherhood.

'Am I never to be let alone?' she asks her son as she sets off on horseback for the further wilderness of the Sierra Madre with the vague purpose of finding the Chilchui Indians who are said to live beyond the mountains. As she rides on, she is neither afraid nor lonely. 'Indeed, the loneliness was like a drink of cold water to one who is very thirsty. And a strange elation sustained her from within.' In telling us that 'her conscious development had stopped mysteriously with her marriage', that her husband, though pleasant, is jealous and keeps her in luxurious but 'invincible slavery', Lawrence is evincing a shrewd understanding of this woman's need for singleness and freedom. The need is anchored in reality, the reality of some unfulfilled part of herself, rather than an intellectually assumed vehicle for her hatred of men. It is also anchored in the social reality of a conventional and empty marriage which she can leave, with Lawrence's apparent blessing, 'without a qualm'.

In her solitary ride a process of shedding begins. During the first cold night before the dawn she feels 'like a woman who has died and passed beyond. She was not sure that she had not heard during the night, a great crash at the centre of herself, which was the crash of her own death.' The next day she has no will of her own, sees but cannot feel the beauty of the landscape, does not know where she is going or what she is going for, and allows her horse to plod dejectedly along a stony little trail. In a sense this death, the death which she continues to undergo, is genderless. It is the death of individual identity, the death of getting (children as well as money) and spending, of the striving sense of purpose which is unmindful of last things and new beginnings, and is inherent in mechanistic Western civilization. And yet, in another sense, it is important that she is a woman; that she, a woman, has taken such an initiative out of intuitive necessity and a sure but uncanny self-knowledge which may well be beyond man the thought-adventurer. The woman is making the same sort of spiritual journey as is Somers in his prolonged and agonized pacing of the Australian shore. But her way towards the dark gods is surer, unmediated as it is by rationalization.

The Indians she meets along the way look at her 'as if she were some strange, unaccountable *thing*' rather than a 'beautiful white woman', and she comes to recognize that her whiteness takes away her womanhood, leaving her 'like some giant female white ant'. Contrary to Kate Millett's claim in *Sexual Politics*, there is no evidence here of the white male fantasy that dark-skinned men are inordinately attracted to white women. It is repeatedly stressed that the Indians find the woman sexually repulsive. Something quite other is happening: one of the last vestiges of her identity, the double pride in her whiteness and the power of her sexuality, is being shed.

Travelling on with the Indians, who have agreed to guide her to the Chilchui, she feels powerless, knows that she is dead, and no longer cares what will happen to her because she is weary and 'beyond it'. But *what* is she beyond? Millett never pauses to ask this question, so intent is she on telling us that it is the Indians who crush the woman's will in order to subject her to all sorts of tortures which she, being a woman, naturally (for Lawrence) enjoys. But the woman has lost her will before she meets the Indians: she surrenders it, as she surrenders the other attributes of her individuality, of her own accord. She does so, not because she is a model of female passivity, but because she has embarked on a spiritual or religious quest. Such a quest can no more be called passive than can the practice of yoga, which in its highest form consists of uninterrupted meditation. It is essentially the quest for union with god, or the cosmos, which in terms of this story amount to the same thing.

The woman is bringing her heart to the god of the Chilchui because she is tired of the white man's god. She is beyond the beliefs and demands of Judaeo-Christianity; beyond her nice marriage, her nice husband and her nice children; and beyond the reaches of the white, daylit upper self. She cannot find union with the god of the white man, but is searching for a darker god, with whom she can communicate in the blood, to whom she can surrender her heart. That she eventually does so literally in the story should not be taken as an illustration, much less an advocation, of female masochism but as a metaphor for all religious-mystical experience. Now, it is perfectly possible to find all such experience unnecessary or absurd, but to describe it as pornographic, as does Millett, really is to miss the point. What is actually going on in 'The Woman Who Rode Away' is far more interesting and pertinent than propaganda will allow.

The Chilchui imprison the woman, taking her quest seriously, and at the same time seeing the symbolic advantage to themselves, their tribe and their race. They see her as a willing emissary from white Judaeo-Christianity, an emissary who comes in a spirit of surrender and sacrifice, an emissary who will bring them redemption. The woman is no less a Christ-figure than the man in 'The Escaped Cock' (sometimes known as 'The Man Who Died') and her death is neither more nor less symbolic than his. The question we have to ask ourselves (as if we were Lawrence's contemporaries

– which in this context we are) is, why is a female Christ-figure
either necessary or desirable?

To find the answer we have to go back to the religion of
Quetzalcoatl. It is a religion in which men and women are sharply
divided, but complementary, as are the sun and moon, the eagle
and the serpent. It is a religion of reconciliation between opposites.
The woman who rode away is segregated from other women in the
Chilchui tribe, from the whole world of women and children. She
is a special woman, an emissary and redeemer whose mission it is
to restore the moon (the source of female power) to the women of
the Chilchui. The white races, we are given to understand, have
stolen both the sun and moon – which is to say, both male and
female potency – from the dark races who formerly held them and
took better care of them in the proper spirit of reverence. It would
seem that only another woman is capable of restoring potency to
the women of the dark races and that, further, the restoration of
dark male potency is dependent on that of dark female potency.
Male salvation is dependent on a prior female salvation. And
women are entitled to their own saviour.

This is a pretty startling line of thought, especially in its latter
proposition, a proposition which has been advocated in various
guises by many a latter-day feminist separatist. Lawrence's interest
differs from that of the separatists in that he sees female self-
realization as a means towards and indivisible from male self-
realization. But it seems to me that Lawrence is, up to a point, in
accord with non-separatist feminist thinking in seeing the two
processes as complementary.

Up to a point. The extent to which Lawrence can endorse a
woman alone as an autonomous agent depends rather heavily on
what he considers to be the content of both male and female self-
realization. The woman who rode away is surrounded by custodians
who

watched over her and cared for her like women. In their soft, insidious
understanding there was something womanly. Yet their eyes, with that
strange glitter, and their dark, shut mouths that would open to the broad
jaw, the small, strong, white teeth had something primitively male and
cruel.

To be male in the proper sense, the sense which the white races of Western civilization have lost and/or abused, means to recognize and be in touch with the feminine side of the self, the anima, as well as with the traditionally macho animus. To be whole as a man means to be able to reconcile the two without mingling them, not shying away from human cruelty (which would be to tilt the balance in favour of the feminine within oneself) nor yet from human nurturance and caring (which would be to tilt the balance in the opposite direction). The question remains: where, seeing that the male has the potential for reconciling opposites within himself, does this leave the woman?

The short answer is: as the agent or catalyst of reconciliation. But such agency will become possible (most importantly through the sexual act) only when woman has got herself sorted out. Men may be allowed to recognize and make use of the anima, but for women the animus is largely forbidden territory, territory on to which the superconscious modern woman has all too flagrantly strayed.

Dosed with emetics and hallucinogenic herbal drinks, the woman who rode away is purged of all the poisons of Western civilization. Surrounded by the distant ritual dancing and singing of both men and women, and as if in a trance, 'she seemed at last to feel her own death, her own obliteration'. As she watches the 'changeless and absorbed women' dance, she sees, with Lawrence, the writing on the wall.

Her kind of womanhood, intensely personal and individual, was to be obliterated again, and the great primeval symbols were to tower once more over the fallen individual independence of women. The sharpness and the quivering nervous consciousness of the highly-bred white woman was to be destroyed again, womanhood was to be cast once more into the great stream of impersonal sex and impersonal passion. Strangely, as if clairvoyantly, she saw the immense sacrifice prepared.

It would seem, to extend the Jungian terminology, that the woman has got in touch with a vast, untapped female collective unconscious. No less than the white Western male, the white Western female has been divorced from her own anima, and it is her duty, both to herself and him, to find it and acknowledge it again. Until she does so, thus making herself whole, he will never be able to achieve wholeness.

So what exactly is going on here? An overt condemnation of female autonomy and independence? Yet another heavy trip laid on women to make us responsible for all the ills of the world? Partially, yes to both questions. But Lawrence is also advocating that both men and women become more feminine. His problem now, having changed the nature of the male principle, is to maintain duality/polarity between it and the female principle.

And there is more here. I find it significant that the passage describing the imminent death of modern superconscious woman follows immediately on from the woman's realization of her own death, which she now 'feels' – that is, truly understands – for the first time. The woman's quest for self-realization or union with God (which amount to the same thing) is less a quest for the meaning of life than for the meaning of life-and-death. That life and death (and eventually rebirth) are part of the same process is a recurrent Lawrentian theme. It is taken up in *St Mawr* where the middle-aged Mrs Witt is unable to 'feel' her own approaching death, and takes a house overlooking a graveyard in order to watch funerals and so understand death. And so understand life.

The woman who rode away has been granted a meaningful death, the death of white Western superconsciousness. The beginning of her journey or quest marks also the beginning of the death process, and the ceremony of sacrifice is only the culmination and overt public sign of what has been going on within. In her captivity, she lives in a kind of daze or half-life, always

in the same relaxed, confused, victimized state, unless the sweetened herb drink would numb her mind altogether and release her senses into a sort of heightened, mystic acuteness and a feeling as if she were diffusing out deliciously into the harmony of things. This at length became the only state of consciousness she really recognized.

It is in this state of 'passional cosmic consciousness' that she is carried to the sacrificial site and her ultimate death, telling herself: 'I am dead already. What difference does it make, the transition from the dead that I am to the dead I shall become very soon.' Yet, significantly enough, 'her soul sickened and felt wan'. Personal consciousness is not quite dead, one tiny flicker remaining until the moment the knife strikes.

It seems to me that the death of personal or superconsciousness is intended by Lawrence to liberate women, to liberate the female principle from its latter-day shackles. The woman is carried on a litter to a platform in a cave, 'a cavity, an orifice' behind a curtain of ice. It seems extraordinary to me that Kate Millett should see this curtain as a phallic symbol when it is clearly a downward flow of water (water is always symbolic of femininity) which has been 'arrested'. (The only sense in which it can be called phallic is that Lawrence describes it as 'an inverted pinnacle' which could possibly signify false male doing on the part of the woman.) The curtain of ice clearly symbolizes the arrested development of the female principle. When the sun strikes the ice and, simultaneously, the knife strikes the woman's body (yes, the sun and the knife are both phallic) the flow of her blood will release the flow of the ice, and the dry pools below be filled with water again. The fertile, newly-fertilized female principle will once again attain its proper power.

In a sense 'The Woman Who Rode Away' can be seen as a modern fertility myth, but there are important departures from the norm. Orpheus, Osiris, Thammuz, the Fisher King and even Jesus Christ were all male, and it was their male blood which was considered to possess fertilizing/redemptive powers. Even in *The Plumed Serpent* it is male blood which is shed. 'The Woman Who Rode Away' points, in contrast, towards a true recognition that it is female blood which is shed in menstruation and childbirth and is thus a primary creative agent. But – and this should give us pause – there is also a hint that it is female blood which is shed in sexual intercourse.

It is clear that the sacrifice constitutes a sexual act between the male and female principles. The sun's rays or 'shafts' must 'penetrate' through the ice to the 'orifice' beyond, 'to the inner-most'. The female principle cannot operate as it should until activated by the male principle. And yet the male principle cannot realize itself until the female principle declares itself ready for self-realization. It is an act of co-operation, each principle behaving after its kind.

Or so Lawrence would have us believe. Although I find 'The Woman Who Rode Away' a powerful and often beautiful mythic tale, I confess I am uneasy about the sacrifice. It seems to me that we are back with Lawrence's difficulties in coming to terms with male sexuality, and that his failure leads him to misunderstand the nature of female sexuality. Once again he is making an overt connection between the male principle and cruelty and bloodshed, between the act of penetration and the infliction of pain or even death. And yet Lawrence consciously knew otherwise, as his portrayal of Connie Chatterley indicates. The connection is so persistent that I can only conclude that it springs from the fantasy of a little boy who hears his mother cry out in the night and fearfully assumes that his father is mistreating her. Such a fantasy would be all the more difficult to relinquish for a boy who has habitually witnessed his mother being abused by his father in other ways. And more difficult still for a boy who identifies strongly with his mother.

Be that as it may, the fantasy has important implications for the Lawrentian treatment of women. And this is the point at which Lawrence seems to be attributing passivity and submission (even sacrifice) to the female principle. He is purporting to advocate a separate-but-equal policy for the sexes, a sort of apartheid of gender. But it is, as all such policies are, hypocritical, in that it fails to take into account the fact that one group holds the great power and that the other group must operate in the shadow and the service of that power. Although Lawrence can see perfectly well that it is possible to be successful as a woman and yet not conform to his particular stereotypical idea of womanhood, he simply refuses to believe the evidence of his own intelligence. This is the hurdle at which all his thought-adventuring stalls: he can go so far and no further.

Because 'The Woman Who Rode Away' is a mythic parable, peopled by nameless characters, Lawrence can ensure that everything (except perhaps that last tremor of nausea on the woman's part) works out to his own satisfaction. But Lawrence was by no means always a mythic writer, and when he tries to put the same ideas into practice in the novel of character, he immediately runs into difficulties. In *The Plumed Serpent*, which is a mixture but never a real blend of the mythic and the naturalistic, those difficulties present themselves most forcefully in the form of the heroine, Kate Leslie.

Kate is a forty-year-old Irishwoman, divorced from her first husband and widowed by her second. No less an odd number than Mrs Norris, she has come to Mexico because in Europe she 'heard the *consummatum est* of her own spirit'. The first half of her life is over, and she is 'no longer in love with love. She no longer yearned for the love of a man, or even the love of her children.' To her, modern life is an impinging and degenerate presence which she professes to have discarded, but against which she rages inwardly:

And then, when she could escape into her own loneliness, the influx of peace and soft, flower-like potency which was beyond understanding. It disappeared even if you thought about it, so delicate, so fine. And yet, the only reality.

She knows that, if her old life is finished, a new one must now begin, and that 'we must be born again'. It is then the promise of rebirth, however vague, which has brought her to Mexico, a promise which she sees as being fulfilled in being 'alone with the unfolding flower of her own soul', but with 'the silence of other unfolded souls around her like a perfume'.

But Mexico is death-laden, full of cries of 'Viva la Muerte!' and she is afraid, while morbidly fascinated by the Mexicans themselves, who touch 'her bowels with a strange compassion'. Women kneeling in a church, 'sunk there in a wild, humble supplication of dread and of bliss', move her to 'tenderness and revulsion. They crouched like people not quite created.' It is the women, 'little and insidious', she fears more than the men, 'the primitive womanliness of the world, that is so touching and so alien'. For the rest of the novel Kate is torn between the superconsciousness of Europe (or what now tends to be called the North) and the alien but insidiously

attractive consciousness of the 'undeveloped' South, with its 'soft,
dark flow' and its impersonal relationships.

Kate is intelligent and sharp, spiky even, and ill at ease with
anything mystical. Yet when she joins in the dance at the Plaza in
Sayula she has what amounts to a mystical experience.

Men and women danced alike with faces lowered and expressionless,
abstract, gone in the deep absorption of men into the greater manhood,
women into the greater womanhood. It was sex, but the greater not the
lesser sex . . .
 She felt her sex and her womanhood caught up and identified in the
slowly revolving ocean of nascent life, the dark sky of the men lowering
and wheeling above. She was not herself, she was gone, and her own
desires were gone in the ocean of the great desire.

The experience, like the night, is timeless and, when the dance is
over, Kate refuses to look at her watch, turning it face down. The
death of superconsciousness, the consciousness which so plagues
Gudrun that she likens her own face to a clock, has now begun.
Kate wants to hurry home with her new secret, 'the strange secret
of her greater womanhood, that she could not get used to. She
would have to sink into that mystery.'

She keeps her secret, luxuriating in it, while outwardly rejecting
the tenets of Quetzalcoatl, of which it is presumably a part. It is
Ramon who challenges her inward belief that she has changed, has
left the first half of her life behind, by asking her why, if she does
not need people, she continues to travel and seek them out.

She was silent, very angry. She knew she could not live quite alone. The
vacuity crushed her. She needed a man there, to stop the gap, and to keep
her balanced. But even when she had him, in her heart of hearts she
despised him, as she despised the dog and cat. Between herself and
humanity there was the bond of subtle, helpless antagonism.

Kate's object in coming to Mexico is neither as straightforward nor
perhaps as spiritual as she would have us believe. She does not
want a man, and yet she needs one, and recognizes that need. She
does not like people, and yet she needs them, and recognizes that
need too. Like Lawrence himself, she is looking for a new kind of
relationship, new forms of connection.

It seems to me that here, in the person of Kate, Lawrence is exploring questions which have only recently been taken up again in the wake of the Women's Movement. Kate is asking, what does it mean to be a woman, particularly a woman of forty and over, a woman who may be widowed or divorced, whose children have grown up and gone away? Now that we are free from the demands of wifehood and motherhood, do we really want to repeat the same sort of relationships we have had in the past, form the same sort of connections? If not, how and with whom should our most intimate connections be made? Why should they be made at all? Is it not better to remain the 'free, proud, single being' so often advocated by Lawrence himself? Once again Lawrence seems to be asking all sorts of pertinent questions, questions we have not yet even begun to resolve. His answers may not be wholly acceptable: they are ultimately not wholly acceptable to Kate herself.

Lawrence clearly approves of Kate's misanthropy, seeing it as the result of too much intimacy, but at this point in the novel he does not allow her to understand it for herself. She can admit to a certain disgust with people:

Her mother, her father, her sisters, her first husband, even her children whom she loved, and Joachim (her second husband) for whom she had felt such passionate love, even these, being near her, filled her with disgust and repulsion after a little while, and she longed to fling them down the great and final oubliette.

But here the authorial voice intervenes in a couple of dramatically-set new paragraphs:

But there is no great and final oubliette: or at least it is never final until one has flung *oneself* down.
So it was with Kate. Till she flung herself down the last dark oubliette of death, she would never escape from her deep, bottomless disgust with human beings.

She must be reborn. But how?
She has had a glimpse in the dance of meeting and mingling on another, less personal plane, of an emergent new self in the 'greater womanhood'. And her relationship with Cipriano is pretty

impersonal, even after they have gone through a form of marriage by Quetzalcoatl. Although Kate is, by her own repeated avowal, 'just a woman', she is marrying more than just a man – no less than 'the mystery of the primeval world' and 'the ancient phallic mystery, the ancient god-devil of the male Pan' who appears in a column of blood rising from earth to heaven. 'Ah! and what mystery of prone submission on her part, this huge erection would imply! Submission absolute, like the earth under the sky ... with the finality of death, and yet more than death ...' If it is more than death, it must presumably be rebirth. Kate sees her marriage to Cipriano as 'the supreme passivity', and at the same time as an abandonment 'of so many things she wanted to abandon'. When Ramon sees her now, he recognizes the change in her at once: 'she had the face of one waking from the dead, curiously dipped in death, with a tenderness far more new and vulnerable than a child's.'

Kate has lost herself, and language – that tool of superconsciousness – has now become meaningless to her. Lawrence would have us believe that she has abandoned her old self for a new and better one, a self which recognizes and submits to godlike male power, and in doing so approaches its own godhead. She has also become infantilized during the process of rebirth. What she has really abandoned is her own mature intelligence, the sort of rationality and know-how which are both based in experience. Once again Lawrence is advocating a repudiation of the past, but the repudiation of maturity, especially female maturity, is a new and significant bias.

That Kate has not altogether abandoned her former consciousness is evident in her relationship with Teresa, Ramon's second wife. Teresa loves Ramon with a 'wild virgin loyalty' for having rescued her from her coarse brothers, and 'saved her sex from insult, restored it to her in its pride and its beauty'. She is small and shy, rather distant with Kate, whom she sees as a 'travelled, experienced, rather assertive white-skinned woman'. Kate thinks that Teresa, sitting demure and still, looks 'rather like a little sempstress'. Teresa despises her, she feels, because she cannot be in love as Teresa is with Ramon. In her turn she despises Teresa as 'the harem type'.

But she is torn between envy of Teresa's 'subtle female power' (and not a little jealousy *vis-à-vis* Ramon) and a robust superconscious scorn.

The hidden, secretive power of the dark female! Kate called it harem and self prostitution. But was it? Yes, surely it was the slave approach. Surely she wanted nothing but sex from him, like a prostitute! The ancient mystery of the female power, which consists in glorifying the blood male.

Was it right? Kate asked herself. Wasn't it degrading for a woman? And didn't it make the man either soft and sensuous, or else hatefully autocratic?

Kate sees her own relationship with Cipriano rather differently. Although she is now finally convinced (she tells herself) that 'the clue to all living and all moving-on into new living lay in the vivid blood-relation between man and woman,' she also believes that the togetherness needs a balance, and that the Ramon–Teresa relationship is weighted on the male side. She and Cipriano want 'moments' from each other, no more. 'Her life was her own! It was not her metier to be fanning the blood in a man, to make him almighty and blood-glamorous. Her life was her own!'

The two women become friends of a sort, having one thing in common besides their many differences: 'that they felt it was better to stand faithfully behind a really brave man, than to push forward into the ranks of cheap and obtrusive women.' But Kate's reluctance to join ranks with other women seems to spring more from snobbishness than from an attitude of subservience towards men: she is too much of a 'lady' rather than too much of a true woman.

Eventually she tackles Teresa on the subject of self-sacrifice, only to have the poor little thing burst into tears, claiming that she has been misunderstood. Later Teresa declares with some pride that Ramon is more than a lover, more than a husband to her: her life. But surely, Kate expostulates, 'it is better to live one's own life', and to keep one's own soul. Teresa replies that it is impossible to keep one's own soul (as if in a purse) without its dying. Neither woman is disposed to learn from the other, Kate because she is used to homage from other women, and Teresa because she sees Kate as 'one of those women of the outside world, who make a very splendid show, but who are not sure of the real secret of womanhood, and her innermost power.' Understandably enough, Kate is angered by Teresa's apparent monopoly of righteousness. 'The slave morale! she said to herself. The miserable old trick of a woman living just for the sake of a man. Only living to send her soul with him, inside his precious body. And to carry his precious seed in her womb! Herself, apart from this, nothing!' But Teresa is very far from perceiving herself as 'nothing', and it is Kate who learns from her, rather than the other way round. Despite herself, Kate cannot help envying Teresa for the 'comfort of a living man permanently in her womb. And the secret, savage indomitable pride in her own womanhood that arose from this.'

But Kate was right first time: it is a miserable old trick, and no amount of dressing it up in fancy clothes can make it new. Nevertheless, Lawrence has a good try and Teresa is, as it were, his trump card. It is as if he knows that women will learn from other women what they will never accept from a man. It is Teresa who, in her acceptance of Quetzalcoatl, prompts Kate's most profound self-doubts. And it is after her conversations with Teresa that she begins to understand 'the old, terrible bond of the blood-unison of man' inherent in Quetzalcoatl, and to recognize its purpose: 'to bring the great opposites into contact and into unison again'. In the face of such concepts, what is the mere individual? Kate is frightened of what is happening to her, feeling that she still belongs in the old world of Europe and that 'she could not make herself over so quickly'.

She agrees to a civil marriage with Cipriano, deciding that after a month she will go back to Ireland alone, presumably to slow herself down. But the now legalized marriage has a strange effect on her:

He made her go all vague and quiet, as if she sank away, heavy and still, away from the surface of life, and lay deep in the under-life.
    The strange, heavy *positive* passivity. For the first time in her life she

felt absolutely at rest .... a final rest within a great opened-out cosmos
... She had become almost like Teresa in sureness.

So Kate has now swung round completely again. But the process
of change is also terrible to her, as she begins to let go of her old
modes of being. Cipriano never talks seriously to her, and she
becomes aware of the 'curious irritant quality of talk'.

Similarly, she begins to understand her former mode of sexuality
as 'frictional, irritant sensation'. When Cipriano refuses to share
'the spasms of frictional voluptuousness' with her,

Her strange, seething feminine will and desire subsided in her and swept
away, leaving her soft and powerfully potent, like the hot springs of water
that gushed up so noiseless, so soft, yet so powerful, with a soft, secret
potency ... she was open to him, soft and hot, yet gushing with
a noiseless, soft power. And there was no such thing as conscious
'satisfaction'.

What actually happens is 'dark and untellable'. Well, so it is. I find
this passage pretty obscure – and indeed Lawrence is not as open
or direct about sex as I had supposed or remembered. It has been
claimed that Cipriano is at pains to deny Kate an orgasm or
orgasms, but I think that this claim (especially when voiced in an
indignant tone) misses the point: that the sexual act is not a
mechanistic process, and that good sex is beyond the capabilities of
language. Lawrence is attempting to describe the indescribable
without resorting to clinical language.

It is clear that Kate achieves some sort of satisfaction, some sort
of orgasm, but that it is not on the conscious level. I suspect that
Cipriano disapproves of any activity which involves the deliberate
stimulation of one partner by the other with the object of producing
a solitary orgasm. In short, that he will not allow Kate to reach
orgasm without penetration and unless they come together. Even
then she will scarcely know what has happened to her. 'What she
had with Cipriano was curiously beyond her knowing; so deep and
hot and flowing, as it were subterranean. She had to yield before
it. She could not grip it into one final spasm of white ecstasy,
which was like sheer knowing.' It is also clear that this new sort of

orgasm is somehow morally superior to those attained by Kate in her ecstatic past.

Lawrence, then, is still at one with Paul Morel in believing that good sex somehow just happens without your having to think about it, and that it will inevitably be good provided that you have the right attitude. Or, to put it in more Lawrentian terms, provided that you bring your dark, passional self to the act, and abandon the striving towards some consciously apprehended goal, all will be well. This is a notion I shall discuss at more length in Part III.

For her part, Kate seems to accept her place in a marriage which is, like Alvina's, 'a mindless communication of the blood'. It is only when Cipriano goes back to his troops that she begins to hanker after Europe again, and books herself a pasage from Vera Cruz to Southampton, with no clear idea of when she will return to Mexico. 'She was alone, as usual. It occurred to her that she herself willed this aloneness. She could not relax and be with these people. She could not relax and be with anybody. She always had to recoil upon her own individuality, as a cat does.' Another turnaround. It is not as easy to kill off the modern woman as Lawrence imagines or hopes in 'The Woman Who Rode Away'. Neither can sex, at any rate Cipriano's brand of sexuality, entirely relieve her of her European consciousness.

Sex, sexual correspondence, did it matter so very much to her? It might have mattered more, if she had not had it. But she had had it – and very finely and consummately with Cipriano. So she knew all about it. It was as if she had conquered another territory, another field of life. The conqueress! And now she would retire to the lair of her individuality with the prey.

I don't find this at all convincing.

If sex with Cipriano is so wonderful, surely Kate will want more of it rather than less. Her blithe assumption that now she has had the best sort of sex there is to be had, she can forget about it, reads to me like yet another male misconception about female sexuality. Lawrence is attempting to explain Kate's apparent indifference to sex with Cipriano by describing her as a predator and a destroyer, a woman who is a natural odd number. But it seems to me that

Kate's attitude could just as well be explained by the supposition that sex with Cipriano is not as wonderful as it is cracked up to be by Lawrence. At any rate, I feel that there is special pleading here: female independence and self-sufficiency must be explained in terms which are not detrimental to the male.

Kate cannot be saved for rebirth in Quetzalcoatl by an act of faith. It is no good, Lawrence belatedly realizes, appealing to her on this plane. She is a rational woman, and can perhaps be argued into it instead. She will argue herself into it:

> Suddenly she saw herself as men often saw her: the great cat, with its spasms of voluptuousness and its lifelong lustful enjoyment of its own isolated, isolated individuality. Voluptuously to enjoy a contact. Then with a lustful feline gratification, to break the contact, and roam alone with a sense of power.

She knows so many women who behave in this fashion, the 'grimalkins', and she shrinks from becoming one of their number. But surely what Lawrence is shrinking from is the prospect of women behaving like unfettered social beings – in short, like men.

When Kate is with Cipriano, her body flowers and she experiences 'the greater sex'; but 'when she spread the wings of her own ego, and sent forth her own spirit, the world could look very wonderful when she was alone. But after a while the wonder faded, and a sort of jealous emptiness set in.' She concludes that she must have both: both Cipriano and her aloneness. With Cipriano, she is limited, 'but then one must be limited. If one tries to be unlimited, one becomes horrible.' Without Cipriano, she will become 'a horrible elderly female' – which could be the worse fate.

> I ought to *want* to be limited. I ought to be *glad* if a man will limit me with a strong will and a warm touch. Because what I call my greatness, and the vastness of the Lord behind me, lets me fall through a hollow floor of nothingness, once there is no man's hand there, to hold me warm and limited.

Cipriano will balance her, ensuring that she remains both ordinarily human and womanly. So much for gods and goddesses.

This is neither a submissive nor even an altruistic conclusion, but one based firmly in enlightened self-interest. Kate will stay in Mexico with Cipriano because the only alternative she can perceive – the life of an elderly single woman in the drawing-rooms of Europe – is repulsive to her. But she will try, as far as possible, to stay on her own terms. 'I will make my submission,' she tells herself as she sets off to find Cipriano, 'as far as I need, and no further.' Neither a victory nor a defeat, then, for the superconscious and independent modern woman, but a sort of truce.

Lawrence recognizes but cannot altogether accept Kate's needs for independence and autonomy in the modern manner. He cannot altogether believe that a woman does not need a man – at least for *something*. And yet perforce he has to examine the possibility. In his essay, 'We Need One Another', he writes:

> Now, if I say to a woman, or to a man: 'Would you like to be purely free of all human relationships, free from father and mother, brother and sister, husband, lover, friend or child?' . . .
> I expect, in almost all cases it is an emphatic 'yes.' In the past most men would have said 'yes' and most women 'no.' But today I think many men might hesitate, and nearly all women would unhesitatingly say 'yes.'

Of course Lawrence is exaggerating and, again, being disingenuous. He has no real objection to a woman's not needing a father, mother, brother, sister, friend or child. What he does object to is her professing not to need a man.

> We may as well admit it: men and women need one another. We may as well, after all our kicking against the pricks, our revolting and our sulking, give in and be graceful about it. We are all individuals: we are all egoists: we all believe intensely in freedom, our own at all events. We all want to be absolute and sufficient unto ourselves and it is a great blow to our self-esteem that we simply *need* another human being.

This is a graceful enough admission of need in itself, but in 'The Real Thing', another posthumously published essay, he expands this theme in a rather more dogmatic manner.

Having conceded that 'perhaps the greatest revolution of modern times is the emancipation of women', he goes on to assert that the fight has now been won and has even become 'a tyranny of women,

of the individual woman in the house, and of the feminine ideas
and ideals in the world'. But women will persist in continuing to
fight.

Today, woman is always tense and strung up, alert and bare-armed, not
for love but for battle. In her shred of a dress and her little helmet of a
hat, her cropped hair and her stark bearing she is a sort of soldier, and
look at her as one may, one can see nothing else.

But even at her most militant (and therefore of course desexed)
woman is not granted primary agency. 'It is not her fault. It is her
doom. It happens when man loses faith in himself and in his very
life.' This is one of the themes played over in both *The Rainbow*
and *Women In Love*, but here Lawrence takes it further. If women
really are still struggling for the recognition of their own autonomy,
why don't they just leave men alone instead of fighting with them?
Sometimes they do, he concedes, but only to move on to another
man and 'resume the fight'.

Why can't she live alone? She can't. Sometimes she can join with other
women and keep up the fight in a group. Sometimes she *must* live alone
because no man will come forward to fight with her. Yet sooner or later,
the need for contact with a man comes over a woman again. It is
imperative.

Is it? There is nothing in Lawrence's unvarnished assertion to
persuade us that this is so. It is in his masterly short novel *St Mawr*
that he explores this question in depth, and comes to conclusions
which are not altogether to be expected.

Lou Carrington and her mother, Mrs Witt, are two of the most
interesting women Lawrence ever wrote about, and two of the
most convincing. They are both immediately recognizable, without
any of the special pleading that Lawrence found necessary on
behalf of the Brangwen sisters, as extraordinary people: and as
women who could just as easily exist in the 1980s as in the 1920s.
Lou especially has all the shrewdness and toughness necessary for
survival in our decade. She is 'of course' American and rich – then
as now two major advantages for a woman in dealing with life's
many obstacles.

Mrs Witt is a widow, a fine healthy woman of fifty-one, who has had nothing to do with men for the past fifteen years. 'She loved men – real men. But, on close contact, it was difficult to define what she meant by "real men." She never met any.' Mrs Witt is handsome, energetic and sardonically inclined; although she says little, what she does say, bites, 'and her terrible grey eyes with the touch of a leer looked on at the hollow mockery of things' in a 'queer, democratic New Orleans sort of conceit'. When Lou announces that she is to marry Henry Carrington, a popular Australian artist who has just inherited an English baronetcy, Mrs Witt is 'exasperated beyond exasperation', because she looks on Rico, as he is known, as little more than a handsome cipher. 'She would almost have preferred Lou to elope with one of the great, evil porters at Les Halles. Mrs Witt was at the age when the malevolent male in man, the old Adam, begins to loom above the social tailoring.'

Mrs Witt is right to have her doubts about the marriage, which soon goes awry. Lou and Rico are fond of one another, but also have an exhausting effect on one another. 'A nervous attachment, rather than a sexual love. A curious tension of will rather than a spontaneous passion.' Theirs becomes a marriage without sex. 'Sex was shattering and exhausting, they shrank away from it and became like brother and sister. But they were still husband and wife. And the lack of physical relation was a source of uneasiness and chagrin to them both.' When Mrs Witt arrives in London and establishes herself in a nearby hotel, she keeps track of everything and 'her small, occasionally biting remarks revealed her attitude of contempt for the menage.'

Lou and her mother go riding in Hyde Park and decide that Rico too must have a horse so that he can join them. St Mawr seems the ideal purchase to Lou:

He was of such a lovely red-gold colour, and a dark invisible fire seemed to come out of him. But in his big black eyes there was a lurking afterthought. Something told her that the horse was not quite happy; that somewhere deep in his animal consciousness lived a dangerous, half-revealed resentment, a diffused sense of hostility.

St Mawr has been raised for stud purposes but, as Lewis the groom reports, 'he didn't seem to fancy the mares, for some reason.' Like Lewis himself, St Mawr is a male odd number, and therefore worthy of respect and admiration. Lou is determined to buy him because he makes her want to cry – something she, as a modern woman, never does. But now,

as if that mysterious force of the horse's body had split some rock in her, she went home and hid herself in her room, and just cried . . . It was as if she had had a vision, as if the walls of her old world had suddenly melted away, leaving her in a great darkness . . . He was some splendid demon and she must worship him.

This is no simple case of sexual frustration, but indicates the repression of the 'greater sex' which is demonic and impersonal, promising rebirth.

The horse haunts Lou, and her human relationships begin to seem superficial by contrast. Rico especially suffers from the comparison, the 'central, anxious powerlessness' of him driving Lou mad. 'He too was rather like a horse – but forever quivering with a sort of cold, dangerous mistrust, which he covered with anxious love.' He is all bluff, and 'attitude', whereas 'that black fiery glow in the eyes of the horse was not an "attitude." It was something much more terrifying and real, the only thing that was real.' The horse is more or less docile with Lou, but springs back violently when Rico approaches him, and eventually throws him in Hyde Park.

Obsessed as she is with the horse, Lou is beginning to become an odd number. Although she has her husband and her mother, she feels detached from them both. Rico and Mrs Witt are 'deadly enemies, yet neither could keep clear of the other. It might have been they who were married to one another, their duel and their duet were so relentless.' When Mrs Witt takes a house in Shropshire for the summer, the Carringtons join her, and Rico immediately becomes involved in the social round. 'Everything intensely thrilling, and so utterly wearisome, Lou felt.' She begins to spend a lot of time alone, learning to do nothing, while Rico consorts with the bright young Manbys, and Mrs Witt takes on the role of

Lady Bountiful among the villagers. All Lou wants is to be
peaceful, but Mrs Witt cannot believe that any daughter of hers
'can be content to lie on a hammock and do *nothing*, not even read
or improve her mind'. Lou replies that she is (like Teresa, but with
a difference) 'the harem type . . . only I never want the men inside
the lattice'. Mrs Witt retorts that she is an *American* – with all of
the anti-harem typology that designation implies. Mother and
daughter, no less than husband and wife, are operating in contrary
modes.

Mrs Witt loves trimming, whether in house or garden, and
arranging things just so. When she insists on cutting Lewis's hair,
poising 'a pair of long scissors like one of the Fates', she is clearly
intended as a castrating figure, but her wit (her name is no
accident) and verve are such that she cannot come across as purely
destructive. Despite himself, Lawrence is fascinated by her energy
and her ability to get things done, to change things – in short, her
power. He never quite convinces me that Mrs Witt is simply a
terrible old woman, a 'grimalkin', who needs a man to balance her.
It seems to me that his attitude to her gradually softens as the
novel progresses. Although she is in a sense cynical and sees
corruption everywhere, something of her peculiar American innocence remains itself incorruptible.

If mother and daughter are at odds on the proper conduct of
one's everyday life, they are even more so on the subject of men.
Mrs Witt thinks that Lewis – no less than her own Navajo groom,
Phoenix – is stupid, but Lou becomes impatient with her.

I think one gets so tired of your men with mind, as you call it. . . . It
seems to me there's something else besides mind and cleverness. Perhaps
it is the animal. Just think of St Mawr! I've thought so much about him.
We call him an animal, but we never know what it means. He seems a far
greater mystery to me than a clever man. He's a horse. Why can't one say
the same of a man: *He's a man?*

The concept of maleness is more elusive and less attainable than
the concept of horseness. And yet Lou seems to have some idea of
what maleness is all about. Clearly it does not consist in intellectual
ability. And neither – this becomes plain as the novel unfolds –

does it consist in sexual prowess. It consists rather in a self-awareness which is not accessible to consciousness.

Lou despises men because the animal (which embodies such self-awareness) in them has become tamed, and is now servile and cringing. For her it is St Mawr and the two grooms who most truly embody the male principle; it is they – the horse, the Celt and the American Indian – who should be the masters rather than the servants they are. Here Lawrence comes so near to saying something profoundly true that it is amazing for him to persist in identifying the male principle with a mindless indifference and, by implication, cruelty. Of course the middle-to-upper-class Englishmen whom Lawrence met so often were products of a system which bred all spontaneous sensuality out of them, and this is bad enough. But what is horrifying, from the point of view of the women with whom such men become entangled, is that they are often hideously out of touch with their own emotions. Animal indifference and impersonal sex do not and never will constitute a bridge over the chasm between the world of women and the world of men. But, in a peculiarly oblique way, Lawrence is on to something here, and Lou's subsequent actions have all the logic of last-ditch female behaviour in the face of an uncomprehending male world.

For Mrs Witt, 'man is wonderful because he is able to *think*,' rather than for his animal attributes, and it is a lack of mind which makes the commonplace. For Lou, men's minds *are* commonplace:

Most men have a deadness in them that frightens me because of my own deadness. Why can't men get their life straight, like St Mawr, and then think? Why can't they think quick, mother: quick as a woman: only further than we do? Why isn't men's thinking quick like fire, mother? Why is it so slow, so dead, so deadly dull?

For me this *cri de coeur* is spoiled only by the phrase 'only further than we do': there is no need for that. Men can't get their life together and then think, can't think as quick as a woman, because men have not been educated to operate intuitively: to trust their intuition and to trust their emotions. But I doubt if their lack can be attributed to suppressing the animal in themselves. Suppressing the feminine, maybe. Skating around the issue, and yet, in sum, managing to get to the kernel of it, Lou is asking the pertinent question: why are men (that is, inhabitants of the modern world of men) so inferior to women that there is little reason for us to respect and admire them?

On this last point mother and daughter are agreed. But Mrs Witt cannot understand Lou's declaration, 'I can't live, mother, I just can't,' retorting, 'I don't see why not. *I'm* full of life.' If men are such unworthy creatures, it is no big deal to Mrs Witt, who indeed takes some grim satisfaction in the fact. But Lou is young, and 'I've got to live. And the thing that is offered to me as life just starves me, starves me to death, mother.' Unlike her mother, she cannot live by 'shattering' people from a position of detachment, and enjoy the process. The knowledge that people, more especially men, are empty and dull, gives her no pleasure; on the contrary, it is driving her very near to despair. Mrs Witt has turned her singleness to advantage in ways which seem fitting to her age, but Lou is not ready to accept her own unsatisfactory experience of life as all that can be expected. She knows at the same time, however, that her mother understands her better than does Rico, and that there is some indefinable bond between them which is as much a matter of shared femininity as it is of heredity. And theirs is the closest bond between women that Lawrence ever describes.

Rico invites the sisters, Flora and Elsie Manby, to stay and the 'whole clockwork of "lots of fun"' begins again. Lou escapes to look at St Mawr. 'He knew her and he did not resent her. He took no notice of her. He would never "respond." At first she resented it. Now she was glad. He would never be intimate, thank Heaven.' Unlike most of Lawrence's women, Lou needs no persuading to recognizably Lawrentian ideas about relations between men and women. She and her mother agree that neither of them has ever met 'the unfallen Pan'. Their shared problem is not, like Kate's or Ursula's, that of recognizing and having to come to terms with the male principle, but of finding the embodiment of that principle in a man. It is not their own shortcomings which make them odd numbers, but the dearth of men who can be considered good enough for either of them. They are not so much unmated as unmatable: matchless in both senses of the word.

When St Mawr throws Rico again, partially crushing him, the bond between mother and daughter is strengthened. Both are on the side of the horse, whom Rico and the Manbys want to have shot. Mother and daughter are now proving themselves real women in defending the male principle. But Lou is also uneasy: if St Mawr is not after all noble, but mean and treacherous, perhaps he should be shot. Watching him, she feels 'a great animal sadness come from him,' and a great woe, 'the woe of human unworthiness. The race of men judged in the consciousness of the animals they have subdued, and there found unworthy, ignoble.' She is flooded with grief and sympathy for the animal, a grief which makes her want to be alone. 'She knew now what it all amounted to. She knew that the horse, born to serve nobly, had waited in vain for someone noble to serve. His spirit knew that nobility had gone out of men. And this left him high and dry, in a sort of despair.'

It is of course Lou's own despair, the despair of a woman who has not found a man worth 'serving'. The terminology is wrong, but the predicament is recognizable: it is the despair of a sensitive and intelligent woman who has never found her equal, a man worth loving. Again, Lawrence is so near and yet so far from understanding. Where he goes wrong is to equate the relationship horse–human being with the relationship woman–man. The despair shared by Lou and St Mawr (and probably Lawrence himself as well) is that of the disappointed idealist or 'the grief of the generous creature which sees all ends turn to the morass of ignoble living'. Life, for such a creature, has become meaningless. As far as Lawrence is concerned in this novel, the way towards meaning lies in submission: a recognition of that which is bigger than ourselves. For both women and horses, this elusive entity should be the adult human male. But this is not how it works out in the end.

Mrs Witt is apparently less despairing than Lou, but essentially engaged in the same sort of quest.

Examining herself, she had long ago decided that her nature was a destructive force. But then she justified herself, she had only destroyed that which was destructible. If she could have found something indestructible, especially in men, though she would have fought it, she would have been glad at last to be defeated by it.

Nobody has ever defeated her, and when she is on the point of crying out, 'Conquer me, oh God, before I die,' she realizes that she feels contempt even for God, that she could make him too kiss her hand. But it is clear that her strength does not make her happy. Nothing in her life has ever really affected her, not even the thought of her own death, which she sees as a passing into mere nothingness 'like a thing made into a parcel and put into the last rubbish-heap'. But something in her longs 'to die, at least, *positively*'. She cannot realize death because she has never fully realized life, never even submitted fully to the process of ageing, but has remained as 'timeless as an hour-glass that turn. morning and night, and spills the hours of sleep one way, and the hours of consciousness another'.

When Rico decides to sell St Mawr to the Manbys – who will have him gelded, if not shot – Mrs Witt is ready with an alternative plan. She and Lewis will take St Mawr across country to some friends of hers, and then leave for America, taking Phoenix and the horse with them. It is on this journey, ironically enough, that she meets her match. Lewis is emotionally inaccessible to her, meeting her eyes 'with that cold, distant look, looking straight into her hot, confused, pained self'. He does his job and keeps his distance: an attitude which angers and challenges her. Twenty miles from their destination she makes him an oblique proposal of marriage which, when pressed, he rejects, his look 'neutral, sombre and hurt'. But inside he is angry with 'an anger congealed like cold lava, set impassive against her and all her sort'.

Mrs Witt is not yet defeated, and insists on knowing his reasons. These turn out to be the usual reasons of the Lawrentian male for steering clear of women: 'No woman shall touch my body and mock me and despise me.' Mrs Witt becomes cutting, looking at him with 'a touch of contemptuous mockery, raillery': what is so precious about his body? But he refuses to answer and rides on.

She was in love with him. And he, in an odd way, was in love with her . . . But he would not have her come physically near him. Unapproachable there as a cactus, guarding his 'body' from her contact. As if contact with her would be mortal insult and fatal injury to his marvellous 'body.'

What a little cock-sparrow!

When the cock-sparrow announces that he is going to hand in his notice to Lou, Mrs Witt is non-committal. But it is at this point in the novel that she begins to change. She becomes listless and wishes for the first time in her life that she had a maid, feeling that her electric energy, her power, has been switched off.

I don't see Mrs Witt's rejection by Lewis as an act of vengeance on the strong, independent woman. Although Lawrence often pairs older upper-class women with younger lower-class men, it is clear from the outset that Mrs Witt and her groom are incompatible. She has no 'respect' for the male body, and is not likely to react to it, as do Alvina and Kate, with an adoring swoon. Mrs Witt seems to me to emerge from the incident with some of her allure and much of her dignity intact. Her proposal to Lewis may be basically foolish and a last-ditch act of desperation, but she does not come across as a silly, insensitive middle-aged woman; rather, as an American woman to whom all things are possible, a woman who is on some sort of quest and is willing to learn. What she seems to have learned is defeat, the defeat which will give meaning to her life and death. The suggestion is that at last she has met a 'real man', and that he has given her what she has really wanted.

Lou is horrified to hear of her mother's proposal to Lewis. For her part, she aches 'in every fibre to be left alone, from all that sort of thing. I feel all bruises, like one who has been assassinated. I do understand why Jesus said, *Noli me tangere*.' Noli me tangere. Lawrence has granted Lou one of his own recurrent phrases, a cry usually allowed only to male odd numbers. Here it is Rico who wants intimacy, or 'at least the pretence of intimacy', whereas for Lou the very thought 'fills me with ashes, and the pretence of it exhausts me beyond myself'. Left in Shropshire with the injured Rico and the Manbys, she feels herself to be in a minority, and writes to her mother: 'It's an awful thought, to think that most all the young people in the world are like this: so bright and cheerful and *sporting*, and so brimming with libido.' It is only Phoenix who seems to understand her, leaving her 'understandingly alone'.

When she talks to Lewis, trying with the utmost tact to persuade him to go to America with St Mawr, she surmises:

I think you and Phoenix and mother and I might live in a far-away wild place, and make a good life: so long as we didn't begin to mix up marriage, or love or that sort of thing into it. It seems to me men and women have really hurt one another so much, nowadays, that they had better stay apart till they have learned to be gentle with one another. Not all this enforced passion and philandering.

Lou is envisaging some sort of asexual, pre-lapsarian community which is nevertheless neither ascetic nor monastic, the sexes living in side-by-side segregation. She makes the four of them sound like babes in the wood, pre-pubertal, and undergoing the same sort of belated adolescent moratorium that Ursula assumed after her teaching practice. This too is a recurrent Lawrentian theme, and one which leads eventually to his advocation of tenderness. But even here, in Lou's proposed utopia, it is plain that to be a sexual odd number is only a defensive and probably temporary measure.

On the voyage from Southampton to Galveston Mrs Witt spends most of her time in her cabin, lying on her bunk, 'silent, shut up like a steel trap, as if in her tomb'. Lou lunches with the captain and feels 'she ought to be flirty', but has no stomach for the exercise. She watches England fade away with no regrets, not even for Rico, all of her life there 'passing in a grey curtain of rainy drizzle, and she with not a feeling left'. Like Kate Leslie, Lou and her mother are going to America to be reborn. Mrs Witt is already in a kind of limbo, looking towards death, her Amazonian ways abandoned for 'a virgin wistfulness'. When they arrive in Texas, she tells Lou that she has come home to die, and that she has made her last decision: never to make another decision. From now on, if Lou wants decisions, she must make them herself. This abandonment of superconsciousness, the sort of consciousness which inflicts itself on reality in order to dominate it, is what Mrs Witt has learned from her relationship with Lewis – and ultimately from St Mawr. But Lou is still the superconscious modern woman, consciously seeking the South and forsaking 'the idealistic,

Christianized tension of the now irreligious North'. Like the woman who rode away, she knows that somewhere there are other gods. For her, the process of reconciling intuition and consciousness has now begun.

It is left to Lou to go and look at a ranch which has been advertised for sale, and it is Phoenix, now a 'sort of half-friend, half servant retainer', who drives the car into the mountains. In this rugged territory he becomes himself, 'impassive, detached, self-satisfied and silently assertive', and begins to entertain fantasies about himself and Lou. He wants to become her lover and then marry her, thus making himself a rich man. In return, he will look after her, and remain loyal in his fashion: his relations with Mexican or Indian women will be none of her business. She is 'one of these white women who talk clever and know things, like a man'. To him she is hardly a woman at all, 'yet it would flatter his vanity and his self-esteem to possess her' while finding the answer to 'the phallic male in him' elsewhere. Lou is straightforward and cannot 'satisfy the furtiveness in him. He needed this plaintive, squeaky, dark-fringed Indian quality, something furtive and soft and rat-like, really to rouse him.' But he is ready to trade in his sex 'which, in his opinion, every white woman was secretly pining for, for the white woman's money and social privileges.'

Far from endorsing the sexuality of the dark-skinned male as best medicine for the white-skinned female, Lawrence is pretty scathing here about Phoenix's attitude to sex and women. Unlike Lewis, who respects his body and is therefore worthy of a woman's respect, Phoenix is prepared to prostitute himself. Lou, divining 'as a woman does', more or less what is going on in his mind, does not judge him too harshly. She too may be at fault in that she cannot be the sort of woman he finds desirable. The daughter is a shrewder judge of character than is her mother. Somewhere, Lou feels, Phoenix is just like Rico in his 'real meaninglessness', but pleasanter because more childish.

The same with his opinion of himself as a sexual male! So childish, really, it was almost thrilling to a woman. But then, so stupid also, with that furtive lurking in holes and imagining it could not be detected. He imagined himself dark in his sexual rat holes. He imagined he was not detected!

Phoenix is 'ridiculously mistaken' in thinking that Lou is looking for 'some secretly sexual male such a himself'. The missing animal in modern man is clearly not a rat.

Lou cannot fool herself into seeing Phoenix as husband or mate. 'There was a certain physical sympathy between them. His obtuseness made him think it was also a sexual sympathy.' The white superconscious modern woman is not devoid of wisdom when she can also be intuitive. For Lou 'mere sex' has become repellent, and she will never prostitute herself again.

She understood now the meaning of the Vestal Virgins of the holy fire in the old temples. They were symbolic of herself, of woman weary of the embrace of incompetent men, weary, weary, of all that, turning to the unseen gods, the unseen spirits, the hidden fire and devoting herself to that, and that alone.

The sum of her relationship with Rico and her former lovers is almost nothing, involving only her top layers. But the 'successive inner sanctuaries of herself' are inviolable. She tells herself that she is not a marrying woman.

I am not a lover or a mistress or a wife. It is no good. Love can't really come into me from the outside, and I can never, never, mate with any man, since the new mystic man will never come to me ... My dealings with men have only broken my stillness and messed up my doorways. It has been my own fault. I ought to stay virgin, and still, very, very still ...

St Mawr may have given her some idea, some revelatory delineation of the 'mystic new man', but now even that illusion has gone.

The hidden fire to which Lou will devote herself is alive and burning out there in the mountains and in the desert. When she sees the ranch, Las Chivas, she wants it at once, although it is rat-infested and practically derelict. The news of the purchase gets Mrs Witt out of bed at last, and the two women drive out to the ranch together. There Mrs Witt, sitting on a fallen tree at the mouth of the canyon, surveys the world beyond, 'a world not of

men. She could not fail to be roused.' When she asks her daughter
what she hopes to achieve at Las Chivas, Lou replies that she
hopes to escape achievement: whatever heart she once had for
living with people has now been broken. Mrs Witt, now gradually
emerging from her lethargy, both argues and understands:

I'm convinced that ever since men were men and women were women,
people who took things seriously, and had time for it, got their hearts
broken. Haven't I had mine broken! It's as sure as having your virginity
broken: and it amounts to about as much. It's a beginning rather than an
end.

On this last the two women are agreed. It looks as though they are
both ready, each in her own way, for rebirth. And without benefit
of any male midwife.

   Lou then has to explain to her mother that 'either my taking a
man shall have a meaning and mystery that penetrates my very
soul, or I will keep to myself'. Mrs Witt's understandably cynical
reply is that her daughter will probably spend her life keeping to
herself. Lou, however, is quite prepared for this possibility, knowing
that there is something else for her there on the ranch: a spirit:

I don't know what it is definitely. It's something wild, that will hurt me
sometimes and will wear me down sometimes. I know it. But it's something
big, bigger than men, bigger than people, bigger than religion ... And to
it, my sex is deep and sacred, deeper than I am, with a deep nature aware
deep down of my sex.

This spirit, which is also something to do with wild America – a
spirit of place – will save her from cheapness in needing her,
craving her. It will keep her virgin or intact, which is to say,
integral. It will give meaning to her life and death.

   Lou is Lawrence's most independent woman, and his most
successfully independent. Her independence and her wish for
solitude are both synonymous with her integrity, which in turn is
inseparable from the quest for meaning. There is no question that
the 'mission' she has sent herself is going to prove beyond her
capabilities. If men refuse to be men, 'babies and playboys, and
poor things showing off all the time, even to themselves', then it is

right that women should forsake them and find new ways to live without them. Such an action is not a denial of sexuality, but a proper respect for it; not a denial of relationship and community, but a refusal to cheapen either; not a negative and cynical move, but a brave and positive one.

So women can be brave and positive? Indeed, they can. A reading of *St Mawr* suggests that it is *only* women who can be brave and positive, only women who can take the lead in the quest for meaning and individual integrity. It may well be that men will follow them, but this is a possibility which is not considered in this novel. On the contrary, it is repeatedly stated that men (except for Lewis and beyond him St Mawr, both of whom are also keeping to themselves) are probably incapable of understanding the aim and import of the journey. There is no doubt here as to which is the more powerful, indeed superior, sex.

But to say that modern women have more real power and integrity than modern men is not to concede that the female principle is any way superior to the male. The men have abused their own power, the phallic power embodied in St Mawr, and allowed women to become powerful, the female principle to assume the ascendant. In *St Mawr* Lawrence seems to have given up on men and invested his hopes for the future in women instead. A reading of his essays shows that Lou is his mouthpiece. But perhaps she is also his self-portrait: one in which he recognizes, acknowledges and even celebrates the feminine side of his nature: in his own terms, the ability to be rather than to do. And yet the whole novel is also a lament for the loss of maleness, which Lawrence attributes to the modern, mechanistic, money-grubbing world – the world of men. It is only in the face of such a loss that women can become powerful and independent. Further, it would seem that only in these circumstances are they entitled to enjoy those qualities which are more properly aspects of the male principle.

For all that, Lou is not happy until the end of the novel, and Mrs Witt is not happy at all. Both women suffer or have suffered because of the defects of men. Mrs Witt's suffering is less assuaged than reoriented after her longed-for defeat. And Lou's release from her suffering amounts to peace rather than any form of joy. Neither woman is basically fulfilled by the exercise of sheer power. Mrs Witt would like to shed her cynicism but, until she can recognize a broken heart as a new beginning, sees no reason to do so. Lou yearns to shed her nervous, frictional tension, but even in her mystic apprehension of Las Chivas, she remains clear-headed, superconscious to the end.

The truth, which Lawrence seems to fight against but eventually has to concede in part, is that it is too late in human history to shed superconsciousness. It is in particular too late for women to cease behaving as rational, analytic beings with a sense of autonomy, and revert to some sort of dark consciousness which will keep us subordinate to men. The stirrings of Lou's new consciousness come from the spirit of place and from within herself rather than from a man or a sexual relationship with a man. Although she claims to dislike men, she is a respecter of the male principle which she has found so lacking in modern men. Strikingly decisive in her thought, she is neither mocked nor punished by Lawrence for her temerity. Her sexual remoteness does not merit castigation and, although she remains superconscious, she is allowed some intuitive insight into it. We have come a long way from Ethel Cane.

4
Motherhood

To be womanly, in Lawrentian terms, does not necessarily mean to be a mother. Indeed, motherhood is often seen as a positive hindrance to womanliness, that is, to a woman's self-realization. Both Letty in *The White Peacock* and Anna in *The Rainbow* are slaves to motherhood, Letty resigned and resentful, Anna triumphant in her acceptance of the female anatomy as destiny. Both women, it is clear, have chosen to narrow their lives, rather than allowing them to expand and flower. Such is Lawrence's overt attitude to motherhood: that it restricts personal growth, especially when it becomes all-absorbing.

But there is a sub-text to this apparently feminist objection to motherhood. Aaron and Lilly both jeer at 'sacred children and sacred motherhood', and Aaron is damned if he will be 'used' by a woman as an instrument to get and rear children. Both men see it as their duty to force women to the recognition that manhood is more important than childhood, that women should care more about the men in their lives than they do about their children. Here the objection to motherhood is not that it hinders women, but that it harms men, in excluding and downgrading them, and is indeed intended to destroy their manliness.

Motherhood gives women too much power. This I believe to be Lawrence's basic attitude, despite his passing sympathy for the tribulations which women actually endure as mothers. He is capable of seeing that motherhood can restrict a woman's power-to-be in the fullest sense, but he seems incapable of understanding the relationship between motherhood and fatherhood. In general the Lawrentian hero perceives fatherhood not as an expression or proof of his manliness, but as a threat to it. At its sourest this view could be expressed as: men want sex and women want children. At its most benign it acknowledges a woman's need for children, while insisting that it remain subsidiary to her need for a man.

What is left out of this triangular relationship is the possibility that a man may also want and need children – and not just as heirs. Because he cannot understand fatherhood, Lawrence comes to misunderstand motherhood, at the same time overvaluing and devaluing it as an institution. And so mothers tend to become either monsters or pitiable apologies for womanhood.

In *Mr Noon* Gilbert and Johanna (only very thinly disguised portraits of Lawrence and Frieda) are delighted to meet Stanley, a young American who is always talking about his mother. The narrator comments: 'But though he was quite a well-bred young man, even I daren't transcribe his language faithfully.' Stanley refers to his mother as a bitch, and denies that he loves her: he is always 'tipping a little fat in his dear mother's steady if neurotic American fire. But there you are – men shouldn't have mothers.' Stanley's mother is an invalid, but he doubts if she will die and claims to be pining for her death, 'mother's little pet lamb' though he is. In her apparent weakness, she is powerful, indestructible, and clearly still holds her son in thrall. For his part, he is not averse to being 'half-smothered' by Johanna, and 'like a queer mother's child, he understood so much of a woman's feelings, particularly of her nerves.' Eventually, and without Gilbert's knowledge, the two of them make love.

Stanley is a transmogrified Paul Morel: charming, childish, rather spoiled and, for all his declared rebellion, still very much the mother's son. And more: a mother's son who commits the Oedipal act, if only by proxy. Revealingly enough, Johanna describes him as 'almost impotent'. The implication is that Stanley's manliness has been destroyed by his overmotherly mother – although the nature and scale of her excessiveness are never made plain.

Pauline Attenborough in 'The Lovely Lady' is another monster-mother, but of a rather subtler kind. When the story opens she is a perfectly preserved woman of seventy-two who can 'still sometimes be mistaken, in the half-light, for thirty'. Pauline lives with her son Robert, and her niece Cecilia, who is financially dependent on her. Ciss, thinks Pauline, is in love with Robert, but she also knows that the stronger relationship is that between mother and son. Herein lies her power and the secret of her everlasting youth. Robert is shy and silent, but secretly passionate.

And how Pauline could play on this! Ah, Ciss was not blind to the eyes which he fixed on his mother, eyes fascinated, yet humiliated, full of shame. He was shamed that he was not a man. And he did not love his mother. He was fascinated by her, completely fascinated. And for the rest, paralysed in lifelong confusion.

He is in his mother's power, but this is not the power of love: rather the power to stun and hold immobilized. If Ciss wants to marry him, she will have to take the initiative.

She discovers that Robert's brother Henry died (or killed himself) after his mother had prevented him from marrying the woman he loved, and that Robert is actually the son of an Italian priest rather than of Pauline's former husband. This information can be used against Pauline, who has in effect murdered one son and, by denying the truth, is well on her way to at least the soul-murder of the other. When found out, she crumples and begins to look her age, as well as becoming openly spiteful towards the young people. They draw closer as Pauline takes to her bed, and one night Ciss asks Robert if he thinks his mother ever loved anyone.

He looked at her fixedly.
'Herself!' he said at last.
'She didn't even *love* herself,' said Ciss. 'It was something else. What was it?' She lifted a troubled, utterly puzzled face to him.
'Power!' he said curtly.
'But what power?' she asked. 'I don't understand.'
'Power to feed on other lives,' he said bitterly. 'She was beautiful and she fed on life. She has fed on me as she fed on Henry. She put a sucker into one's soul and sucked up one's essential life.'
'And do you forgive her?'
'No.'

Mothers are supposed to feed rather than feed on their children, and to nurture their self-awareness rather than empty them of their manliness. Robert's bitterness resembles that of Mrs Morel towards Miriam, a bitterness which Miriam and Paul might both have felt with more justification towards her.

It is not only sons who are overpowered by their mothers. In 'Mother and Daughter', Virginia Bodoin, aged thirty, is deserted by her fiancé, Henry Lubbock, 'for two good reasons. He couldn't stand her mother. Her mother couldn't stand him.' Mother and daughter are a sort of couple, much as Lou and Mrs Witt, but Virginia is no match for Rachel, and finds herself abetting the older woman's attempts to humiliate Henry 'in a helpless sort of family loyalty'. Virginia doesn't really want to join in,

But when her mother egged her on, she couldn't help it. For ultimately her mother had power over her; a strange *female* power, nothing to do with parental authority ... another much subtler form of domination, female and thrilling, so that when Rachel said: 'Let's squash him!' Virginia had to rush wickedly and gleefully to the sport.

Women, Lawrence concludes, 'very often hypnotize one another' into destructive behaviour towards men. In a perversion of the maternal relationship, Virginia and her mother are both witches. 'She was a young, weak, spendthrift witch, accomplice of her tough-clawed witch of a mother.' This is of course standard misogynistic paranoia, but Lawrence reserves his revenge, as so often, for the older woman.

Mrs Bodoin wants Virginia to marry, but the man must be one she can consider worthy of her daughter. When Virginia meets a sixty-year-old Armenian, her mother refers to him as 'the Turkish Delight', and feels 'disgust at being forced into contact with such scum'. For his part, M. Arnault sees Mrs Bodoin as a handsome figure, while his inner voice is asking, 'But what under holy heaven, are you as a woman? You are neither wife nor mother nor mistress, you have no perfume of sex ... No man on earth could embrace you.' Mrs Bodoin is unforgivable because she is unwomanly. She is unwomanly because she cannot be seen either as a mother (from which role she should be superannuated by now) or as an object of sexual desire. Although Arnault is supposedly expressing the views of the Eastern male, it is clear that his summation of Mrs Bodoin is intended as a general condemnation.

When she is told that Virginia and Arnault are to marry, Mrs Bodoin is at first incredulous, then sarcastic, and finally moves out into a hotel. Unlike Virginia, she is not woman enough to recognize and respond to Arnault's 'reptilian' virility. She openly and contemptuously accuses her daughter, as Kate inwardly accuses Teresa, of being 'the harem type'. But Virginia is not fazed, and when her mother tells her, 'You have *all* my pity,' replies, 'Thank you, dear. You have just a bit of mine.' There is, however, no doubt as to which woman Lawrence thought to be the more deserving of our pity.

Both Pauline Attenborough and Rachel Bodoin are monsters partially because they, like Mrs Morel, seek to prevent their offspring's marriages. They are both sexless and loveless old women, the one delighting in her own beauty, the other in her own cleverness, who get their kicks from the exercise of power. What Lawrence fails to see in Mrs Morel, he sees all too damningly in other mothers, other women over fifty. These are the 'grimalkins' who cause such fear and repulsion in Kate Leslie that she is induced to accept, at least in part, a marriage which resembles that of Virginia Bodoin. Lawrence's hostility towards the older woman seems to grow with the years. It is difficult to know what he expected of such women, and more difficult to resist the impression that what he chiefly resented was their very existence, their continuing existence. In other words: their capacity for survival and their indestructibility.

Just as Stanley resents his mother's longevity, so Lawrence can curse the health and strength of his mother-in-law, the Baroness von Richthofen. In a 1929 letter to Pino Orioli, the woman with whom he once had such an affectionate correspondence has now become 'that terrible old woman', on a par with every other huge German female who is as terrifying as she is greedy. 'Truly old and elderly women are ghastly, ghastly, eating up all life with hoggish greed. I know my mother-in-law would secretly gloat if I die at 43 and she lived on at 78. She would feel an ugly triumph.' These are of course the words of a sick and dying man, but their virulence is still remarkable, and all the more so because Lawrence's strictures about the old (which may very well be true enough) apply only to old women, and not to old men. They apply even more particularly to mothers who live on and on, threatening to outlive their children. They are reluctant to relinquish their power, their stranglehold on life, and on the lives of their children.

The Baroness in *Mr Noon* (based on Frieda's mother) is much the same sort of monster. Johanna has left her husband and children to elope with Gilbert, and it is her mother who reminds her of her duties, especially her maternal ones. She expresses herself volubly, and Gilbert can only gaze at her, shrinking and incapable of speech. Later Johanna berates him for his lack of manliness in failing to stand up to her mother. Thus Gilbert is unmanned twice over, first by the Baroness and then by her daughter. Each in her own way is formidable, but whereas Johanna is accessible to Gilbert through sex, the Baroness is not (nor would he want her to be) and therefore remains triumphant. Her bulk, her rank, her articulacy, all indicate her power; her distance from Gilbert ensures that she keeps it. He is too much in awe – albeit resentfully – of mothers in general to be able to challenge her.

But at the same time Gilbert is challenging the importance of Johanna's own motherhood, as Lawrence challenged Frieda's, in expecting her to abandon her children for him. Johanna's husband Everard, like Frieda's husband Ernest Weekley, writes bitterly abusive letters to his wife, calling her a whore and insisting that her immoral union with Gilbert has rendered her unfit for motherhood. He, being the injured party, will keep the children and not allow them to see their mother, who will be a bad influence on them.

This is the moral dilemma which Lawrence and Frieda had to face themselves, and it was obviously agony for both of them, as well as the cause of many a quarrel. Ultimately the decision had to be Frieda's, and it seems that Lawrence gave her very little help towards it, disdaining as he did to persuade or cajole. In the foreword to *The First Lady Chatterley* she wrote:

The price I had to pay was almost more than I could afford with all my strength. To lose those children, those children, that I had given myself to, it was a wrench that tore me to bits. Lawrence suffered tortures too. I believe he often felt: have I really the right to take this woman from her children?

Take her he nevertheless did, while managing to absolve himself of the ultimate responsibility: she had made her decision, and she must abide by it without repining. Easier said than done, and the children ('duds' Lawrence called them) remained a cause of contention between them. It seems more than probable that Lawrence was jealous of Frieda's children and that he believed, like Aaron and Lilly, that motherhood would give the woman too much power within the marriage, swinging the balance in favour of the female. It is not surprising that Lawrence's attitude towards children tends to become increasingly more callous. The early novels and stories are full of babies and children, all described with sympathy, tenderness and a kind of lingering fascination. There are no children at all in the later novels until we come to *Lady Chatterley's Lover*, where Mellors's little girl by the wife who has misused him (or so he believes) is treated with extraordinary malevolence. When her gamekeeper father shoots a cat, the child is upset and weeps, but her tears are not seen by Lawrence as an instance of tenderness or compassion. They indicate instead that she is a 'false little female' and 'already as full to the brim of tricks as a little monkey' in using tears to win sympathy or, as in this case, sixpence from Lady Chatterley. The child has become the enemy of the man, in league with women (her mother, her grandmother and perhaps Connie herself) against him. As the property of his estranged wife, she has learned from her mother the tricks and the self-assurance which guarantee that she will get the better of men. This is surely a perverse attitude towards a child's tears for the death of a cat.

Lawrence's central couples are all childless, and for most the question of parenthood never even arises. Again and again Lawrence insists that the crown of womanhood is not motherhood but wifehood. It is sexual desire which is the flame of human life, as the scarlet petals of the poppy described in the 'Essay on Thomas Hardy' proclaim its own peculiar and consummate existence. The poem, 'Rose of All the World', using the same metaphor, asks the questions:

How would you have it? – the rose is all in all,
Or the ripe rose fruits of the luscious fall?
The sharp begetting or the child begot?
Our consummation matters or does it not?

There is an element of the rhetorical in those questions, plainly
addressed to a woman, and Lawrence leaves us in doubt as to his
male-oriented answer:

To me it seems that the fruit is just left over
From the red rose flower's fiery transience . . .

And he goes on to urge, 'Blossom, my darling, blossom, be a rose',
a flower with no other purpose than to be itself, just as Ursula is at
her best when she is flower-like, just as Kate is at her most
womanly when she allows the petals of her soul to unfold.
   But, as every schoolgirl knows, the aim and end of each plant is
to bear fruit. The need to deny supremacy to motherhood (a state
which either reduces the male to helpless dependence or leaves
him out of the picture altogether) is so strong that Lawrence is
prepared to distort botany in the attempt to prove his point. There
are many women as well as men today who would agree with him
and place sexual coupledom well above parenthood in their scheme
of things. This is of course a convenient and self-enhancing belief
for men. Why women are prepared to go along with it is a different
matter, and one which would benefit from some soul-searching
investigation. Of all Lawrence's central loving couples only Connie
and Parkin/Mellors are allowed to have a child – and that posited
in the future – because they exemplify the fulfilment of Lawrence's
life's work: 'sticking up for the love between men and women'.
Lou Carrington thinks that men and women should stay apart until
they have learned to be gentle with one another: Connie and
Parkin/Mellors are shown in the process of learning this very
lesson. In a letter to Catherine Carswell, Lawrence describes a

disastrous act of love . . . which is pure thrill, is a kind of friction between
opposites, interdestructive, an act of death. . . . But there must be an act
of love which is a passing of the self into pure relationship with the other,
something new and creative in the coming together of lovers, in their

creative spirit, before a new child can be born: a new *flower* before there can be the seed of a child.

Lady Chatterley and her lover discover this new flower in themselves, in each other, and in their relationship, and so the flower can be allowed to fruit. Because a child is not necessary, a child can (just about) be allowed.

I say 'just about' because Lawrence seems to have modified his views on motherhood throughout the three different versions of the novel, starting off with a sympathetic attitude and gradually reverting to something approaching his more usual position of hostility. In *The First Lady Chatterley* Connie misses sex and motherhood in more or less equal proportions. She is in her late twenties and married to Sir Clifford Chatterley, a mine-owner of forty or so, who has been wounded in the 1914–18 war and is now confined to a wheelchair, an impotent cripple. From the beginning of this version of the novel Clifford is worried not only about his inability to father an heir for Wragby Hall, but also about his wife's suppressed sexuality, which he thinks will lead to trouble later on. Speaking 'bravely and a little glibly', he advises her, 'Have a lover, if you have to!'

Later she asks him if he would mind if she had a child. His answer is what he sees as the only pertinent question: 'Whose child?' This is the one question that Connie refuses to answer: does it matter whose child it is? It does indeed matter to Clifford, who wants to bring up any children there may be as his own. To Connie, Clifford is 'plucky but not human'. She cannot think of a child, as he does, as merely a son and heir, but as 'a fresh fountain of life', which may 'be able to discover a new immortality in which the disembodied ideal had some sort of body again'.

To her lover, the gamekeeper Parkin, she says, 'There is something beautiful in you. I should be glad to have your children.' For her the passionate connection with the man and the desire to bear his children are both part of the same process, the process which is evident in the soft flow of natural life in the woods where they make love. During her pregnancy she flowers and begins to loathe both Clifford and Wragby: 'the cold emptiness of that way of life, the toughness, the insentience, the negative sort of tyranny'. She knows it will be impossible for her to have Parkin's child and then hand it over to Clifford to become 'a Chatterley and a baronet and a gentleman and another cold horror'. Parkin is the fire of life at which she has warmed her hands, and 'I *won't* spit in the fire.'

Nevertheless Parkin is not particularly interested in the prospect of a child, and seems not to mind handing it over to become a little Chatterley. The child, he tells her friend Duncan Forbes, is Connie's business, not his. He cannot altogether trust her maternal feelings, especially when they threaten to spill over in his direction. Lawrence takes it upon himself to comment:

But a maternal tenderness only occupies the breast of a woman. It does not go deep down into the sources of her being. There in the depths only the tenderness of the unknown can penetrate, and the warm gleam of the man, the male she loves ... With Constance, again, the deeps of her female self were closed up, and the mysterious stream of desire was stopped. She was living from her upper, superficial, maternal self.

It seems to me significant that this almost complete turnaround in the novel's attitude towards motherhood should come to us, not through Parkin and still less through Connie herself, but directly through the authorial voice. Lawrence knows perfectly well that Connie cannot think of her maternal self as superficial. What woman can? And who can know better than Lawrence himself the profundity of maternal tenderness? There is probably a twofold denial going on here: a denial of the importance of his own relationship with his mother; and a denial of the importance of Frieda's relationship with her children. If he grants the former, he is bound to grant the latter.

Connie has already told Duncan that when the child comes, she is afraid that she will love it. 'And suddenly as she spoke, her breath went, and her heart ran hot. The colour swept up in pain to her face and throat.' Just as Mrs Morel loved Paul at once and against her will, in tenderness and pain. As the pregnancy proceeds, 'a deep, voluptuous, almost lascivious indolence and contentment had come over her, a strange female contentment that had something vindictive in it.' The vindictiveness is presumably intended for the male of the species.

Let no one disturb her! Particularly let no man disturb her or lay his thoughts on her. She felt she could tear him open with one stroke of her paw if he tried. Parkin or Duncan – *à la bonne heure!* Let them keep out of her way. It was her hour now, absolutely her own womb-filled female hour.

Motherhood represents the triumph of the female over the male, and with it the female's loss of sexual desire for the male.

This reads to me like another paranoid male fantasy. Maybe there are women who feel vindictive towards men during pregnancy, but I doubt if there are many of them. Again, Lawrence seems to understand so well up to a point, then draws the wrong conclusions. Connie's catlike and voluptuous feeling of existing only in and for her own pregnant body is utterly convincing. Pregnancy does bring with it a peculiar form of self-absorption. But it is not directed against men: rather, it is directed in favour of the coming child. If men choose not to be emotionally involved in the process, that is their problem, and their failing.

Similarly, it is all very well to describe the contentment of pregnancy, but what about the doubts and fears? Not many women can undertake pregnancy – let alone a first-time and illegitimate pregnancy – in a spirit of complete fearlessness and self-confidence. Certain questions will inevitably be asked. Will it be a difficult birth? How much pain will I have to suffer? Will the child be all right? And so on. Pregnancy is a time when one needs a great deal of emotional support, however trivial the daily social round may seem. It seems to me that here Lawrence underestimates the vulnerability of women in depicting the pregnant female body as an impregnable fortress. And, in doing so, he overestimates the power of motherhood.

Connie, however, does not exclude Parkin entirely. When Clifford addresses her as a virgin mother, a Madonna and a wonderful woman, whom he worships, she is nauseated by his behaviour and begins to feel frightened, cold and dead.

Just to suit himself, his own selfish egoism, she had now become a stainless mother, a virgin big with yet another virgin birth. How horrible! A virgin birth in itself was an obscenity when she felt the warmth of the man inside her. How insulting to charge her with a virgin birth!

Clifford has committed the unforgivable sin of leaving the man out of the reckoning because he himself is out of it anyway. He is also cutting Connie off from Parkin and, because she has been missing him, Clifford has hit home. Now, again, she wants 'the tender rosy thing that was between them', and feels she has betrayed it by telling Clifford about the child.

Fool that she had been to trifle with her very life, and the whole life of the child. She might as well have tried to break the great blood-vessel that fed the child in her body, and let herself bleed to death, and the child be a clod of clay. For the child's sake, even, how could she think of that death-in-life, dooming it to Wragby!

She will divorce Clifford and become Mrs Parkin, taking her new husband seriously in his 'manly fucking'.

In this version of the novel the woman is seen to be capable of reconciling the potentially conflicting demands of child and man, and of obviating any sibling rivalry between them. Or, at least, she is seen to be tentatively embarking on such a course. She can do so because she has a proper respect for the man as a sexual being as well as for herself as both wife and mother.

In the second version, *John Thomas and Lady Jane*, Connie is somewhat ambivalent about motherhood from the start. 'Even if she had children, she did not imagine they would *really* have mattered deeply to her: not to her own individual life.' And she compares the dutiful motherhood of her sister Hilda with her own dutiful housewifery. 'There was nothing at all profound in it. There was even no real experience in it.' But when she listens to Clifford and his male guests discuss the immortality of the body in their abstract, philosophical terms, she begins to yearn for a child. At this stage, it is not Parkin's child she wants. The implication is rather that, for a woman, immortality comes in the form of motherhood, whereas men achieve it through actions which are not dependent upon the life of the body. Because she is a woman, the male concept of immortality is repugnant to Connie. And here Lawrence seems to be on her side.

Once the affair with Parkin is under way, the desire to have his child grows unconsciously in Connie. She pays a visit to Mrs Flint, a neighbour of her own age who has a ten-month-old baby. There she enjoys the 'quiet female atmosphere' as the two of them sit 'talking about the baby, and everything that came up'. On her way back from this visit she meets Parkin by accident in the wood, and they experience their first simultaneous orgasm. All at once Connie is able to admit her now conscious desire to bear his children. 'At the thought of him a flame went through her bowels. She wanted his children.' The chain of events is subtly and convincingly linked, and at first it seems that this Connie too will be able to reconcile the demands of child and man, of motherhood and wifehood.

But *John Thomas and Lady Jane* is a more complex novel than its predecessor, and Lawrence does not leave the matter there. This Connie has not yet learned from her lover that the events in which the penis takes part occupy centre stage, while those which take place in the womb constitute a sideshow. Thinking of Parkin, she finds that

he did not touch her heart. That, as usual, remained free. Nobody touched her heart, except, perhaps, children. Yes, her heart belonged to children. Clifford, she was attached to him personally. The other man held her with passion. Nothing and nobody held her altogether and she did not want it.

Connie is partially operating from her superficial, maternal self, and the distinction between it and her dark, passional self is both clear and convincing without the jarring intervention of the authorial voice. This Connie is altogether tougher and sharper than either her predecessor or her successor, and it is entirely credible that she should divide herself consciously in this manner.

Parkin is dumbfounded when she reveals to him her conversations with Clifford about the possibility of a child. He has assumed that she has been taking some sort of contraceptive measures. With some embarrassment he asks her if this is what she has wanted him for: a child. But 'she was silent, so confused, she did not know.' Eventually she manages to say that she wants him *and* a baby. After they have made love, he speaks his piece.

'Whether tha gets thee a childt or whether tha doesna, we'n 'ad summat for ouselves,' he said with that darkening glow of afterwards. But there was a tension on his brow. And she felt his heart accused her.

He himself has no particular desire to be a father. He is one already, and there is a hint that Connie is jealous that he should have a child with another woman.

If the world were different, she and Parkin agree, she would live with him as his wife, and have his children. As it is, any child she bears will have the advantage of being raised as the heir to Wragby. Clifford now has another stipulation to make: that the father of the child must be English 'and of at least *decent* descent'. He has changed and become bitter and sarcastic on the subject of Connie's proposed maternity, warning her that if she falls in love, he will not necessarily grant her a divorce. His attitude frightens Connie, but she is more frightened by Parkin and his influence over her: the influence to which her dark, passional self responds. But she is not frightened of having a baby. It seems that a child would serve as a buttress, not only between herself and Clifford, but between herself and Parkin.

On holiday in Italy with Hilda, Connie begins to change her mind. When she suspects that she is pregnant, she is not glad, but uneasy, almost wanting to put the whole thing off. But when Hilda advises her that it would be better to end the 'intrigue' if she has a child, Connie is mortally insulted.

Why she didn't know if it was even conceived. And if it was, she felt she almost hated it in advance for foisting itself on her. The child! It would be another *substitute*. It would once more be margarine, when she asked for butter. And everybody, her family even, and Clifford, would think that now, now, with the child, the margarine for the rest of her life, she should be purely satisfied.

The butter is presumably sexual passion, for which motherhood is no substitute. She concludes that, faced with such a choice, she will have to leave Clifford.

Parkin's wife has reappeared and caused a scandal in the village by insisting that he take her back, meanwhile revealing in public the details of their marital life. Once back in England, Connie tries to comfort him, but finds that she does not want him sexually – only to be near him and to touch him. When he asks if her attitude is the result of her pregnancy, she tells him, 'But I care more about *you* than the child . . . I want *you* more than a child.' She has made her commitment, to his satisfaction as well as her own.

But in the deadening atmosphere of Wragby she feels abandoned by him, concluding that 'he was selfish, like all men, and only aware of himself.' She knows now with certainty that 'she must go, for her own sake, for the sake of her own decency. Parkin or no Parkin, child or no child, she must go.' This Connie is capable of seeing herself more consistently than do the others as separate from both child and man. She is being dragged under by Clifford and his nurse, being 'made to produce children to keep their uncanny game going in the next generation'. It is no longer sexual passion but self-preservation which motivates her. And with it comes the need to preserve or save future generations from all that Clifford and Wragby stand for.

The novel ends uncertainly, with the lovers parted, and Parkin willing to accept the child – if only for Connie's sake.

She put her fingers to his face, and he turned his head and kissed them softly, laying his hand with sure instinct on her belly, where the fret was, and the coming child. Softly he seemed to gather her belly and her womb into the safe warmth of his hand that pressed so still across her navel. And it was like the sudden warmth of the sun after a bitter winter.

This Parkin is capable of accepting the coming child in tenderness, however bleak the future. It is a tentatively hopeful conclusion, but the hope lies in the lovers' eventual reconciliation, with parenthood very much a subsidiary consideration.

In *Lady Chatterley's Lover* (the third and, until recently, the only available version of the novel) it is Clifford rather than Connie who first mentions the possibility of a child. When they are taking an outing in the wood, he recognizes that it is here more than anywhere else that he minds not having a son (and it is a *son* he mentions) who will be a link in the chain of property-owning Chatterleys. It is with 'a curious impersonality' that he asks Connie to consider the possibility of having a child by another man. For his part, he does not 'believe very intensely in fatherhood', but rather that a child reared by Connie and himself would become their own. Even sex is not particularly important, and the matter should be arranged quite simply, like going to the dentist. What counts in marriage is companionship, 'the long, slow, enduring thing : . . . that's what we live by.'

In this version of the novel men are the movers, and Connie an uncertain and confused woman who reacts slowly. What shakes her is that 'the child, her child, was just an "it" to him. It . . . it . . . it!' She then asks Clifford about the putative 'other man'. Would he not mind who he was? In view of the fact that Connie is currently having an affair with Michaelis (a character who does not appear in either of the earlier versions) and a man of whom Clifford heartily disapproves, his reply is ironic: 'I should trust your natural instinct of decency and selection. You just wouldn't let the wrong sort of fellow touch you.' Neither will he want to know the identity of the man involved.

This Clifford is more self-confident than his predecessors and (like the third version of the gamekeeper) rather nastier, more of a bully, his very confidence constituting a threat. He does all the talking and Connie listens hesitantly, 'a little overwhelmed', as she will later be by Mellors. It is clear that she has given no thought to the future, but has been taking life as it comes. Now, however, she begins to wonder if she will in fact be spending the rest of her life with Clifford. Children are, in any event, a remote possibility.

Even when she thinks later about motherhood, it is in terms of 'one of the sensations' she has yet to experience. Although she knows several men 'who would have been quite possible as lovers', there is not a man in the world whose child she wants. The desire for a child is contingent upon finding the right man, and because she is in no hurry, the idea of motherhood remains 'at the back of her mind'. After she has become aware of the gamekeeper, Mellors, it begins to edge itself forwards.

Once the affair has begun, Connie goes to visit Mrs Flint, as in *John Thomas and Lady Jane*. But here, as befits the increasingly male-centred version of events, the relationship between the two women is underplayed. Connie finds Mrs Flint, like Mellors's daughter, 'a false little thing', and their conversation is dismissed as 'real female chat'. Mrs Flint is 'flaunting her motherhood', and Connie is 'just a little bit jealous'. When she takes the child on her

knee, getting 'a deep, voluptuous pleasure out of its soft young
warmth', she is led at once to speculate on the fear and narrowness
in most people's lives. Rather than being moved not-quite-
consciously by a womanly desire to have a child, she begins to
theorize like a typically bilious Lawrentian hero. She cannot after
all be allowed the pure moment of maternal desire unless it has
been overlaid with Mellors's contempt for the modern world. This
is an altogether more pointed and upfront version of the episode.
And the point seems to be to place the man more firmly in the
picture.

Again, as in the previous version, this episode is followed by the
accidental encounter in the wood, from which Connie and Mellors
gain mutual satisfaction. Again, Connie is led immediately to a
conscious desire to bear the gamekeeper's child. But this Connie
is sure where her primary loyalty lies.

'If I had a child!' she thought to herself, 'if I had him inside me as a
child!' – and her limbs turned molten at the thought, and she realized the
immense difference between having a child to oneself, and having a child
to a man whom one's bowels yearned towards. The former seemed in a
sense ordinary; but to have a child to a man whom one adored in one's
bowels and one's womb, it made her feel she was very different from her
old self, and as if she was sinking deep, deep to the centre of all
womanhood and the sleep of creation.

This child is, in the most blatantly Freudian sense, a substitute for
the penis. And it is only once she has abandoned the superconsciousness of modern woman for a 'helpless adoration' for a man
that this Connie is ripe for motherhood.

Now of course children are brought into the world for all sorts
of reasons, some more worthy than others. And of course there is
all the difference between having a child 'to oneself', and having a
child which is born out of love and is a mutual undertaking. In the
first, and to a lesser extent the second, versions of the novel I find
evidence by implication of both love and mutuality in the conception
of the child. But here, perhaps because Lawrence is so explicit
(and indeed insistent) I think there is something else going on. It
amounts almost to superstition: that good fucking makes good

children. Further, that good fucking entails helpless adoration, which is to say, submission, on the part of the woman. Thus does the man get in on the act, as it were, of procreation, arrogating to himself the role of prime mover. Such an assumption would be all very well if any of Lawrence's gamekeepers were capable of seeing himself as an actual father, more so if any were openly desirous of such a role. But no – all three declare the child to be the woman's business. The man is a son of God, a visitation, but the woman is a daughter of men who must endure pregnancy and childbirth alone. Such is Lawrence's limited understanding of fatherhood.

Mellors alone makes some attempt to justify his attitude. After a Birkin-type diatribe against modern industrial civilization, he tells Connie, 'It seems to me a wrong and bitter thing to bring a child into the world.' This is a poor excuse. The world is in a rather worse state today than it was in the 1920s, but this fact has not noticeably prevented the human race from reproducing itself: even the Greenham women, whom we must assume to be more than usually mindful of the threat of nuclear holocaust, have babies. Connie too is less than convinced and begs Mellors to tell her that he wants a child in hope. At the end of the novel he seems to have gained some hope from her, but he is still insisting that there are bad times just around the corner for the industrial masses, and that 'you can't insure against the future, except by really believing in the best bits of you, and the power beyond.' The best bits in himself and Connie consist in 'the little flame between me and you', and the baby is 'a side issue'. Connie never goes so far as to call her child a side issue, but she seems by default to accept Mellors's judgment. We learn little of her feelings about her pregnancy, and all her rhapsodizing is reserved for the joy of fucking Mellors and the power of the penis.

This is false, even in Lawrence's own terms. In all three versions of the novel the affair between Connie and the keeper is precipitated by the same episode: the hatching of the pheasant chicks in the wood. In all three it is the sight of the vulnerable newborn creatures which moves her to tears. Here is a woman who yearns, however unconsciously, for motherhood. It is Connie's longing for children quite as much as sexual desire which leads her into a relationship with the man. The novelist knows better than the propagandist. But if we take the propagandist seriously, we are left, at the end of *Lady Chatterley's Lover*, to draw the conclusion that the Connie who wept over the pheasant chicks now knows better, and has learned to devalue childbearing in relation to the power of male sexuality.

We are back once again with the notion (which in fact Lawrence never abandoned despite *St Mawr*) of the prime human relationship being a sexual one between one man and one woman, to the partial or total exclusion of all other relationships. After all his thought-adventuring, Lawrence has returned to a conventional belief in heterosexual monogamy. He called the relationship marriage, whether or not it was formally recognized by Church or State, and he believed in it passionately, almost desperately. It seems to me that Lawrence's view of marriage entails the elevation of psychological needs into a religion.

Those are of course male psychological needs, and more especially those of the mother's son fighting to establish and maintain his own separate male identity. It is paradoxical that Lawrence, like Stanley the mother's son, is capable of understanding and sympathizing with women so well when he chooses to do so, and yet at the same time so often incapable of accepting and absorbing the meaning of either his understanding or his sympathy. But I think it also makes sense: women must remain the other, must be kept firmly on the other side of a sexual division in order to give definition to the elusive concept of maleness. Thus men and women are constantly at war, jarring opposites. It is only in marriage that the opposites can be truly reconciled and both warriors arrive at some sort of peace – even if it is only a truce.

PART THREE
Marriage

1
Theory/essays

The whole thrust of Lawrence's work is towards wholeness: the unity of being and of experience. This means not only the integrity of the microcosm which is a human being, but the integrity of the universe, the macrocosm of which the human individual is inevitably a part. In seeing the modern world as fragmented and mechanical, Lawrence was accusing it of a lack of integrity. For him, order was not to be produced out of chaos through the workings of the mind, however rational, nor yet through the products of the mind, however technically perfect. On the contrary, order and meaning already exist in the universe and can be apprehended only through intuitive sympathy or blood-knowledge, a process from which modern men and women have alienated themselves. Because they are out of connection with themselves, they are also out of connection with one another, and hence with the whole series of shifting complexities which constitute life as part of the natural world.

It follows that 'getting into connection' – whether with oneself, another, others or the flow of all natural life – is the major life task of every human being. In his *Study of Thomas Hardy* Lawrence contrasts the poppy, 'this flame of the phoenix', with the cabbage, 'hidebound, a bunch of leaves that may not go any further for fear of losing its market value'. It is the poppy, flaming scarlet and excessive, which is true to its own nature, whereas

a cabbage seen straddling up into weakly fiery flower is a piteous, almost indecent sight to us. Better be a weed and noxious. So we remain tight shut, a bunch of leaves, full of greenness and substance.

But the rising flower thrusts and pushes at the heart of us, strives and wrestles, while the static will holds us immovable. And neither will relent. But the flower, if it cannot beat its way into being, will thrash destruction about itself. So the bound-up cabbage is beaten rotten at the heart.

To be true to oneself, to achieve integrity, means to blossom ('Blossom, my darling, blossom, be a rose') – and to do so extravagantly. 'The final aim of every living creature or being is the full achievement of itself.' Here is Lawrence's 'free, proud, single being', whether male or female, in metaphorical terms.

But the supreme achievement of selfhood also consists in the recognition of duality/polarity. 'And necessarily accompanying this more perfect being of myself is the more extended knowledge of what is not myself.' This is the primary duality of self and not-self which forms the basis of individual consciousness. So far, so acceptable to most people, I imagine. But somehow or other, sooner or later, Lawrence's division between self and not-self manages to express itself in the division between male and female. 'But, except in infinity, everything of life is male or female, distinct.' Well, you either believe as much or you do not: like most beliefs, this one is susceptible neither to proof nor to refutation. And, again as with most beliefs, it is more important to understand what purpose it fulfils than to argue for or against it.

If everything and, as Lawrence claims, 'every impulse that stirs in life, every single impulse, is either male or female', then the universe is transformed at one stroke from fragmented chaos into an object, or rather a process, of two distinct halves. The thrust towards wholeness is therefore simplified in that the two halves – which are opposite as well as distinct – hold out some promise of reconciliation, hence of order and meaning. Duality/polarity allows us to preserve our sense of individuality and separation, while also allowing us the out necessary to overcome the ensuing sense of isolation or loneliness. The impulse towards individuation can be reconciled with the impulse towards connection. Each can be justified in itself, while admitting dependence on the other. Thus, each can enhance the other. For Lawrence, both the symbol and the literal embodiment of this primary reconciliation consists in sexuality within a permanent and committed marriage.

Later in the Hardy essay Lawrence explains his absolute distinction between male and female.

In every creature, the mobility, the law of change, is found exemplified in the male; the stability, the conservatism is found in the female. In woman

man finds his root and establishment. In man woman finds her exfoliation and florescence. The woman grows downwards like a root towards the centre and the darkness and the origin. The man grows like the stalk, towards discovery, light and utterance.

This is the age-old division between the mysterious, earthy female and the rational, enlightened male: a division which only a man could make. It leads Lawrence to the bizarre conclusion that it is in the body that men and women are most alike, and that 'in genitals they are almost one'. I would have thought that it was, if anything, the other way round, and that men and women are most alike (barring the accidents of history) in their minds, and least in their bodies, least of all in their genitals. But Lawrence seems to believe that where we are most 'complementary', we are most alike.

Starting from the connection, almost unification of the genitals, and travelling towards the feelings and the mind, there becomes ever greater difference and finer distinction between the two, male and female, till at least, at the other closing in the circle, in pure utterance is a perfect unity, the two in one, united by the Holy Spirit.

This union constitutes the 'Law of Consummate Marriage' in which recognition and reconciliation of opposites play equally important parts. Further: recognition and reconciliation are interdependent.

Lawrence seems to be saying that the sexual act makes us equally aware of our unity and our separateness: that the more aware we are of our separateness, the more capable we are of unity; and the more capable we are of unity, the more we are aware of separateness.

It needs that a man shall know the natural law of his own being, then he shall seek out the law of the female, with which to join himself as complement. He must know that he is half, and the woman is the other half: that they are two, but they are two-in-one.

In becoming purely either male or female, men and women are forced to recognize that they are only halves, that they cannot be anything other than halves, and that their unity is dependent upon those very recognitions. 'Desire', he writes earlier in the essay, 'is the admitting of deficiency.' But what sort of deficiency? Sometimes Lawrence seems to be saying that it lies in being insufficiently well balanced between male and female. At other times he seems to be saying that it lies (for a man) in being insufficiently male, and (for a woman) in being insufficiently female. Both deficiencies, it would seem, can be cured by sex. Such tangles are the inevitable result of drawing too rigid distinctions between male and female.

In the essay 'The Two Principles' Lawrence insists that 'all life depends upon duality and polarity,' and that it is from the union of opposites that all new life springs. The *Study of Thomas Hardy* makes it clear that new life does not necessarily come in the form of children. 'That she bear children is not a woman's significance. But that she bear herself, that is her supreme and risky fate: that she drive on to the wedge of the unknown and beyond.' It is of course union with a man which will lead her to give birth to herself. 'It is so arranged that the very act which carries us out into the unknown shall probably deposit seed for future security to be left behind. But the act, called the sexual act, is not for the depositing of seed. It is for a leaping off into the unknown, like Sappho into the sea.' What both men and women seek in sex, each meeting the other's deficiency, is that further union with the unknown. Lawrence distinguishes here between two ways of loving a woman: the one in which the man claims that the woman is 'administered unto' him; and the other in which the man says, 'she is the unknown, the undiscovered, into which I plunge in discovery, losing myself.' Union with the unknown brings both loss and discovery of self, both death and rebirth.

The idea of rebirth was of great importance to both Lawrence and Frieda, and it is clear that they consciously helped each other towards such a goal. They believed that a man is born twice, once of his mother, and again through his wife or the woman he loves. Through her he is able to father both himself and her, as she is able to give birth to both herself and him. In *Not I But The Wind* . . . Frieda writes: 'Being born and reborn is no joke, and being born into your own intrinsic self, that separates and singles you out from all the rest – it's a painful process.' And again, 'To grow into a complete whole out of different elements that we are composed of is one of our most elemental tasks.' The process of rebirth involves, like Jung's individuation process, a separating and singling out, but is at the same time a drawing together of the disparate parts of the self. Paradoxically, it is within marriage (and perhaps only within marriage) that individuation is achieved.

'We have our very individuality in relationship,' Lawrence writes in 'We Need One Another'. 'Let us swallow this important and prickly fact. Apart from our connections with other people, we are barely individuals, we amount, all of us, to next to nothing.' These strictures are particularly true of relations between men and women. 'It is in relationship to one another that they have their true individuality and their distinct being: in contact, not out of contact.' There is no allowance here for other sorts of relationship, but at the same time it would be a mistake to interpret the primary relationship too narrowly. 'This is sex, if you like. But it is no more sex than sunshine on the grass is sex. It is a living contact: give and take: the great and subtle relationship of men and women, man and woman.'

But at the same time, as Lawrence writes in one of his essays on Melville, 'Each soul is alone, and the aloneness of each soul is a double barrier to perfect relationship between two human beings.' Each soul, Lawrence insists, *should* be alone. He then goes on to quote La Bruyère's maxim (which he cites repeatedly throughout the *Studies in Classic American Literature*): *Tous nos malheurs viennent de ne pouvoir être seuls.* All our problems arise from the inability to be alone, and a perfect relationship, in the sense of perfect correspondence, *should* be impossible.

Every relationship should have its absolute limits, its absolute reserves, essential to the singleness of the soul in each person. A truly perfect relationship is the one in which each party leaves great tracts unknown to the other party.

No two persons can meet at more than a few points consciously. If two people can just be together fairly often, so that the presence of each is a sort of balance to the other, that is the basis of a perfect relationship. There must be separateness as well.

By romantic standards, this does not sound like much of a marriage. But Lawrence's point is that marriage is a matter of balances within balances. Not only does it balance male and female, but also individuality and relationship. It is out of this system of balance or reconciliation that rebirth becomes possible.

So sexuality without procreation is still a creative process. The *Study of Thomas Hardy* goes further in claiming that the sexual act can also give birth to artistic creation. Once the man has recognized that he and the woman are two but two-in-one,

Out of this final knowledge shall come his supreme art. There shall be the art which recognizes and utters his own law; there shall be the art which recognizes his own and also the law of the woman his neighbour, utters the glad embraces between them, and the submission of one; there shall be the art which knows the struggle between the two conflicting laws and knows the final reconciliation where both are equal, two in one, complete. This is the supreme art which yet remains to be done.

Duality/polarity is capable of seeing the male and female principles in conflict, but reconcilable only in terms of the submission of one to the other. A reconciliation in equality may be 'supreme', but it is still seemingly unattainable. The three sorts of art described here constitute a pretty accurate account of the scope and ambition of Lawrence's own work: its difficulties and shortcomings as well as its successes.

There is no mention of the art which recognizes and utters the woman's own law, and no intimation that a woman may be capable of producing any art at all, let alone one which 'knows the final reconciliation'. Nowhere does Lawrence claim that the sexual act may inspire a woman towards creativity, and indeed he wrote to Catherine Carswell (herself a novelist!) that 'there is something tragic and displeasing about a woman who writes.' As the agent for setting both maleness and femaleness to rights, sex presumably makes men better writers than they would otherwise be, and prevents women from writing at all – and a good thing too! For women, writing or any other art is a sort of disease, of which we may be cured by sex. Or, if not entirely cured, then diverted to an ancillary role within the creative process, being allowed to represent the inchoate material out of which true art is fashioned by the male.

Despite the 1914 letter to A. W. McLeod in which Lawrence claimed that 'the only resourcing of art, revivifying it, is to make it more the joint work of man and woman,' it is clear that, whatever the woman's contribution in the way of ideas, or inspiration, she will not be the one who is actually putting pen to paper. In his autobiography, Bertrand Russell claimed that Lawrence himself was his wife's mouthpiece. And in *The Von Richthofen Sisters* Martin Green claims that Lawrence was a co-writer, Frieda's secretary. Both seem to believe that they are giving Frieda all due credit as a writer. Were they themselves women writers, they would not be able to believe any such thing. A writer is a person who writes, and Frieda was not a writer but a sort of Muse, a provider of both sex and ideas – notably ideas about sex.

Martin Green traces the influences Frieda brought to her relationship with Lawrence, and makes a convincing case for their central importance in Lawrence's life and work. Frieda was one of three sisters, daughters of the Baron and Baroness von Richthofen, minor members of the German aristocracy. All three were involved, in varying degrees, in the turn-of-the-century German erotic movement, which probably came into being as a reaction against Prussian militarism and patriarchal values. One of its chief exponents was Otto Gross, by all accounts an extraordinary and charismatic character, who became the lover of both Frieda and her elder sister, Else. Gross had rebelled against his upbringing, more particularly against his father, Hanns, a criminologist and author of the *Handbook for Examining Magistrates*. Otto Gross rejected his uptight bourgeois background for adventures in the psyche: he knew Freud, but became estranged from him; his book *The Secondary Function of the Brain* (1920) was the forerunner of Jung's *Psychological Types* (1920); and he himself became a psychoanalyst, albeit of an unorthodox kind.

Gross insisted on the erotic drive as the mainspring of all meaningful and creative life, and called for a sexual revolution to save the world. He believed that erotic love does not entail identification with the other, but with a third, transcendental element, the relationship itself. And it is this relationship which alone can overcome man's existential loneliness. In these respects (and, indeed, many others) he and Lawrence are of one accord, and it seems probable that Frieda, who had become a radiant exponent of 'free love' under Gross's tutelage, was responsible for the centring of Lawrence's life and work in this area.

But there are also important differences between the two men. Gross was, like Frieda, a hedonist who believed (as Green puts it) that 'only by entering the paradise lost of polymorphous perversity can man renew himself,' whereas Lawrence remained a puritan to the end. Gross was against monogamy, whereas Lawrence endorsed it; Gross advocated homosexuality, whereas Lawrence came to find it abhorrent; Gross was a drug addict, dying self-destructively young, whereas Lawrence was abstemious in all things and died of tuberculosis. Compared to the members of the German erotic movement, Lawrence and Frieda were, no less than Clifford Chatterley, 'conservative anarchists'.

It seems to me that Lawrence would go along with Gross's ideas only to a limited extent, just as he could venture so far and no further into the world of women. Indeed, the two processes often amount to the same abortive journey. But at the same time, there can be no doubt about the importance of Frieda's continuing influence on his work, nor of the ensuing conflict between her feminine or matriarchal values and those of his own neo-patriarchal protest. It is hardly surprising that Lawrence should have arrived at a belief in duality/polarity between the male and female principles, nor yet that he should have recognized the necessity of trying to reconcile the two. In view of his own working-class origins and the peculiar circumstances of his early years as a mother's son, it is also less than surprising that he should, by his own oblique admission, have progressed no further in the attempt than to conclude that the submission of one principle to the other is, at present and in practice, the only solution to the problem.

Even so, Lawrence often goes further than this solution–which then comes to seem like a fall-back position to which he retreats when under threat. In his essay, 'A Propos of *Lady Chatterley's Lover*', he discusses marriage in terms which have less to do with duality/polarity than with a cyclical progression, shifting according to its own seasons and in harmony with those of the natural world. Having posited that 'the sense of the eternality of marriage is perhaps necessary to the inward peace, both of men and women,' he goes on to assert that

Marriage is the clue to human life, but there is no marriage apart from the wheeling sun and the nodding earth, from the straying of the planets and the magnificence of the fixed stars. Is not a man different, utterly different, at dawn from what he is at sunset? And a woman too? And does not the changing harmony and discord make the secret music of life?

Marriage is placed here in some sort of context which will illustrate its variations as well as its constancy. Then, when Lawrence goes on to expand the metaphor, he can also allow that the cyclical process is one of continuing growth.

Is there not some peculiar harmony, through youth, the period of childbirth, the period of florescence and young children, the period of the woman's change of life, painful yet also a renewal, the period of waning passion but mellowing delight of affection, the dim, unequal period of the approach of death, when the man and woman look at one another with the dim apprehension of a separation that is not really a separation: is there not, through it all, some unseen, some unknown interplay of balance, harmony, completion, like some soundless symphony, made out of the soundless singing of two strange and incompatible lives, a man's and a woman's?

This is indeed a paean to marriage, beautiful in its acceptance of unity-in-difference as well as reconciliation-in-equality, and notable for its recognition of the changes which take place in the world of women as well as in the world of men. Here is no special pleading against childbirth or motherhood, and even the menopause is given its due without any of Lawrence's more usual resentment of the older woman. A symphony is a far cry from the noise of the battlefield.

The essay was written very near the end of Lawrence's life, and the above description of marriage reads like a final peace offering. It is of course an idealized as well as a generalized one, the 'phallic marriage' which has significance beyond itself and is part of the order of the universe. It is essentially not a personal relationship:

Now this affinity of mind and personality is an excellent basis of friendship between the sexes, but a disastrous basis for marriage. Because marriage inevitably starts the sex-activity, and the sex-activity is, and always was and will be, in some way hostile to the mental, *personal* relationship between man and woman.

The personal marriage constitutes a meeting or, worse, mingling between two upper, daylit selves, and because it is based upon ego and tied to individuality, is bound to end in hatred. Lawrence never really relinquished this idea: that sexual passion was impossible between two people who could talk to each other.

But how can two intelligent and articulate people not talk to each other? Or, and this is perhaps the more pertinent question, why is the idea of two intelligent and articulate people, one a man and the other a woman, talking to each other such a threat to Lawrence? It seems to me that here we are back yet again with the concept of the frailty of the male, who needs must entertain some idea, any idea, of male superiority in the face of self-evident female strength. Just suppose that, in conversation, a woman might prove herself to be the more intelligent and articulate of the two. Such a supposition is more than the frail male ego can bear. What Lawrence is really saying is that women should not be intelligent and articulate. If we are, we will prove so much of a threat to the male that he will become unmanned. And so not fancy us. Therefore, in being intelligent and articulate, we women are doing ourselves a disservice.

Phallic marriage is essentially a matter of desire, but unlike marriage itself, desire is not constant. Lawrence concludes his essay with the exposition: 'The powers that enter me fluctuate and ebb. And the desire that goes forth from me waxes and wanes. Sometimes it is weak and I am almost isolated. Sometimes it is strong and I am almost carried away.' It is tempting to see more special pleading here: the irony of the priest of love (or rather, sexuality) covertly admitting to a weak erotic drive, which leads him to resent and therefore ignore female sexuality as an active agent. There is some truth in this conclusion, but at the same time something rather more valid is going on here. In the same essay, Lawrence writes: 'A great many men and women today are happiest when they abstain and stay sexually apart, quite clean: and at the same time, when they understand and realize sex more fully.' Chastity is the obverse of desire, and an enhancement of both it and its fulfilment. Once sexual activity becomes forced, that is, a product of the will as in 'personal' marriage, satisfaction is diminished. 'The important point is that sex itself comes to subserve the personality and the "personal" love entirely, without ever giving sexual satisfaction or fulfilment. In fact, there is probably far more sexual activity in a "personal" marriage than in a blood-marriage.' Quantity is not to be confused with quality, because sexual experience is beyond quantification, and the desire which is its true concomitant arises from mysterious and probably unknowable sources.

Setting aside for the moment Lawrence's confusion about what constitutes the 'personal', his assertion that chastity can help us to 'understand and realize sex more fully' seems to be particularly in tune with the mood of the 1980s, that is, a mood which is a reaction against the failed sexual revolution of the 1960s.

Ours is the day of realization rather than action. There has been so much action in the past, especially sexual action, a wearying repetition over and over, without a corresponding thought, a corresponding realization. Now our business is to realize sex. Today the full conscious realization of sex is more important than the act itself . . . When people act in sex nowadays, they are half the time acting up. They do it because they think it is expected of them. Whereas as a matter of fact it is the mind which is interested, and the body has to be provoked.

Lawrence would no doubt be horrified by the latter-day proliferation of sex shops, packed with sexual aids designed to provoke the body in the service of the mind which is convinced, however vaguely, that sexual activity is per se A Good Thing and, by extension, that the more of it we engage in, the better. Needless to say, such a view of sexuality is not based on the flow of spontaneous desire recognized and endorsed by Lawrence, but on 'sex in the head', which constitutes a betrayal of individual integrity as well as a perversion of the individual's ideally harmonious relationship with the natural world of the cosmos. It seems to me that it is only now in the 1980s that we are beginning to take such an idea on board. But, ironically enough from Lawrence's point of view, this has only become possible in the wake of the Women's Movement which has taught women how to say no to any action which is not in accordance with our own desires.

The betrayal which Lawrence envisages consists above all in the split between mind and body – a split which we should be attempting to heal. 'A Propos of *Lady Chatterley's Lover*' lists the perversions which follow on as: the hush-hush puritanism of the past, the modern 'smart licentiousness', and the 'dirty mind'.

In the past 'the mind's terror of the body' ensured that sex remained 'a dirty little secret' like the excretory functions. Lawrence cites Swift's poem to Celia with its astonished and 'maddened refrain, "But Celia, Celia, Celia shits"' and goes on to comment:

Of course Celia shits! Who doesn't? And how much worse if she didn't. It is hopeless. And then think of poor Celia made to feel iniquitous about her proper natural function by her 'lover.' It is monstrous. And it comes from having taboo words, and from not keeping the mind sufficiently developed in physical and sexual consciousness.

Judaeo-Christian morality has taught us to deny that we are bodies in any meaningful sense: it is in our souls, rather, that we should find meaning and identity. Swift's poem is also cited by Ernest Becker in *The Denial of Death*, where he has some illuminating comments to make on the Swiftian madness. According to Becker, 'excreting is the curse that threatens madness because it shows man his abject finitude, his physicalness, the unlikely reality of his hopes and dreams.' The mind's terror of the body is thus not, as Lawrence suggests, merely the product of a single historical moral system, but an existential problem. To deny that we are bodies means to deny that we are mortal, to deny death.

Lawrence does not go as far as making explicit the connection between puritanical disgust and the denial of death. He himself saw immortality, not as a matter of life after death for the body, but as a lifetime's achievement. In 'The Crown' he writes: 'I am not immortal until I have achieved immortality. And immortality is not a question of time, of everlasting life. It is a question of consummate being.' And consummate being means living fully in the body as well as in the mind, unsplit and whole. Here, I think, is another clue to the meaning of 'phallic marriage', in which men and women are 'linked up with the sun and the earth, the moon and the fixed stars . . .' Thus do we attain eternity, infinity, and immortality: bodily death is not denied, but rendered irrelevant. Such an achievement is a matter for rejoicing and for celebrating in creativity. This is an attitude far removed from the guilty delights of the 'dirty little secret' which attempts but fails to deny mortality, and is therefore imbued with death.

But modern 'smart licentiousness' is no answer to the hypocriti- cal secrecy of the past. 'From fearing the body and denying its existence, the advanced young go to the other extreme and treat it as a sort of toy to be played with, a slightly nasty toy, but still you can get some fun out of it before it lets you down.' Straightforward terror has been replaced by trivialization which in turn amounts to another form of fear: the mind's attempt to subdue the body and keep it in its own subordinate place by failing to accord it due serious attention. As a result, the body becomes literally profaned: both desacralized and desecrated. Any sexual act between two such bodies is either purely functional or else functional with an overlay of sentimentality.

Purely functional sex, which uses the body as an instrument for self-gratification, is repellent to Lawrence. 'That ghastly crudity of seeing in sex nothing but a functional act and a certain fumbling with clothes is, in my opinion, a low degree of barbarism.' Here the body is being used as a machine is used, specific actions being directed consciously to specific ends in the deliberate provocation of 'sensations'. This is of course the language of sex manuals and of Masters and Johnson, and betrays an essentially behaviouristic view of the world: that all can be apprehended and, by extension, controlled in simple terms of stimulus and response. In his essay, 'Pornography and Obscenity', Lawrence has the following comment to make on this sort of sexuality:

The unhappy 'free and pure' love of so many people who have taken out the dirty little secret and thoroughly disinfected it with scientific words is apt to be more pathetic even than the common run of dirty-little-secret love. The danger is, that in killing the dirty little secret, you kill dynamic sex altogether, and leave only the deliberate and scientific mechanism.

It is a danger, but not, as Norman Mailer seems to suppose, an inevitable one.

At this point it is worth going back to the argument between Millett and Mailer – which is really an argument about the nature of sexuality. Mailer admits that the image of the woman on the laboratory table experiencing multiple self-induced orgasms (the sort of sexuality advocated as liberating and feminist by Millett) gives him the horrors. 'Why', he asks in what seems to be genuine perplexity as well as the old male fear of female voraciousness, 'did that woman desire such endless satisfaction? ... A man could spend his life looking to answer that question.' Not only a man, Mr Mailer. The image is surely less the expression of poor, starved female sexuality than that of the poor, starved (and lost) soul which, split into body and mind, regards the former as a machine and the latter as its operator.

Is this really the sort of image of womanhood which feminists can wholeheartedly endorse? I think not. One does not have to be a swooning Alvina or Kate to find it both unattractive and sad. Is it even at all representative? Although I often get the feeling that the present-day sexually-frank novel (and not just the popular variety) is actually imbued with a hatred of the body, I should like to believe otherwise. I should like to believe that women (and indeed men too) were getting rather more out of sex than Millett's image implies. And I should like to believe that being a feminist does not necessarily impose limitations on one's sexuality. There is still a lot of thinking and writing to be done in this area.

As the above paragraphs suggest, functional, self-gratificatory sex also carries connotations of masturbation. Lawrence devotes a large portion of 'Pornography and Obscenity' to a condemnation of 'the act of self-abuse', which he sees as the aim and end-result of pornography. It is 'the one functional result of our sex-secrecy' and inevitably produces 'a feeling of shame, anger and futility' which deepens as the years go on 'because of the impossibility of escape. The one thing that it seems impossible to escape from, once the habit has been formed, is masturbation.'

The doctrine of the dirty little secret tacitly accepts the existence of masturbation, hypocritically finding it harmless (because even more secret) when compared to sexual intercourse as an expression of sexuality. Lawrence cannot agree.

The great danger of masturbation lies in its merely exhaustive nature. In sexual intercourse, there is give and take. A new stimulus enters as the native stimulus departs. Something quite new is added as the old surcharge is removed. And this is so in all sexual intercourse where two creatures are concerned, even in the homosexual intercourse. But in masturbation there is nothing but loss. There is merely the spending away of a certain force and no return. The body remains, in a sense, a corpse.

Masturbation is on the side of death rather than life, the ultimate act of sex-in-the-head where the mind must remain in conscious control. Lawrence's view verges on that of the hydraulic model: what is spent out of a presupposedly limited store is lost forever instead of being replaced. This is surely a very male view of masturbation. But his main point is that masturbation excludes mutuality and the reciprocity to be found in sexual intercourse, the reaching out to another person, and thence to the rest of the natural world. Life in the body is essentially a matter of connection.

In making a distinction between the sort of sexuality which is purely functional and the sort of sexuality in which the body is not subjected to the mind, Lawrence is also making a value judgment, which we are free to accept or reject. If I have given the impression that I totally accept it, I must now make a few qualifications. Of course Lawrence is essentially right, that is, he would be right if human beings were perfect creatures living in an ideal world. The trouble is that Lawrence lived on a higher plane than most of us (although he would have denied as much!) and in doing so, often failed to take human frailty into account, let alone extend it any compassion. But it seems to me that both 'loveless fucking' and self-induced orgasms are not necessarily destructive, and have their place from time to time in the scheme of things. Of course, again, if such a functional attitude contained all we ever felt about sex or sexuality, our lives (and not just our sex lives) would thereby be impoverished.

Lawrence was, if anything, even more scornful of the sort of sexuality in which the functional is overlaid with sentimentality, the suggestion being that here is yet another layer of hypocrisy manufactured by the mind in order to keep the body under its control. 'Never was an age more sentimental,' he asserts in 'A Propos of *Lady Chatterley's Lover*', 'more devoid of real feeling, more exaggerated in false feeling, than our own.' That is a matter of opinion, but this surely is not: 'You can fool yourself for a long time about your own feelings. But not forever. The body itself hits back at you, and hits back remorselessly in the end.' All modern humanistic (as distinct from behaviouristic) theorizing about psychic health, as well as the techniques for its furtherance, are based on those very premises.

Lawrence goes further in positing sex as the revealer of hypocrisy, the touchstone of truth.

Sex is the one thing you cannot really swindle; and it is at the centre of the worst swindling of all, emotional swindling. Once come down to sex, and the emotional swindle must collapse. ... Sex lashes out against counterfeit emotion, and is ruthless, devastating, against false love.

People who pretend to love each other (he continues) or pretend to feel more than they actually do, always end up hating each other, sex having shown them up in their mutual swindling. But the process works both ways. 'The element of counterfeit in our love at last maddens, or else kills, sex, the deepest sex in the individual. But perhaps it would be safer to say that it *always* enrages the inner sex, even if it at last kills it.'

Falsity of emotion is a difficult concept to convey in abstract terms, and beyond lashing out at 'intimacy' or 'meeting and mingling', Lawrence does not attempt to do so. The relationship between Gudrun and Gerald in *Women In Love* is presumably an example of counterfeit emotion and emotional swindling. They both feel as the convention of being 'in love' expects them to feel: readily, passionately and overwhelmingly. The short story 'In Love' provides another illustration. Hester and Joe, who have known each other for years, are now engaged to be married, but Hester is beginning to have her doubts.

But now, alas, since she had promised to marry him, he had made the wretched mistake of falling 'in love' with her. He had never been that way before . . . Once he started cuddling and petting, she couldn't stand him. Yet she felt she ought to. She imagined she even ought to like it. Though where the *ought* came from, she could not see.

To see Hester's aversion to cuddling and petting as a sign of frigidity (and it is difficult not to) is to miss Lawrence's point. What is important is that Hester is being drawn into activity which is not in accordance with her feelings. When it turns out that Joe too has been acting according to what he believed was expected of him, Hester's attitude changes. 'And she saw the patient honest love for her in his eyes, and the queer, quiet, central desire . . . A hot flush went over her heart. She felt herself responding to him.' Now that neither of them is acting according to the dictates of the mind, which tells them how they *ought* to behave, even 'cuddling and petting' become permissible.

The third consequence of the split between mind and body is what Lawrence calls the 'dirty mind'. This is the sort of mind which, rather than shrinking in fear from the body or trivializing it, actively denigrates it and derides it. Pornography, 'this furtive, sneaking, cunning rubbing of an inflamed spot in the imagination', is at once the product and the food of such a mind, constituting an 'insult to the human body . . . to a vital human relationship'. In a very revealing passage in the pornography essay Lawrence writes:

It was one of my fond illusions when I was young, that the ordinary, healthy-seeming sort of men, in railway carriages, or the smokeroom of a hotel or pullman, were healthy in their feelings and had a rough, devil-may-care attitude towards sex. All wrong! All wrong! Experience teaches that common individuals of this sort have a disgusting attitude towards sex, a disgusting contempt of it, a disgusting desire to insult it.

These are the men who despise a woman after sex, who 'tell dirty stories, carry indecent postcards, and know the indecent books.' So much for the robust working-class heroes whose ranks Lawrence so often yearned to join. And here, I suspect, is the reason that Mellors becomes so much more of a gentleman than either of his gamekeeper predecessors.

The dirty mind is the one that shits on sex. 'Pornography is the attempt to insult sex, to do dirt on it.' Lawrence finds this unpardonable, and his metaphor then takes on a literal force.

The sex functions and the excretory functions in the human body work so close together, yet they are, so to speak, utterly different in direction. Sex is a creative flow, the excrementory flow is towards dissolution, decreation, if we may use such a word. In the really healthy human being the distinction between the two is instant, our profoundest instincts are perhaps our instincts of opposition between the two flows.

But in the degraded human being the deep instincts have gone dead, and then the two flows become identical. *This* is the secret of really vulgar and of pornographical people: the sex flow and the excremental flow are the same to them ... Then sex is dirt and dirt is sex, and sexual excitement becomes playing with dirt, and any sign of sex in a woman becomes a sign of her dirt.

Brave and, in a sense, optimistic words. There is much here that is admirable, not least Lawrence's implied attitude towards women.

But that distinction between the healthy and the degraded human being gives me pause. Again, Lawrence's rhetoric seems to leave compassion for human frailty out of account. There is no hint that the connection between sexual function and excretory function may be primary, and that the connection is one which we may have to fight from childhood to overcome – especially if we are male: females are less likely to confuse sex and excretion. Much less is there any intimation that, as Becker puts it, 'all the talk about blood and excrement, sex and guilt is true ... because all those things reflect man's horror of his basic animal condition, a condition that he cannot – as a child – understand, and a condition that – as an adult – he cannot accept.' This is as pessimistic a position as Lawrence's is optimistic, and it seems to me that the truth lies somewhere in between: that childish connections between sexual and excrementory functions can be overcome through adult experience.

The flaw in all Lawrence's thinking about sex is that he can see only one sort of sexuality as good and right, and that he divides people into sheep and goats accordingly. But he also deserves credit for attempting to describe this good and right sexuality in action. As every writer knows, it is much easier to write about bad sex than good sex, to be analytical and detached rather than celebratory, and prurient (or, conversely, sentimental) rather than brave and honest. As a novelist, Lawrence is undoubtedly courageous; as a moralist, he is often all too honest for his own good, so much so that he subverts his own case. Nowhere in his work is this process more evident than in his fictional account of phallic marriage.

Individuality and relationship. Chastity and sexuality. Mind and body. Give and take. Male and female. These are the polarities which balance the Lawrentian phallic marriage and are reconciled within it. Or so Lawrence would have us believe. If we now move from theory to practice, that is, from essay to novel, we shall be in a better position to judge whether or not such a marriage is workable – or even desirable. After all, it is in the lives of men and women like ourselves that Lawrence's ideas must be tested and embodied, if they are to prove their worth and convince us, as he would have wished, to attempt to live by them. So now I shall take a look at the four (or is it two?) novels which are most closely concerned with phallic marriage: *Mr Noon* and the three versions of *Lady Chatterley's Lover*.

2
Practice/fiction

The progression of the affair between Lawrence and Frieda
towards marriage is related in the second part of *Mr Noon*
through the personae of Gilbert Noon, an educated working-class
Englishman and Johanna Keighley, a German-born aristocrat with
whom he elopes. Johanna is married to an American doctor and
has two young sons, but is very far from being a devoted wife. She
has love affairs to which her husband turns a blind eye, preferring
to see her as a 'snowflower', and place her on a pedestal so that he
may worship her. She sees herself, on the contrary, as a 'born
dandelion' who loves love and hates worship. All this and more she
conveys to Gilbert within minutes of their first, accidental meeting
at the house of a German professor in Munich.

Johanna is 'glowing' and forthright, and Gilbert is immediately
smitten. 'She was full-bosomed, and full of life, gleaming with life,
like a flower in the sun and like a cat who looks round in the
sunshine and finds it good.' She tells Gilbert about her first lover,
Eberhard (a recreation of Otto Gross) who was a genius and
taught her so much.

He made me believe in love – in the sacredness of love. He made me see
that marriage and all those things are based on fear. How can love be
wrong? It is the jealousy and the grudging that are wrong. Love is so
much greater than the individual. Individuals are so poor and mean – And
there can't be love without sex. Eberhard taught me that. And it is so true.
Love *is* sex. But you can't have your love all in your head, like the saints
did. But I call that a sort of perversion. Don't you? Sex is sex, and ought
to find its expression in the proper way – don't you think? And there is no
strong feeling aroused in anybody that doesn't have an element of sex in it
– don't you think?

Gilbert has heard such ideas before, but has 'never given them
serious attention', and is now troubled by them. 'It all saddened
him, and he did not agree, but did not know what to say.' The

duality/polarity between the lovers is set up at once, and what remains of the novel is concerned with the attempts at reconciliation between the two principles they represent.

That love is both sex and sacred is something Gilbert learns gradually from his relationship with Johanna. The novel is frank about sexual failure, and the couple's first night together (the same as the night they meet) is 'not a success for either of them. The passion did not get free in either, and therefore neither of them felt satisfied or assuaged or fulfilled.' But in the morning they are 'happy, just being together', and Gilbert tells Johanna that she must not go back to America, but stay with him. It is only the following evening that the 'cyclone of actual desire' breaks 'now for the first time upon Gilbert'. Lawrence, in this novel a very intrusive narrator indeed, insists on apostrophizing:

Oh wonderful desire: violent, genuine desire! Oh magnificence of stormy, elemental desire, which is at once so elemental and so intensely individual! Oh storms of acute sex-passion, which shatter the soul, and re-make it, as Summer is made up out of the debacle of thunder! Oh cataclysm of fulminous desire in the soul: oh new arising from the cataclysm.

Here already is the notion of rebirth or 'resurrection' through sexuality, both Johanna and Gilbert going afterwards to dinner, 'fresh in the face' and somehow rejuvenated.

A few days later Johanna confessed to Gilbert she was rather frightened that he would not be a good lover, adding, 'But it isn't every man who can love a woman three times in a quarter of an hour – so *well* – is it?' Gilbert almost blushes, muttering his ignorance of such matters. At first he is put out that 'That's the price she takes me at. Which thought was followed by a second: Yes, and I'd rather!' Lawrence then proceeds to address his women readers, asking, 'at what better price can a woman take a man for good?' Sex is immediately taken as a firm basis for marriage. 'I can see absolutely no sounder ground for a permanent marriage than Johanna's – three times in a quarter of an hour – and so *well*. Then you know what you're in for. Now you're down at the bed-rock of marriage.' This is no personal marriage, based on 'all sorts of spiritual, aesthetic, ethical and intellectual miracles' which a

man and a woman may see in each other, but the burgeoning of
phallic marriage.

The growth towards such a marriage is by no means a smooth
process for Johanna and Gilbert. Besides the difficulties with her
parents, husband and children (which Gilbert finds humiliating
and Johanna confusing) there are arguments between the couple
themselves as to the nature of love between a man and a woman.
Johanna takes sex as her religion, believing that 'one should love
all men; all men are lovable somewhere.' This is what Eberhard,
who loves all women, has taught her. But Gilbert, as his hasty
projection from sex to marriage indicates, is in favour of 'particular
love' rather than the general variety. When Johanna claims that
'the noblest thing is to overcome jealousy', he retorts that jealousy
'is as natural as love or laughter.' She still believes that it is 'mean
and horrible – and marriage is vile and possessive'. Gilbert then
makes his bid for phallic marriage.

If there is physical love, it is exclusive. It *is* exclusive. It's only spiritual
love that is all-embracing. And I'm off spiritual love. – I don't want it. It
stinks. I want exclusive physical love. – There may be aberrations. But the
real fact in physical love is its exclusiveness: once the love is really *there*.

How impersonal such a marriage can actually be, in its exclusiveness, is open to question. This I take to be another Lawrentian
paradox.

There are indeed a couple of 'aberrations' during the affair
between Johanna and Gilbert – and both on Johanna's part. The
first takes place during a week when the two are living apart at the
insistence of her parents. She is unfaithful with a cavalry officer,
Rudolf von Daumling, who has doubts about his own virility,
and writes poetry 'like pus' flowing from a wound. Lawrence's
comments, once more addressed to his women readers, are biting.

But I ask you, especially you, *gentle* reader, whether it is not a noble deed
to give a poor self-mistrustful Rudolf substantial proof of his own virility.
We say substantial advisedly. Nothing ideal and in the air. Substantial
proof of his own abundantly adequate virility. Would it not have been
noble, under the circumstances, to give him the baby's dummy-teat of
ideal sympathy and a kind breast?

So jealousy and possessiveness are both rampant, although Lawrence pretends otherwise. His feelings may well be patriarchal, but
it is surely a mistake to claim that jealousy and possessiveness are
the exclusive properties of either the world of men or the world of
women. They belong rather to the world of frail humanity, here
getting its due recognition for once from Lawrence.

By the time of the second aberration, Gilbert has evolved more
subtle means for dealing with his jealousy. When Johanna confesses
to infidelity with the mother-fixated Stanley, he is at once all
forgiveness, kissing her and clinging to her 'passionately, in a
sudden passion of self-annihilation', and telling her, 'We do things
we don't know we're doing. And they don't signify . . . I love you –
and so what does it matter?' Johanna is unresponsive, resenting
Gilbert's assumption that her aberration does not signify, and
feeling that now she has been put in an even falser position. That
night,

he loved her with a wild, self-abandon. But she kept something hard
against him in the middle of her heart. She could not forgive him for his
forgiveness of her. After all, forgiveness is a humiliating thing to the one
forgiven. And she did not choose such humiliation. Moreover, she did not
like his convulsion of selflessness by means of which he soared above a
fact which she faced him with: thereby leaving her still saddled with the
same self-burdening fact. He seemed to have put her more in the wrong,
and assumed a further innocent glory himself.

There is no doubt here as to whose is the moral victory: Gilbert is
practising what Johanna has been preaching in overcoming his
jealousy, and in the process has confounded her. He can go along
so far with Eberhard's estimation of jealousy, and 'stand aside for a
moment', but a true disciple of the erotic movement would not
have made Gilbert's vengeful bid for moral superiority. And there
is a hint that infidelity and the attendant jealousy will constitute a
recurring problem within the relationship.

Lawrence makes a virtue of the constant argument between the
lovers, warning the gentle reader that 'I have *not* got two turtle
doves in a cage for you.' There is a sort of peace between them, 'a
bridal peace', but it is the peace of 'one who has found his

opposite, his complementary opposite, and his meet adversary.' In Johanna, Gilbert has found 'his soul's affinity and his body's mate: a she-cat who would give him claw for claw, a bitch who would give him snarl for snarl, a falcon who would demand an eye for an eye.' Theirs is the love of two splendid opposites.

Opposition! Wonderful opposition! The whole universe rests on the magical opposition of fire and water, sun and rain . . . Is not the marriage bed a fiery battlefield as well as perfect communion, both simultaneously. Till we know this, we know nothing. And till we fight our fights like splendid royal tigers, in the wonderful connubial rage, we are nothing. We are at deadlock: either waterlogged or gone woody and dry.

Duality/polarity is as much a part of marriage as of the universe in which it belongs. A personal marriage may be 'lovey-dovey' in its intimacy, but the phallic marriage thrives, as does all vivid life, on the tug and clash between opposing principles.

   Gilbert is still admittedly 'but an acolyte at the dionysic or Priapic altar', striving towards becoming a master of the Priapic craft. This is indeed a worthwhile ambition because the 'great eternity of creation does not lie in the spirit, in the ideal. It lies in the everlasting and incalculable throb of passion and desire.' The key word here is 'incalculable', the ambition being incapable of fulfilment by willed, deliberate means.

The Priapic mysteries are not tricks. They can't be learned with the head, nor dictated from the mind, nor practised by deliberate intent. You can no more bring about deliberately, a sexual storm between yourself and your woman than you can bring about a thunderstorm in the air. All the little tricks, all the intensifications of will remain no more than tricks and will-pressure. You have got to release from mental control the deep springs of passion: and after that there has got to be the leap to polarized adjustment with the woman. And these two things are deep mysteries. It takes us a long time, us, to release the profound desires from mental control.

True sexuality is something which can be learned in time – but only through experience on an unconscious level.
   Here I think is the answer to those who claim that Lawrence's men are at pains to deny orgasm – or sometimes the more narrowly defined clitoral orgasm – to their women. It would seem that

Lawrence considers deliberate and prolonged stimulation of the clitoris or any other thus dissociated part of the body as a trick not worthy of the Priapic mysteries, and that any sexual act which requires such mechanical means for its fulfilment does not proceed from the deep springs of passion, but is still under mental control. This does not mean the denial of orgasm. There are orgasms and orgasms, some more mechanical than others. Once again Lawrence is making a value judgment between what he sees as two sorts of sexuality. That the division exists is surely undeniable, but Lawrence's asumption of the superiority of the one over the other carries an unendearing certainty which can end in bragging and smugness.

He continues in the same paragraph to connect the passional, superior type of sexuality with marriage, claiming that the former

needs a basic courage and a strange concerted unison between the two protagonists, which life alone can give ... The deep *accustomedness* of marriage is the only way of preparation. Only those who know one another in the intricate ways of physical custom can pass through the seven dark hells and seven bright heavens of sensual fulfilment. And this is why marriage is sacred.

This is the imagery of the Apocalypse, explicitly connecting sex to marriage and, through marriage, to the sacred. Johanna's husband, Everard, has given her more sensual satisfaction than any of her other lovers, including, at this apprentice stage of his Priapic career, Gilbert himself. But sex is no sacred mystery to Everard: it is a dirty little secret, whose obverse is the worship of woman-as-snowflower. If Everard were capable of recognizing the sacred in sex, Johanna would not be 'racing round looking for sexual love, and taking it from men who could not give her half the passional gratification and fulfilment Everard had given.'

The following implication is that Johanna's marriage has failed, in spite of fulfilling sex, because of Everard's unmanly humility.

If we are sensual, and deeply, utterly so, then let us not be humble about it. Man has his native right to his dark, flaming sensual fulfilment. It is incumbent upon him, and upon his honour he must get his fulfilment.

Shall he creep then for it, and grovel for it: even under the permission of the law?

Sexual fulfilment has become not only sacred, but a sacred crusade, and one which Everard is ill-equipped to undertake. Johanna has been thrown off balance by his humbleness which makes her 'distraught and at last even vindictive. For is it not a maddening thing for a woman to have the deep sensual relation so insulted, written Number 0, like a WC.' Everard, it seems, both cringes before and shits on Johanna – rather like a domestic animal. At any rate, his lack of pride has rendered him less of a man – and less of a man than Gilbert, for all the latter's inexperience. Although such a situation is perfectly possible (in sexual relations anything is possible), this line of argument reads to me like yet another instance of special pleading on Lawrence's part.

Mr Noon is indeed full of special pleading: it insists repeatedly on trying to demonstrate that the sexual relationship between Johanna and Gilbert is of such supreme quality that it sets them apart from the rest of humanity. Given the circumstances of their elopement and the ensuing battles to be fought with the massed and censorious forces of conventional morality, it is easy to see why such attempts are necessary. But there are often elements of self-congratulation in Lawrence's depiction of the relationship – and not just the sexual relationship. These are elements which occur in more blatant form in *Lady Chatterley's Lover*: a bitter and embattled hatred for the rest of humanity, who fail to understand and live out Lawrentian principles and practice. Whereas in *Lady Chatterley* the hatred finds its outlet in a series of diatribes against modern industrial civilization, in *Mr Noon* it more often takes the form of a semi-facetious haranguing of the reader.

One of the main difficulties in the relationship between Johanna and Gilbert is the question of Johanna's children. She misses them, and Gilbert cannot or will not understand. There is pleading in his voice when he reminds her that she has promised not to return to America for another three months. That night, in their 'narrow, passionate bed', he is woken by her sleeplessness, and she retires to the other bed, wanting to be alone. Gilbert spends a night of sleepless horror, much like Gudrun's, and the next morning they both admit that the night was a failure. Lawrence immediately attempts to justify the situation, reminding us of the difference between tigers and doves. We too are urged to abandon our 'lovey-doveyness', and are addressed as 'you sniffing mongrel bitch of a reader, you can't sniff out any specific why or wherefore, with your carrion-smelling, psychoanalysing nose, because there is no why and wherefore. If fire meets water, there's sure to be dust. That's the why and wherefore.'

Sometimes Lawrence's disingenuousness is breathtaking. Here is a woman longing for her absent children, and inwardly resenting the man who not only cannot sympathize, but is also partially responsible for her sense of deprivation. This seems to me to constitute a pretty solid why and wherefore, without the necessity to invoke cosmic forces. Lawrence's resentment of motherhood has led him to reject cause and effect. Some desperate defensive strategy, this.

In the morning, we are told, both Johanna and Gilbert have forgotten the bitterness of the night. But have they? Has Gilbert? A day or so later, they are sitting on their balcony watching a column of soldiers cross the valley below. One of them, 'a strong, young, handsome fellow,' has a spur on one heel. 'And Gilbert noticed that the belly of the bright bay was wounded with the spur, bloody.' In a strangely vivid little scene, which is as clear an indication as any of Lawrence's ambivalence towards male sexuality, Gilbert watches the rider drink from a water-tub, then furtively bathe the horse's wound, scuffing over the drops of blood in the dust. As the soldiers leave, Gilbert stares after them with

a deep regret. He forgot the woman at his side – and love and happiness. And his heart burned to be with the men, the strange, dark, heavy soldiery, so young and strong with life, reckless and sensual. He wanted it – he wanted it – and not only life with a woman ... to be away from woman, on the borders.

The world of men holds pleasures which the world of women can neither offer nor understand, as the ensuing conversation with Johanna emphasizes.

As women have children (a process from which men are

excluded) so men must have a comradeship which excludes women. 'But man must remain man, and woman woman. There is something manly in the soul of a man which is beyond woman, and in which she has no part. And there is something in woman, particularly in motherhood, in which man has no part and can have no part.' Once again Lawrence, in the person of Gilbert, is turning male inadequacy to an advantage and, in the process, finding further evidence for a central duality/polarity. For either men or women to trespass into the other's territory is 'poison' or 'misery', and the 'dual life-polarity' is the 'basis of the life-mystery', as the 'universe swings in a same dual polarity'.

Johanna and Gilbert are for the most part happy in their dual polarity, but often each tugs at the leash which holds them together, and then there is war instead of equipoise between them. The fight, which is basically that between the values of the world of women and those of the world of men, must be fought out until the two participants are once more restored to equipoise.

For a woman doesn't want a man she can conquer: no, though she fight like hell for the conquest. And the same with a man. Oh horrible submission, especially in marriage are you the foulest of treacheries. Never submit, never abandon yourself completely. This is the last word to every man and woman.

Here is one of Lawrence's rare moves towards the third sort of art cited in his Hardy essay. The equality in reconciliation seems to be a matter of 'the incalculable ebb-and-flow of the two principles'. But this is theory. In practice the ebb-and-flow between Johanna and Gilbert often expresses itself in the form of idiotically trivial quarrels. It may be very honest of Lawrence to describe such disagreements in detail, but it is hardly impressive.

It would seem (though Lawrence himself never actually claims as much) that one of the main objects of the quarrelling is to arouse sexual desire. After a particularly murderous bout, Gilbert is moved by an 'awful fire of desire' when Johanna puts a timid, apologetic hand on his knee.

Ah God, the terrible agony and bliss of sheer passion, sheer, surpassing desire. The agony and bliss of such an embrace, the very brink of death, and yet the sheer overwhelming wave of life itself . . . Gilbert afterwards lay with his soul shattered, his old soul, his old mind and psyche, shattered and gone. And he lay prostrate, a new thing, a new creature . . .

He and Johanna then sleep 'as a new-born child sleeps at the breast', reborn. This is 'the perfect consummating sleep of true, terrible marriage', which is only possible when the whole individual has been shattered in the sexual act, and a new being engendered in its place.

This process, and not 'the accident of childbirth', is the 'real creation' because every man has to be born into manhood by a woman, and every woman into womanhood by a man, as the true, the second birth.

And the man-birth and the woman-birth lasts a life long, and is never finished. Spasm after spasm we are born into manhood and womanhood, and there is no end to the pure creative process. Man is born into manhood forever: and woman into further womanhood.

And it is no good trying to force it. It must come of itself. It is no use having ideals – they only hinder. One must have the pride and the dignity of one's own naked, unabatable soul: no more.

Neither technique nor forced emotion nor, least of all, highflown notions about perfect love and intimacy, can effect the sexual consummation which leads to rebirth.

The mode of love between Johanna and Gilbert is (as Martin Green claims for that between Lawrence and Frieda) triumphant: affirmative, creative and all-powerful. But there is little in such a description of sexuality that can be described as tenderness. It is only in the aftermath of lovemaking that the essentially tender relationship between mother and child is evoked. Within the relationship, Johanna and Gilbert tend to express tenderness in different terms. Johanna's tenderness towards Gilbert tends to be wistful and flowerlike, as is Ursula's towards Birkin, whereas Gilbert's towards her tends to be expressed as maternal solicitousness.

Threatened by her apparent intention to leave him, he has to admit the extent of his dependence upon her. 'It is a horrible thing for a man to realize, not so much in his mind as in his soul, that

his very life, his very being depends upon his connection with
another being.' His lovemaking with Johanna consequently
becomes 'gripped and intense and almost cruel'. She accuses him
of cruelty, of not loving her, sobbing with abandonment and 'with
the strange, irrational continuance of a child'. Knowing that his
cruelty has arisen from superfluity rather than lack of love, Gilbert
takes her gently in his arms, and

he wrapped the bedclothes round her closely, and wrapped her with
himself drawing her onto his breast, and putting his cheek down upon her
round, soft head, so that he seemed to have folded her altogether . . . She
nestled nearer and nearer in his arms, seeming to get smaller, whilst he
seemed to grow bigger in the darkness.

The description reads like that of a mother cradling her child. The
terror, then the petulance, of the little boy who fears abandonment
by the powerful figure of the mother, have been overcome by the
acquisition of some of her female strength. I am not saying that
men cannot or should not express protective tenderness, but it is
interesting at the very least that it is always Gilbert rather than
Johanna who is its exponent in *Mr Noon*.

   The novel was never finished, but there are indications towards
the end of the text that the central relationship was indeed travelling
towards tenderness. Again, the intimation of what that journey
entails comes from Gilbert.

Quite suddenly in the night one night he touched Johanna as she lay
asleep with her back to him, touching him, and something broke alive in
his soul that had been dead before. A sudden shock of new experience.
Ach sweetness, the intolerable sensual sweetness, the silken, fruitlike
sweetness of her loins that touched him as she lay with her back to him –
his soul broke like a dry rock that breaks and gushes into life.

Here is another spasm in the continuing process of Gilbert's
rebirth. Now, he has 'cracked the womb', that is, the old encasing
womb of his first birth, and defeated 'the matrix of the old mother-
days and mother-idea' which is 'hell beyond hell at last'. The
spiritual, daylit world of the upper self, as exemplified by mothers,
has been vanquished by a recognition of the paradoxically 'sensual

soul', and Gilbert is a 'new creature in a new world'. He has grown up.

The new creature manages to fuse that which has previously belonged to the soul with that which has previously belonged to the senses, so that there is no opposition between the two. According to Lawrence, the fusion can come about only through the rejection of womb-oriented values. He might equally well (indeed better) have suggested the rejection of the patriarchal values inherent in war and modern industrial civilization. He might at the very least have shared the blame for the deathly hindrances of the old world between the two sets of values. But he does no such thing: on the contrary, he applauds the Germans for starting the 1914–18 war, adding 'Death to the old, enshrouding body politic, the old womb-idea of our era!' Such a distortion of history approaches the pathological.

Neither passion nor tenderness can be allowed to the world of women, which remains instead a haven of suffocating spiritual values. Instead, both are arrogated to the new male operating in an eternal ebb and flow of conflict and connection with the female principle in a world which surpasses that of the old split consciousness of humanity, mind against body, body against mind. Gilbert and Johanna, reborn, are the new man and the new woman who will inhabit such a world. So too are Lady Chatterley and her lover.

Tenderness was the original title of Lawrence's last major work. But its impact at the time of its private publication in 1928 was rather that of shock, and today its reputation still rests upon sexual explicitness and the frank use of words which are not even now admissible in polite society. Of the three versions, the last is the most explicit and, at the same time, the least tender. This is not, I think, because tenderness and explicitness cannot be combined, but because the novel, undergoing its various metamorphoses, steadily becomes more didactic, more sexist, and more despairing.

'Ours is essentially a tragic age,' runs the opening sentence of all three versions, 'and so we refuse (emphatically) to take it tragically.' The struggle between the tragedy of modern industrial civilization and the triumph of tender and passional sexuality becomes increasingly bitter, and Lawrence's position correspondingly more embattled. Much of his bitterness comes from his own treatment at the hands, tongues and vicious pens of outraged conventional morality. Some may have accrued from his illness (which he persisted in calling bronchitis rather than the tuberculosis it actually was), his impotence and the certainty of his approaching death.

Clifford Chatterley is the embodiment of all that is opposed to the passional and transcendent sexuality advocated by Lawrence, and his marriage to Connie is one of the personal sort which is based in mental and spiritual communication. It is difficult to see how it could be otherwise, given that he is paralysed from the waist down and, literally, exists only in his upper self. That he is a symbolic figure needs no stressing; but that Lawrence identified with him as well as with Parkin/Mellors (according to Frieda) sets him in somewhat sharper perspective. In the increasingly unsympathetic portrait of Clifford we can see some of the self-hatred of *Women In Love*. It is as though the Midlands background, with its rigid class divisions and bleak industrial landscape, necessarily aroused such feelings in Lawrence. After all, it is his background too, and in a sense he always remained a part of it. Rebirth, as Frieda says, is no easy matter. And to repudiate the past is an attempt to repudiate an important part of oneself.

In *The First Lady Chatterley* Clifford is allowed from the start to recognize his wife's 'heavy, craving physical desire', and to show concern for her emotional welfare. There is some pathos in his clumsy masculine concern for her, as there is in her protective pity for him. In *John Thomas and Lady Jane* his attitude towards Connie is devoid of tenderness, and becomes one of 'hard triviality' and sarcasm. For him, 'sex is only an incident, as dinner is an incident', and his 'cold arrogance' leads him to believe that the bond between himself and his wife is stronger than any which is based in the erotic. In *Lady Chatterley's Lover* sex has become for Clifford something which can be arranged like going to the dentist, and he himself, like practically everyone else in the novel a maker of speeches, all too easily convinced by his own rhetoric. He is also much more of a man of property, delighting alike in the exercise of power and the accumulation of wealth. Thus the marriage between the Chatterleys becomes more and more heavily contrasted with the 'marriage' between Connie and the gamekeeper, the contrast accruing more and more symbolic weight in the process. By the time we get to the third version, the central relationship between Connie and Mellors has come to seem like a good deed in a very naughty world, the lovers totally isolated among the philistines or non-believers in their phallic marriage.

It is not only Clifford who becomes increasingly stereotypical, and in the process less sympathetic. Three of the subsidiary women characters suffer a similar fate, their metamorphoses indicating a growing sexist bias. In the first version the relationship between Connie and her only sister, Hilda, is one of 'an old, wild warmth' which is beyond Clifford's understanding. Hilda has left her 'devoted' husband for good Lawrentian reasons: he 'pawed her and petted her but never for a moment came forth naked to her out of his amiable and would-be manly shell.' She dislikes Clifford's 'cold, limited egoism', and is a consistent supporter of Connie. Like the Brangwen sisters, the two of them discuss men with some candour, and although Hilda has never experienced, as has Connie, 'something new in the conection between men and women', their conversation remains amicable. Hilda despises men and thinks marriage a mistake, and so is offended by Connie's declaration that she *must* live with Parkin. But her only reaction is to ask her sister quietly, 'Aren't you being rather foolish?' And at the end of the novel it is Hilda to whom Connie turns for comfort and support.

In *John Thomas and Lady Jane* Hilda becomes bossier and altogether more decisive. It is she who insists on taking the careworn Connie to see a doctor and on Clifford's employing Mrs Bolton as a nurse. She is 'determined to take her sister away from Clifford'. When Connie tells her about the affair with Parkin, Hilda disapproves openly. '"But won't you regret it later?" she said with a tone of distaste, even contempt.' She is wearily impatient when Connie describes her sexual relationship with Parkin as 'wonderful' because 'she herself was through with sex'. Her considered comment to the lovers is: 'I only wonder if it's worth it, that's all. I don't blame anybody or think anybody is wrong. But I do wonder if it's worth it.' As far as she is concerned, a woman does not exist 'merely for lovemaking'. But although she disapproves of Parkin's lowly status, she is 'in instinctive sympathy with the passion itself'. The relationship deteriorates when Hilda asks Connie to 'realize that Parkin's penis doesn't rule the world', whereas property, money and social class all do. She is scathing about Connie's claim that 'the penis is the most godly part of a man,' but concludes, 'I suppose you're in love, that's all.' Although the relationship between the sisters is more acerbic than in the first version, they never quarrel openly and Hilda is still around at the end of the novel to help Connie through her pregnancy.

In both *John Thomas and Lady Jane* and *Lady Chatterley's Lover* Hilda represents the reality principle, but in the latter that principle has in itself become more hostile to the pleasure principle which informs the phallic marriage. Hilda now has 'the very hell of a will of her own, as her husband has found out', and is 'violently angry' with Connie. Although she has previously disliked her brother-in-law,

On the strength of her anger, Hilda warmed towards Clifford. After all, he had a mind. And if he had no sex, functionally, so much the better: so much less to quarrel about. Hilda wanted no more of that sex business where men became selfish little horrors. Connie really had less to put up with than most women, did she but know it.

She can relent slightly as far as Mellors is concerned when she finds out that he has been a lieutenant in the Army. When she actually meets him, she is openly hostile, chiding him for his use of the local dialect, which she finds fraudulent. She is 'frankly baffled and furiously annoyed' when Mellors attempts in uncompromising and offensive terms to justify his relationship with Connie. When Connie says later that Hilda has 'never known either real tenderness or real sensuality', Hilda's reaction is 'For mercy's sake, don't brag about your experiences!' But Connie remains calm, refusing to be dominated by her older sister, as she has been all her life. 'Now, though somewhere inside she was weeping, she was free of the dominion of *other women*. Ah! that in itself was a relief, like being given another life: to be free of the strange dominion and obsession of *other women*. How awful they were, women!' She cannot confide in Hilda that she is pregnant, but tells her father instead.

Clifford's nurse, Mrs Bolton, comes in for similar treatment. In *The First Lady Chatterley* she, another sensual woman, is totally on Connie's side, delighting at being in on the secret of the affair with Parkin. She has been twenty years a widow, her husband having been killed in a pit accident. When she tells Connie about her marriage, she confirms for her 'that a man could be, in his body, the living clue to all the world to a woman.' Although Connie feels that there may well be something sinister in Mrs Bolton's complicity, there is a real pact between the women because, as Mrs Bolton puts it, 'you're a woman, and a true woman, and a body's heart burns for you and not against you.' Clifford can command her attention and teach her some of the accomplishments of the gentry, like playing chess, but this Mrs Bolton remains as loyal to her own sex as she does to her own class.

In *John Thomas and Lady Jane* Mrs Bolton becomes a more complex character. When she describes her marriage and widowing, she is still portrayed as the repository of native female wisdom, but, in allowing her to tell her story to Hilda rather than Connie, Lawrence weakens the bond between the two sensual women. There is still sympathy and even complicity between her and Connie, but for this Mrs Bolton the relationship with Clifford gradually assumes precedence. At first she dislikes him, as she dislikes all gentry. Then she becomes fascinated by him and, by pretending submission, soon begins to wield a subtle power over him and especially over his body. When she shaves him, they get 'voluptuous pleasure' from the physical contact. 'It was almost a sort of marriage.' But in Lawrentian terms it is, of course, a perversion of marriage and of sexuality. Clifford educates her in the ways of the gentry, and she reciprocates by telling him all the local gossip. It is through these latter conversations that he is led to reorganizing the mines. By the end of the novel Mrs Bolton is Clifford's 'daimon or familiar spirit', and he is 'quite unaware how he was no longer an individual, how he was part of duality with Ivy

Bolton'. They are no longer master and servant but embody a 'powerful impetus' which derives from 'the unison of their two souls'. No longer the ally of other women, this Mrs Bolton has made it her main concern to assume power over a man.

In *Lady Chatterley's Lover* Mrs Bolton makes a similar progression, but is more devious and treacherous in her divided loyalties. Her gossip becomes more malicious and sickens Connie, but later the two women can weep together over Ted Bolton's death. She is more bitter about her widowhood and about the 'masters' whom she blames for her husband's death. By the end of the novel she is less the driving force of the second version than the Magna Mater so feared and hated by Lawrence himself. When Clifford weeps at Connie's departure, Mrs Bolton comforts him and kisses him until he becomes perverted into a 'child-man', kissing her breasts in exultation.

And they drew into a closer physical intimacy, an intimacy of perversity, when he was a child stricken with an apparent candour and an apparent wonderment, that looked almost like religious exultation ... While she was the Magna Mater, full of power and potency, having the great blond child-man under her will and stroke entirely.

And, concomitantly, 'in some corner of her female soul, how she despised and hated him!' Here is the ultimate perversion of the true relationship between a man and a woman: the man has become infantilized and the woman assumed potency. It is too close for comfort to the primary relationship between an all-powerful mother and a weak and sickly son. Mrs Bolton has become a monster.

The third woman to undergo a similar set of changes is Bertha, the gamekeeper's wife. In all three versions she is a trouble-maker: vulgar, self-assertive and sexually treacherous. And in all three it is clear that the keeper has married beneath him. In *The First Lady Chatterley* Connie looks at Bertha's photograph and finds her 'common'. Parkin tells her that Bertha is 'not a nice woman, an' 'er niver was', but is otherwise uncommunicative. When Connie is on holiday with Hilda in France Clifford writes to tell her (among other things) of Bertha's behaviour. 'She has aired in minute detail every incident in her married life with Parkin that respects to his discredit.' The incidents consist of 'minor perversities' which are never elucidated. But Connie knows 'that every woman, and hence every man, had private sexual secrets which no one had any right to betray.' In her treachery, Bertha is both morally and aesthetically unpleasing, a lower-class loudmouth who, whatever the havoc she causes, can eventually be dismissed as unworthy of serious attention.

The Bertha of *John Thomas and Lady Jane* has assumed enough importance within the narrative to be able to provoke Connie's jealousy, and Parkin is not allowed to get away with a refusal to talk about her. When Connie persistently questions him as to why he ever had anything to do with Bertha, his reply is, ''Appen she made me.' Parkin and Bertha knew each other as children, she being five years the elder. One evening, 'she lifted up her clothes and showed me – you know what.' Again, he has to be pressed, but eventually confesses, 'She wanted me to come and feel. But I never knowed afore then as women had hair there. Black hair! An' I don't know why it upset me an' made me hate the thoughts of women from that day.' In keeping with his character as the most vulnerable of the gamekeepers, this Parkin is indeed a sexual casualty.

The childhood incident established some sort of bond between Parkin and Bertha, and later they married. But, until he shaved off her pubic hair, he was impotent. Thus did she gain a sort of power over him, and for a while, he admits, he loved her. Soon, 'she wanted it all her own way, I was nowhere; as if she was the man, an' me the woman.' Although he has now managed to overcome his aversion to pubic hair, this Parkin certainly has problems, not the least of which is his blithe assumption that a man's part in the sexual act is to have everything his own way. Lawrence is implying that the marriage has broken down because Parkin was unmanly enough to allow himself to be dominated by Bertha; that she was responsible for having unmanned him in the first place; and that later, having attempted to make amends, she took continuing advantage of her power to unman. If Parkin hates and fears women, it must be the fault of women themselves – or, rather, of a specific woman.

Mellors has a different tale to tell about his wife. There is no childhood trauma to account for his attraction to Bertha, but rather her own straightforward sexuality. After his unsatisfactory experiences with women who wanted everything from him except sex, Mellors tells Connie, 'I wanted a woman who wanted me, and wanted *it*.' Bertha may have been common, but she wanted him, so 'I fucked her like a good 'un.' No sexual casualty this, but a bit of a stud. Bertha, however, probably despised him 'for being so pleased about it'. After a while she began to treat him 'with insolence' and become sexually selfish:

And she got so's she'd never have me when I wanted her: never. Always put me off, brutal as you like. And when she'd put me right off and I didn't want her, she'd come all lovey-dovey and get me. And I always went. But when I had her, she never came off when I did. Never! She'd just wait. If I kept back for half an hour, she'd keep back longer. And, when I'd come and really finished, then she'd start on her own account and I had to stop inside her till she brought herself off, wriggling and shouting . . . Gradually I got sick of it: and she got worse. She sort of got harder and harder to bring off, and she'd sort of tear at me down there, as if it was a beak tearing at me. By God, you think a woman's soft down there, like a fig. But I tell you the old rampers have beaks between their legs, and they tear at you with it till you're sick. Self! Self! Self! all Self! tearing and shouting!

A more blatant and more hysterical piece of misogyny it would be difficult to encounter. It is impossible to believe that here is a man speaking to the woman he loves. Mellors seems to have no idea that his wife's lack of satisfaction could be due to his own sexual inadequacy, nor that his demand that she should 'come off' when he is ready is just as selfish as anything Bertha either does or fails to do. What Bertha is really guilty of, as a lover, is insensitivity rather than the dreaded female voraciousness. And Mellors's account does not illustrate the awfulness of women, but the terrible failure of two people to communicate.

As far as his attitude towards women is concerned, this is one of the most damning passages Lawrence ever wrote. And it gets worse. Mellors goes on to divide women as sexual partners into five categories, all unacceptable. First, there are the oldfashioned sort who are basically indifferent to sex, and just let the man get on with it. Then there are women who enjoy petting, but not penetration, 'going off every kind except the natural one'. Third, there is the hard sort who are 'the very devil to bring off' like Bertha, and want to be the active party. Fourth, there are those who are simply dead inside. And, fifth and worst, there are women who

go on writhing with their loins till they bring themselves off against your thighs. But they're mostly the Lesbian sort. It's astonishing how Lesbian women are, consciously or unconsciously. Seems to me they're nearly all Lesbian ... When I'm with a woman who's really Lesbian, I fairly howl in my soul, wanting to kill her.

Women can't win: if they're passive, they're boring; if they're active, they're threatening. And any woman who does not behave exactly as a man wants must be a Lesbian. Can Lawrence really expect his women readers to find this man an attractive proposition as a lover? And can a man who wants to kill Lesbians have any credibility as an exponent of tenderness? Lawrence really should know better. Whether he does or not must remain an open question.

Bertha has progressed from a vulgar loudmouth, through a sexual tease only too willing to exploit male fears of female sexuality, to a rampant and castrating monster, deadly in her effectiveness. The first Parkin can be seen as justified in his revulsion from his treacherous wife. The second Parkin can be seen as a rather pathetic creature who could do with some sexual therapy in the form of A Good Woman. But Mellors is supposedly on the right path in that he has the strength to resist being dominated by a woman. To judge solely by their attitudes towards their wives, it is impossible to imagine either Mellors or the second Parkin having any sort of satisfying sexual relationship with a woman. And yet this is exactly what Lawrence expects us to imagine.

Something has gone badly wrong. Lawrence's intention is presumably to highlight the phallic marriage, as embodied in the relationship between Connie and the gamekeeper, by contrasting it with as many as possible inferior variants. But in the attempt he has only succeeded in raising serious doubts about the desirability for women of phallic marriage. Similarly, in portraying both the second Parkin and Mellors as sexual misfits, he is presumably hinting at the possibilities for rebirth and growth within the phallic marriage. But what woman in her senses would, on this evidence, have anything to do with either of these men? It is not, of course, all the evidence that Lawrence provides, but it is quite enough to give us pause.

Even so, the progression of Hilda, Mrs Bolton and Bertha to the unsympathetic or grotesque is not the whole story. As they sink in Connie's estimation or cease to be valuable to her, so does her father, Sir Malcolm, assume an obverse ascendancy. In *Lady Chatterley's Lover*, when Connie chooses to confide in her father rather than in Hilda, the primary bond within the family becomes that between father and daughter rather than that between sisters. Although Sir Malcolm advises Connie to stick by Wragby as the one permanent feature in her life, ' "I hope you had a real man at last," he said to her after a while, sensually alert.' Connie is his favourite daughter because 'he had always liked the female in her', and he is as pleased about her pregnancy 'as if the unborn child were his child'. It would seem that quasi-incest between father and daughter can be endorsed, if not that between mother and son. At first Sir Malcolm suspects Mellors of being a gold-digger, but when the two men meet, he becomes 'Scotch and lewd'. The only outcome of their conversation is that they establish 'the old freemasonry of male sensuality between them'. Sir Malcolm, Mellors and Connie are three of a kind, the aristocratic kind who are fully realized sexual beings. It is thus, and not according to class divisions, that people should be categorized and evaluated.

Connie is the only woman in the three versions of the novel who is in the end acceptable to and can be endorsed by the world of men. That is, in essence, she is the only woman who is woman enough to accept a male view of sexuality. But her acceptance comes gradually, as the novel evolves towards its final version. In finally accepting Mellors's view of sexuality, and hence of the world at large, she has isolated herself from the world of women and female friendship and solidarity. Instead she is left with a male mentor in a heterosexual dyad whose exclusivity can be broached only – and only rarely – by other male mentors of similar temperaments.

In all three versions it is Connie's sexual awakening and subsequent experience which provide the main thrust of the narrative. And, although the character of the gamekeeper becomes progressively more prominent, Lawrence could in a sense be said to be writing for women. Perhaps such a preference or bias indicates that he is, once again, placing his main hope for the future in women rather than in men. But it seems to me that he is, rather, admitting that men cannot change unless women do (men need women); and claiming at the same time that the change will come from an acknowledgment by women of their dependence on men (women should need men). It is the latter half of the proposition which is the more in need of demonstration. Thus women become the prime targets for Lawrence's preaching. And Connie becomes the vehicle through which we must be convinced of the supreme value of phallic marriage.

The constituents of the phallic marriage are already observable in *The First Lady Chatterley*, where Lawrence is still capable of delineating them with some restraint. They are, briefly, sensuality, tenderness and an acknowledgment of the power of the penis. Lawrence has not lost sight of the duality/polarity he advocates in *Mr Noon*, but he no longer sees the reconciliation between opposites as a matter of constant fight, and his lovers are less tigers than shy deer, lost and found in their own forest. They have arrived at that stage in their emotional lives envisaged by Lou Carrington: where men and women have learned to be kind to one another, rather than struggling for supremacy in the to and fro of destructive friction. Each is, for different reasons, isolated and unadmittedly lonely. They are both ripe for pleasure and for a relationship which will assuage not only the loneliness of the individual within his/her social setting, but the isolation of the human species within the universe, the two being essentially interconnected.

Much of this process is understated in *The First Lady Chatterley*, where sensuality and tenderness are both evident in the spare, lyrical natural world and the working people are all of a piece. In seeing in her lover 'something tender and fragile, yet really him, and beautiful as an open crocus flower', she can also feel tenderness for a countryside despoiled by the mining industry, and for the 'disfigured, strange, almost wraithlike populace' from which Parkin has sprung. In that her feelings are tender and compassionate, they belong to the world of women which has no interest in ravishing the countryside in the name of profit. In this world the power to conquer and subdue nature is meaningless.

Towards the end of the novel Parkin still looks like 'a very fresh sensitive flower', a look which makes Connie 'mad with love for him' because it is so 'vulnerable'.

And in all the sensitive unfoldedness a quiet repose of power, the power to live and to set life flowing. In the long run he was the master because life was with him. And Clifford, though he had a diabolic will and cleverness, had lost the softness and mystery of life. But, for the time being, the external power was in Clifford's hands, and Parkin was powerless.

The new world which the lovers have entered rejects the brute power of the modern industrialized world of men. But the male is not therefore rendered powerless, except in terms which are acceptable to that latter world. Instead, he has acquired the sort of power which is more usually attributed to the world of women.

But Lawrence cannot let things rest there. If this sort of power is desirable for the male within the phallic marriage, how does a man differ from a woman, and what happens to duality/polarity? The answer lies in the body and, of course, in the phallus itself. Parkin is 'not ashamed of what I've got atween my legs'. Remembering this declaration, Connie begins to ponder 'the mystery of the penis'.

And she knew, as every woman knows, that the penis is a column of blood, the living fountain of fullness in life. From the strange rising and surging of the blood all life rises into being . . . And with the mystery of the phallus goes all the beauty of the world, and beauty is more than knowledge . . . and it is the penis which connects us sensually with the planets. But for the penis we should never know the loveliness of Sirius or the categorical difference between a pomegranate and an india-rubber ball.

How on earth can one begin to comment on such a mind-boggling series of statements? It really is absurd to cite a fascinated adoration of the penis as an instance of 'what every woman knows'. Whatever women may know profoundly about life in the body belongs to the female body, and not to the male. It is even more absurd to suggest that anyone who does not possess or has not experienced a penis is incapable of aesthetic appreciation of the universe. On the contrary, if there is a portion of the human anatomy which connects us to the movements of the planets, it is to be found within the female body and expressed in the lunar menstrual cycle. Not that it matters. To claim primacy and/or superiority for the female body in its monthly shedding of blood seems just as absurd to me as Lawrence's claims on behalf of the penis. We make such claims only when we feel threatened or cornered by the opposite sex.

And this, surely, is just the point. Lawrence's struggles towards finding and defining optimum relationship between men and women are often valiant on behalf of equality and reciprocity. But, like the proverbial horse (which he himself has brought to water) he then simply refuses to drink. Having demonstrated that, contrary to prevailing stereotypes, tenderness is not an exclusive property of the world of women, nor sensuality of the world of men, but that the qualities can co-exist fruitfully in both worlds, he is in danger of losing duality/polarity which sets maleness apart from femaleness. What this really means is that he is losing sight of maleness, the more elusive of the two principles. Maleness appears to be getting swallowed up in femaleness, as a little boy is absorbed into the world of his more powerful mother. And yet, the world of men, devoted as it is to constructs of the mind like wealth, property and social status, offers no real compensation for having been born male. The new man, caught between two worlds, must find new means towards self-definition, while still maintaining a relationship of duality/polarity with the new woman. Thus the new man is in a sense the new penis: an instrument which has abandoned its propensity to rape in favour of a generative rite which connects not only man and woman, but all the disparate elements of a complex, ever-flowing, ever-ebbing universe.

No mean task for one small organ. And no mean claim, although a somewhat desperate one. The three versions of the Lady Chatterley novels read like an increasingly desperate attempt to convince women that the claim is justifiable, and the task one capable of accomplishment. The four short paragraphs on phallic power in *The First Lady Chatterley* are expanded in *John Thomas and Lady Jane* to a recurrent theme, and in *Lady Chatterley's Lover* the theme becomes insistent, threatening to swamp or cancel both sensuality and tenderness altogether.

The lovers in *John Thomas and Lady Jane* have both been damaged by their experience of other people, and hate 'ugly egoistic sexuality'. When Connie looks at her naked body she weeps bitterly, and Parkin has been avoiding women for years. From the start they are less certain about each other than they were in the previous version. Their approach to each other is consequently cautious and gradual but, as in the first version, of a piece with the motion of the natural world. Going to the wood in April, Connie finds it a 'sanctuary of life itself'.

Life is so soft and quiet, and cannot be seized. It will not be raped. Try to rape it and it disappears. Try to seize it and you have dust ... But with quietness, with an abandon of self-assertion and a fulness of the deep, true self can one approach another human being, and know the delicate best of life, the touch. The touch of the feet on the earth, the touch of the fingers on a tree, on a creature, the touch of hands and breasts, the touch of the whole body to body, and the interpenetration of passionate love: it is life itself, and in the touch we are all alive.

This passage, coming immediately before the episode with the pheasant chicks and the first sexual encounter between Connie and Parkin, sets the tone for their relationship. It is this version of the novel which best deserves the title of *Tenderness*.

It is not until their fifth meeting that Connie asks Parkin, 'Tell me it isn't only fucking.' But he is baffled. 'Only the erect phallus seemed sure, cocksure, a strange, wildly alert presence between the two beings.' It is like another being, and only when it is inside Connie can the man ask, 'What is there more? What is there more than fucking?' Well, if you ask such a question at such a time, you are not likely to get much of an answer – except perhaps from the superconscious modern woman. But not from Connie. 'And for the moment, she submitted, and was gone.'

Later, lying sleepless beside him and saddened by 'his desire for woman and his hatred of women', she arrives at an answer. Parkin has been wounded by life in 'the soul of his phallus, the overweening blind male soul of him', and his wound is that of 'the pain and hatred of sex'. But with her 'submissive in the circle of his flesh', he is healed. Vaguely now she begins to realize that

to him there could never be 'only fucking.' Because his phallus rose in its own weird godhead, with its own swarthy pride and surety, and 'fucking' went to the phallic roots of his soul. It was not just sensational excitation worked from the ego and the personality. His phallus was not the vulgar organ, the penis. And with the life or death of his phallus he would live or die. That too she realized. Men like Clifford, and a vast number of modern men, lived in the petty triumph over the phallus. They have a nasty penis which they play about with, like dirty little boys. But when it comes to the act, in spite of all the gush about love, it is merely fucking, the functional orgasm, the momentary sensational thrill, the cheap and nasty excitation of a moment.

Here, in essence, is the Lawrentian hero, the suitable partner for the new female in the phallic marriage. And here too is a rare description of a woman's sympathetic attempt to understand maleness.

But are we in fact any nearer a definition of maleness? It is clearly not just a matter of possessing a penis: rather a matter of how the penis is used, of a man's relationship with his penis. A man who fucks from his phallic soul is a whole man who finds mere localized thrills repulsive, and has no need to talk about love because his organ is a loving organ, and his performance a loving performance. At the same time both organ and performance are beyond love in that they are an expression of life itself, and of the act of creation. In these last lies the godlike power of the phallus, an organ of flesh with its roots in the soul. It seems to mean something which is at the same time the essence of a man and separable from him, an alter ego. In connecting himself to Connie through the phallus Parkin has completed a perfect circle 'of the male and female, phallic body'. It is as though the phallus belongs, in and immediately after the sexual act, to both male and female. The perfected unit is one which no one else can enter, and in which the man and woman remain both safe and free. It is the phallus, Connie feels, which has conquered her 'fear of life, fear of society, fear of what would happen, fear of what would not happen'. But her root-fear has been the fear of the phallus itself, which is the 'root-fear of all mankind'.

If Lawrence were merely saying that sex is good for you, and good sex even better, there would be few to quarrel with him. Similarly, if he were saying that men and women should learn to accept each other in their maleness or femaleness. But in fact he is attributing all the good in sex to the male organ, which is its sole source. Although Connie learns to accept, and indeed revere, the male genitals, Parkin makes no reciprocal gesture in her direction, going only so far as admiring her 'arse'. Lawrence wants us to take sex seriously, as seriously as we take religion, but he seems unaware that his description (which is really a prescription) takes as little account of the female as most latter-day religious creeds. Given the premise that sex is centrally and crucially important in life (and such is the basis of all his arguments on the subject), Lawrence's attitude towards the phallus is perfectly justifiable. It is not that he is writing nonsense, but that he is writing only one side of the story. And that he seems to believe that it is the whole story.

I see this failure as yet another instance of Lawrence's stopping-short – or indeed another instance of the same stopping-short. The ensuing lovemaking between Connie and Parkin has nothing of male domination or bullying in it, but remains tender and convincing. And Connie's description of the shrunken penis as 'so little now, like a bud, and innocent', is another acknowledgment of the frailty of the male. It is allowed to be maternal. And Parkin is even allowed to kneel in front of his lover without losing his manly dignity. The power relations implied or stated in Connie's dissertation on the phallus are nowhere in evidence. In this version of the novel, Lawrence does not insist on phallic supremacy, although he often hints at it. He is much more likely to plead for it.

That there are seven sexual encounters between the lovers indicates that here Lawrence had in mind the seven sensual heavens and hells referred to in *Mr Noon*. The encounters consti- tute a learning process, especially for Connie, and we are given to understand that the sexual relationship gets better and better, as tenderness and sensuality are combined in an acknowledgment of the power of the phallus. But Parkin the man remains to some extent separable from his all-conquering penis, and can scarcely be described as a representative of macho manliness. After the scandal caused by Bertha, Connie realizes that he is not tough. 'Nothing can be more easily wounded, in our day, and mortally wounded, than the passionate soul. It is the passionless soul which is tough and rubbery, almost indestructible.' When they meet in the wood, 'everything was green, green, with aching, over-riding vegetation', but Parkin's heart is dead.

He refuses Connie's offer to buy a farm for him, determined as he is to make his own way in the world, like any other man. But he then concedes that to be beholden to a woman is better than to live in misery: his mother always told him that he was only half a man, so maybe he will have to take himself at her estimation, and manage as such.

He spoke with intense bitterness. The idea that he was too womanly was terribly humiliating to him: and manliness meant stupid, unimaginative insentience to him.

'Why do you mind?' she said, tears coming to her eyes. 'It's foolish! You say you have too much of a woman in you. You only mean that you are more sensitive than stupid people like Dan Coutts. You ought to be proud that you are sensitive, and have that much of a woman's good qualities. It's very good for a man to have a touch of a woman's sensitiveness. I hate your stupid, hard-headed clowns who think they are so *manly* – '

She was angry, angry at the implied insult to womanhood, and his stupidity regarding himself.

In the phallic marriage men are allowed to be sensitive, and Parkin is a man, not because he is a macho male, but because he has 'the gift of life' which he expresses in his sexuality. Connie will respect his sensitivity and allow him to feel that he is in some way bigger than her because she recognizes that he is 'nothing but a man. And if his dignity as a man was really hurt, he would die.' She loves him, so she will not hurt him; she loves him as he is, so she will not destroy him.

'They that have power to hurt, and will do none' could serve as an epigraph to *John Thomas and Lady Jane*. Parkin is the very picture of male vulnerability, and this is indeed a strong part of his attraction for Connie, as I suspect it would be for many women. Similarly, his first reaction to her is to perceive that 'the woman suffered: that she was, so to speak, drowning.' A large part of their relationship consists in the recognition and sharing of one another's pain as well as one another's joy. In this sense it resembles the primary relationship between mother and son described at the beginning of *Sons and Lovers* At the end of the novel it is Connie who has to rally Parkin out of his misery and provide the impetus into the future, making a bid as she does so for the values of the world of women. Although the events in *Lady Chatterley's Lover* follow a similar narrative line, the central relationship between the lovers shifts away from the mother/son dyad based in pain and helplessness towards the more acceptable father/daughter dyad in which the man is the teacher (and preacher) and the woman his pupil.

The Connie of the third version is a more sophisticated woman than either of her predecessors. She has had a fair amount of sexual experience but, it is suggested, she has not learned the right lessons from it. What she has learned is described on the fourth page of the novel, striking an ominous note.

A woman could take a man without really giving herself away. Certainly she could take him without giving herself into his power. Rather she could use this sex thing to have power over him. For she had only to hold herself back in sexual intercourse, and let him finish and expend himself without herself coming to the crisis: and then she could prolong the connection and achieve her orgasm and her crisis while he was merely her tool.

Sexuality is immediately seen in terms of power relations, and bad or unsatisfying sexual relations as the fault of the woman.

It becomes evident during the description of Connie's affair with Michaelis that it is not power relations themselves which are objectionable: it is, rather, that power has been concentrated in the wrong hands. Michaelis has something of Parkin in him, in that he arouses Connie's compassion as well as 'a wild, craving physical desire'. But he cannot satisfy her, always 'finishing' too quickly. 'But then she soon learned to hold him, to keep him inside her when his crisis was over. And then he was curiously gentle and patient; he stayed firm inside her, giving to her, while she was active ... wildly, passionately active, coming to her own crisis.' He gets some pride and satisfaction from this procedure, but remains essentially isolated. This pair of lovers reaches orgasm separately and each remains separated, unconnected. In doing so, each maintains his/her own power, and there is no exchange. Connie has 'a subtle sort of self-assurance, something blind and a little arrogant'.

The affair ends when Michaelis asks bitterly, 'You couldn't go off at the same time as a man, could you? You'd have to bring yourself off! You'd have to run the show!' Connie is shocked because 'that passive sort of giving himself was so obviously his only real mode of intercourse.' Lawrence makes it quite clear that it is Michaelis, the less than phallic male, who is to blame because his premature ejaculation has 'forced the woman to become active', thus upsetting the first law of sexuality. But it seems strange that Mellors, who makes the same demand for simultaneous orgasm, is not therefore suspect as a lover. Presumably his phallic maleness gives him the right to make any demands he chooses.

The 'novel masculine information' provided by Michaelis, the brutality of it, kills something in Connie. Sometimes she weeps bitterly for its loss. After a visionary glimpse of Mellors washing himself outside his cottage, she sees her own body as 'meaningless, going dull and opaque, so much insignificant substance. It made her feel immensely depressed and hopeless.' As in the previous version, she weeps, but here she is angry as well as despairing. 'Unjust! Unjust! The sense of deep physical injustice burned to her very soul.' The curious thing is that in this last version the episode takes place after the affair with Michaelis, and so cannot be said to describe the consequences of suppressing one's sexuality. Although Connie's reaction is stronger here, it makes less sense. But Lawrence wants us to believe that it makes more sense, in that no sex at all is preferable to the wrong sort of sex which was evident in the affair with Michaelis. We are one step nearer to the glorification of the Lawrentian hero who will embody the right sort of sexuality.

When Mellors has sounded off about women and lesbians, he finally admits that a 'right relation with a woman' is the core of his life, but at the same time that he mistrusts women. Connie, 'protesting nervously against him', accuses him of talking coldly about sex, 'as if you had only wanted your own pleasure and satisfaction'. He protests that his pleasure is inseparable from the woman's pleasure, which must nevertheless be the perfect match for his own. Up until this point in the novel, Mellors seems to be obsessed by the notion of simultaneous orgasm, so much so that he is prepared to forgo any sexual acts which do not culminate in this way. He seems unaware that it is possible to get pleasure from someone else's orgasm. People do, both men and women. And why not? Mellors's blinkered view of sexuality still prevents him from even suspecting that his years of sighing for 'a woman who'd come naturally with a man' might have been unnecessary, and his suffering remediable through his own efforts.

As ever, Connie's accusations and questions alienate him, but at last she prompts him to the recitation of his creed.

I believe in being warm-hearted. I believe especially in being warm-hearted about love, in fucking with a warm heart. I believe if men could fuck with warm hearts, and the women take it warm-heartedly, everything would come right. It's all this cold-hearted fucking that is death and idiocy.

Of course Mellors is right, in that to be warm-hearted is better than to be cold-hearted, but he still sees sex as something which the man gives, and the woman takes. The underlying and undeclared suggestion is that he who gives calls the tune.

This is hardly any advance on Paul Morel's belief that, if one only has the right attitude, everything will work out for the best, the optimum satisfaction. As of course it often does. But this is hardly the whole story, and sexuality can no more be centred in the heart than it can in the head. If Lawrence wants us to be whole human beings every time we engage in sexual acts, he should accept that our thoughts, our feelings and our bodies are all of a piece. Sometimes he seems to be doing just that. At other times he insists on a tripartite view of the human being: mind, body and some mysterious entity called soul, the mind being the poor relation in the richest acts of love. This is all very well in itself, but Lawrence does not leave the matter there, and his thinking is in fact tendentious, its end being the glorification of the penis as the mysteriously powerful phallus which alone is the source of true sexuality. Such a belief leaves the woman no other role than to submit to the man: she can attain full sexuality (and orgasm) only through the temporary gift of the penis.

There is desperation here, male desperation: women should need men; women *must* need men. The unadmitted subtext is that men need women and hate the need. Although Connie's attitude may seem embarrassingly submissive to a modern woman reader, Mellors is not satisfied, and accuses her,

you like a good, sharp, piercing cold-hearted fucking, and then pretending it's all sugar. Where's your tenderness for me? You're as suspicious of me as a cat is of a dog. I tell you it takes two even to be tender and warm-hearted. You love fucking all right: but you want it to be called something grand and mysterious, just to flatter your own self-importance. Your own self-importance is more to you, fifty times more, than any man, or being together with a man.

There could hardly be a more unfair accusation. When Connie protests, with rather more justification, that this is exactly what she feels about him, he becomes distant and suggests that they stay apart. In other words, he sulks, like a little boy who has not got his own way, a little boy who is still demanding the unconditional love of the mother from all other women, while reserving the right to impose his own conditions on the relationship. This sort of behaviour gives us a glimpse into the nature of that much-vaunted male logic, while affording us a deeper look into male neurosis. Mellors's attitude is probably recognizable to most women. But to recognize is not to endorse, any more than to understand is to forgive.

Of course lovers quarrel, of course all couples are not alike, and of course it is difficult to be prescriptive in all honesty about such matters. Nevertheless there is a principle at stake here, the principle of equality and reciprocity in relations between men and women. If Lawrence really believed in it, now would be the time to introduce it, exposing the mistrust between the lovers as understandable but mistaken, and Mellors's behaviour as a cliché of male emotional incompetence. But there is no evidence that Lawrence even recognizes the cliché. Connie weeps, Mellors calls her 'ma little lass', and they comfort each other. 'And she nestled up to him, feeling small and enfolded, and they both went to sleep at once, fast in one sleep.' Even in this reconciliation-in-tenderness it is apparent that Mellors is still the larger, dominant being.

The next morning Connie realizes again the beauty of the male body, but this time her realization is centred on the penis, which Lawrence now calls the phallos. '"So proud," she murmured, uneasy. "And so lordly! Now I know why men are so overbearing! But he's lovely, *really*. Like another being! A bit terrifying! But lovely, really! And he comes to *me*!" She caught her lower lip between her teeth, in fear and excitement.' Connie is not the only one who is uneasy. I find this passage, with its multiple exclamation marks, Connie's bitten lip and the implication of her own unworthiness, embarrassingly close to the pornographic. That is, I feel I am being shown a glossy closeup photograph of an erect penis, in which the rest of the man is not visible. I also know that it is not women, but homosexual men, who get excited by such photographs. Is Mellors, then, a late-surfacing (or re-surfacing) of Lawrence's homosexual narcissism?

As so often with Lawrence, the answer is probably, yes and no. That there is narcissism in his portrayal of Mellors is undeniable, but I suspect that homosexuality is present only on an unconscious level. This does not make it any the less real; in fact, it could be argued that it is therefore *more* real. I think it is real enough to lead Lawrence to a mistaken view of a woman's perception of the male body. It is surely homosexual men rather than women who are fascinated or indeed obsessed by the penis rather than by the whole man. The notion of dissociating a man from his genitals is not a feminine but a masculine one. Women tend not to dissociate themselves from their own genitalia, and often find it difficult to believe that men are capable of achieving such a split. But when Mellors goes on to address his penis as 'John Thomas', Connie finds nothing odd in the dissociation, and in fact goes along with it.

John Thomas is more 'cocky' than Mellors, who addresses him thus: 'Ay, th' cheek on thee! Cunt, that's what tha's after. Tell Lady Jane tha wants cunt.' Warm-hearted fun and fucking this may be, but it is hardly in keeping with Lawrence's own professed belief that in sexual acts the split between mind and body should be healed, and that sex makes us whole human beings. However, the reason for the dissociation soon becomes apparent. After they have made love, Connie uncovers Mellors again 'to look at the mystery of the phallos'. She finds it tiny now, and 'soft like a little bud of life'. She tells Mellors, 'You must *never* insult him, you know. He's mine too. He's not only yours. He's mine!' A woman is incomplete without a penis, and her completion consists in the gift of a penis from a man.

This should be enough for her, without any of the 'gush' about love. When Connie then asks Mellors, as she often does, if he loves her, he is as usual evasive. He cannot bring himself to make any such admission because it would constitute a slur on his virility. Here is another glimpse into male neurosis: the male fear that the expression of emotion will unman. And although Mellors finally concedes that he loves Connie with his balls and with his heart (in that order) it is clear at the same time that she is to make no further emotional demands on him.

The lovers' next meeting celebrates the marriage of John Thomas to Lady Jane. They run naked and make love in the rain, then deck each other with flowers and foliage. As a prelude to this latter pagan rite Mellors makes some acknowledgment of the beauty of the female body and 'the nicest, nicest woman's arse there is'. He is glad that Connie shits and pisses. It would seem that the female genitalia cannot be altogether dissociated from their excretory functions: an association which Lawrence himself defines elsewhere as pornographic. And it is Connie's arse which claims the greater part of Mellors's admiration. In denying that Connie's cunt is the fulcrum of her sexuality, Mellors is denying female sexuality itself. This denial leads me to believe that the next sexual encounter between him and Connie includes anal intercourse.

Lawrence does not make it clear exactly what is going on. As in *John Thomas and Lady Jane*, this episode is described as embodying a 'sensuality which burns the soul to tinder'. And, again as in the previous version, Connie is led to speculate on what Abelard meant by 'the refinements of passion', which she now recognizes as belonging to the senses rather than to the emotions. But here Lawrence has inserted an extra paragraph.

Burning out the shames, the deepest, oldest shames, in the most secret places. It cost her an effort to let him have his way and his will of her. She had to be a passive, consenting thing, like a slave, a physical slave. Yet the passion licked round her, consuming, and when the sensual flame of it pressed through her bowels and her breast, she really thought she was dying: yet a poignant, marvellous death.

The woman cannot respond or manoeuvre and finds pleasure, not only in passivity but in pain. All this is necessary in order to 'smelt out the heaviest ore of the body into purity'. This is a rather more specific description than the one in *John Thomas and Lady Jane*.

It prompts the question: necessary for whom? It is absurd to claim that women find anal intercourse or (if Lawrence is not actually being that specific) passivity accompanied by pain in any way necessary. To claim as much is to claim that female sexuality is essentially masochistic. And, although anal intercourse is not an exclusively homosexual practice, it is an act which is possible between two men as well as between a woman and a man. It is an act in which it is of no consequence that the woman is a woman, and so constitutes a denial not only of the nature of female sexuality, but of female sexuality itself. No, it is Mellors and not

Connie for whom this episode is necessary. And it is necessary for him because, despite his avowed commitment to the cause of simultaneous orgasm, something in him needs to dominate, subdue and perhaps even humiliate a woman in the sexual act. That Connie is prepared to be the recipient of these needs is less than convincing. Whatever happened to tenderness?

Lawrence would have us believe that Connie now admires Mellors for his courage. 'To find a man who dared do it, without shame or sin or final misgiving! If he had been ashamed afterwards, and made one feel ashamed, how awful! What a shame most men are so doggy ...' Mellors's manliness consists ultimately in his ability to subdue a woman by means of his penis. Towards the end of the novel he too refuses Connie's money, telling her, 'I can't just be your male concubine.' Where Parkin pleaded, Mellors asserts and is blunt about it: 'I'm not just my Lady's fucker after all.' When he surmises, as did Parkin, that there is too much of the woman in him, it is impossible to believe him – as it is to believe Connie when she tells him that he, unlike other men, has 'the courage of his own tenderness'.

Of the three versions of the novel, *Lady Chatterley's Lover* uses the word 'tenderness' most often, insisting upon it as though Lawrence believed that the mere repetition of the word were capable of demonstrating its substance. It is as though he had forgotten that primary lesson for all novelists: 'Don't tell: show.' If we readers cannot perceive tenderness in action, we are not likely to be persuaded of its existence by means of rhetoric. This is not to say that there is no tenderness in *Lady Chatterley's Lover*. There is: especially in Lawrence's description of the wood, the landscape and all natural life. But, as on that first night between Johanna and Gilbert, the passion (and tenderness is a passion) does not get through. It remains to a large extent outside the central relationship between Connie and Mellors, a diffuse presence which never quite manages to take shape at the proper focal point: the centre of their relationship. Compared to the former two, this version of the novel never quite coheres.

The fault lies mainly in the character of Mellors, and in the Lawrentian authorial voice with which it is so often compounded.

His attitude towards women is basically hostile – which he can sometimes admit. It is also basically one of fear, and this can never be admitted. He can overcome his fear and mistrust of connection, but not of female sexuality which, unless it takes the form he thinks it ought, is essentially destructive of the male in its voraciousness. Nothing less than total submission on the part of the woman can convince him of his own manliness, and we women are supposed to find him worthy of such submission, rather than question his insecurity as a man.

Parkin is insecure too, but he does not therefore become a bully. The change in the central male character from the one version to the other is often quite startling. Why did Lawrence find it necessary? Of course one can only speculate, but my feeling is that Parkin is a lot more like Lawrence himself than he was prepared to admit in public. A pity: it is Parkin's feminine and son-like qualities which are so often Lawrence's own saving grace. But in the character of Mellors he seems to have moved away from self-portraiture and back to that of the inadequately internalized father who now has more than a dash of Birkin in his makeup. That the result is a mess indicates that Lawrence had problems with the concept of maleness until the end of his life.

It would be good to be able to believe that *John Thomas and Lady Jane* is a truer representative of Lawrence's beliefs than is *Lady Chatterley's Lover*. But although I find the former the more honest work (its readiness to admit weakness and its lesser need of rhetoric both persuade me so) it would be too simple to conclude that it is therefore truer to the final Lawrentian statement on men, women and marriage. Nor is it necessarily the falser. It seems to me that all Lawrence's thinking on the relations between men and women is full of inconsistencies, and that he never arrived at a position which could be called final.

Perhaps the inconsistencies are inevitable, and not just the outcome of Lawrence's own peculiar psychological history. For both his men and women the inward struggle is fundamentally that between connection and independence. In a 1918 letter to Sallie Hopkin he wrote: 'And it is the human contact that means so much to one, really . . . only the human warmth, when one can get it, makes the heart rich.' And earlier he had written to his teaching colleague A. W. McLeod: 'I think the one thing to do is for men to have the courage to draw nearer to women, to expose themselves to them, and be altered by them: and for women to accept and admit men.' And yet in 1920 he wrote to his friend Godwin Baynes, who was going through a divorce:

One has to learn that love is a secondary thing in life. The first thing is to be a free, proud, single being by oneself: to be oneself free, to let the other be free: to force nothing and not to be forced into anything. Liberty, one's own proud liberty, is worth everything else on earth: something proud within oneself ... It is an ignominious thing, either exacting or chasing after love. Love isn't that important: one's own free soul is first.

It is difficult, but not impossible, to reconcile those first two statements with the third. As Thomas S. Szasz has put it:

Human relations are problematic because men are driven by opposing but often equally powerful needs and passions, especially the needs for security and freedom. To satisfy the need for security, people seek closeness and commitment, and the more they attain these, the more oppressed they feel. To satisfy their need for freedom, people seek independence and detachment, and the more they attain these, the more isolated they feel. As in all such things, the wise pursue the golden mean; and the lucky attain it.

It seems to me that Lawrence was always willing to recognize such conflicting needs in men, but only sometimes and then reluctantly in women. In his wisest pronouncements, such as his litany devoted to the complexities of marriage, he arrives at his own version of the golden mean, but he goes further than Szasz in understanding that its attainment is not merely a matter of luck. It is rather a matter of honesty and sensitivity in recognizing the nature of the conflict, and of courage in being able to live with it.

Conclusions

For Lawrence men are the weaker sex, however strong their muscles and however robust their intellects. They are not weaker by nature but only in the contemporary social context which they themselves have created. Thus their comparative weakness is all their own fault. In devoting themselves to the pursuit of wealth, property and maximum industrial efficiency in the world of men, while accepting the domestic values of the world of women as sacred, they are living only in their upper, daylit selves, and thus are less than whole. The dark lower self of phallic wisdom has been neglected and suppressed. But this latter self is the true repository of manly qualities, especially manly virtues, such as courage, sensitivity, sensuality and a vitally active desirousness. If it were to be acknowledged and cultivated, men would become true men and thus (being now the stronger sex) induce women to become true women.

Women are now the stronger sex but their strength is not inherent. It is rather the result of men's craven abnegation of their own manliness, especially in their attitude towards women. Women have taken over some of the qualities rightfully belonging to men as well as various forms of masculine behaviour. At the same time they have kept their maternal qualities, thus rendering men almost superfluous. In following intellectual and/or solitary pursuits, on the one hand and, on the other, elevating motherhood to a position of central importance, women too are living only in their upper, daylit selves and are thus less than true women. In neglecting their dark lower selves women have lost sight of such womanly qualities as courage, sensitivity, sensuality and a vitally passive desirability. If they were in touch with their lower selves, they would not dominate men and, in doing so, upset the laws of nature.

The laws of nature are based in duality/polarity, the principle which at once moves the universe and keeps it held together. The same principle operates in human life, but men and women have lost sight of it, as they have lost the awareness of their connection with the rest of the natural world. In order to regain this awareness and thus integrate themselves into the universal ebb and flow, men and women must recognize that they are not only different, but opposites, and therefore opposed. But opposition implies complementarity and the possibility of reconciliation. What this means in practical terms is that men and women should both come together and stay apart as reciprocal need arises. Connection and separation will each serve to enhance the other. The upper daylit selves, male and female, must be kept separate, while connection can only take place between the dark lower selves.

Connection is essentially a matter of sexual connection, more particularly heterosexual connection, in which alone the union of opposites is possible. Sexual desire is the desire for completeness, an admission of need. Its fulfilment entails the assuagement of need and the alleviation of the loneliness which human beings feel, not only as individuals but as a species within the universe. In the sexual act, the individual dies, abandoning his/her individuality to the universal flow of the life-force. The end result will be peace, out of which the individual is reborn and made new, ready once again for separation and the daylit world of the upper self. But the death must precede the rebirth. Any device – such as deliberately induced orgasm – which indicates that the individual remains in conscious control will inhibit the process and, further, prove the connection a destructive rather than a creative act.

Marriage is the best, perhaps the only possible, context for connection, and hence for the constant process of rebirth which is necessary for human growth and equilibrium. This, and not the getting and rearing of children, is the true purpose of marriage: that each partner create and recreate the other while creating and recreating him/herself. Casual sexual encounters will not achieve the desired result which depends upon habituation, trust, and on having found the right partner in the first place. He/she will not be an intellectual companion, nor an object of worship or romantic love, but an embodiment of the desire which prompts and answers your desire. He/she will need and know how to be free, proud and single as well as a sexual complement. The optimum marriage consists in a perfect balance between two equal partners, but this is a precarious state and is not easily attainable. It has to be fought for again and again, the battle often ending in the submission of one partner to the other or in stalemate, because no other solution seems pragmatically possible. Equality is the ideal but, just because it is an ideal rather than a self-evident fact, few if any marriages attain it.

Such I believe to be, in necessarily oversimplified form, a summary of Lawrence's views on men, women, sexuality and marriage. They are the views of Lawrence the moralist, as propounded again and again in his essays and other non-fiction. Sometimes they are also propounded overtly in his fiction where the intrusive authorial voice can set up an instant resistance in the reader. But I have found that the opposite process is also at work. In the fiction the words of Lawrentian rhetoric become flesh and, being flesh, become more approachable, but at the same time less amenable to the manipulations of the moralist. Every serious novelist is of course a moralist, but to be a moralist and to moralize are not necessarily the same thing. Although Lawrence's fiction is often marred by his obtrusive moralizing, it seems to me that the sure instinct of the novelist just as often works to subvert the easy polarities – and indeed, the hubris – of the moralist. Lawrence makes it difficult for us, but I think the most rewarding way to read his fiction is to listen to the instinctive voice of the novelist rather than the tub-thumping moral generalizations.

'You can't fool the novel,' as Lawrence himself wrote in an essay of 1925. And indeed even *The Plumed Serpent*, that novel in which Lawrence's views on men and women are elevated into a religion and codified in a system of laws and rituals, remains resolutely unfooled by itself. In the same essay Lawrence claims:

In a novel everything is relative to everything else, if that novel is art at all. There may be didactic bits, but they aren't the novel. And the author may have a didactic 'purpose' up his sleeve. Indeed most great novelists have ... And since every novelist who amounts to anything has a philosophy – even Balzac – any novel of importance has a purpose. If only the purpose be large enough, and not at odds with passional inspiration.

He then goes on to complain that 'It is such a bore that nearly all great novelists have a didactic purpose, otherwise a philosophy, directly opposed to their passional inspiration.' The implied claim is presumably that for Lawrence himself philosophy and passional inspiration are at one. It is a large claim and one which cannot be substantiated. Lawrence's passional inspiration depends, as does that of every other novelist who is not writing genre fiction, on the depth and breadth of his perceptions of human feeling and human behaviour. And it is those very perceptions which are so often at odds with his 'philosophy'.

Whether you find, after a close reading of Lawrence's work, that the novelist triumphs over the moralist or vice versa is probably a highly subjective conclusion. I am in favour of the novelist. And I am in favour of the novelist because I, like Lawrence, am in favour of the novel. He thought it 'the highest form of human expression yet attained' because 'it is so incapable of the absolute'. In his essay 'Morality and the Novel' he wrote:

The novel is the highest example of subtle inter-relatedness that man has discovered. Everything is true in its own place, time, circumstance, and untrue outside of its own time, place, circumstance. If you try to nail anything down in the novel, either it kills the novel, or the novel gets up and walks away with the nail.

This is a shrewdly professional piece of self-appraisal as well as a convenient let-out for one accused of being prescriptive rather than descriptive. Of course the novel deals with the particular, and often the more particularly it does so, the better. But we readers cannot help extrapolating in the light of our own knowledge and experience from the particular to the general. While seeing Connie Chatterley as an individual in descriptive terms, we cannot but also see her as Woman in prescriptive terms.

Lawrence is surely right, however, in warning both writers and readers against being hot for certainties. In the same essay he goes on to exemplify: 'It is no use thinking you can put a stamp on the relation between men and women, to keep it in the *status quo*. You can't. You might as well try to put a stamp on the rainbow or the rain.' In his own novels, and never more busily than when writing of the relations between men and women, Lawrence is forever knocking in nails, only to prise them out again. And although he comes close, particularly in *Aaron's Rod* and *Lady Chatterley's Lover*, to nailing the lid to the coffin, it seems to me that the corpse within will be found to be breathing after all.

Lawrence's novels should not be read as tracts but as a series of tries or trials. He was a pioneer and we should not dismiss him for not getting everything right – as if anyone ever could. He recognized that relations between men and women are problematic, and he attempted to identify and analyse those problems in the light of his own experience and that of others. But unlike most of his contemporaries (and ours) he was not content with analysis and its concomitant pessimism and cynicism. He tried, both in his life and his work, to find solutions, while recognizing that the most satisfactory were probably humanly unattainable. In the process he risked ridicule and vilification, not only from the literary establishment but from outraged public morality. Nevertheless he went on trying until the end of his life, pushed on against all odds by his basically unflagging vitality and optimism.

It is difficult to forgive Lawrence for Ethel Cane. As it is difficult, in another sense, to forgive him for Birkin, Aaron or Mellors. But when Paul Morel tells his mother that nothing else matters as long as she doesn't find life a paltry thing, he is expressing Lawrence's deepest and most enduring belief. This, after all, is what remains of Lawrence. Neither the intermittent misogyny nor the outbursts of painfully-rooted misanthropy. Not the half-cock theorizing about phallicism and the blood. And not the missionary value judgments. But the courage to value life for itself with all its pain and darkness as well as its joy and enlightenment, affirming again and again in the face of nihilism and philistinism that life is meaningful and valuable, if only we are brave enough to bring meaning and value to it.